Selected
Final Pension Payment Vouchers
1818-1864

PENNSYLVANIA:

Philadelphia & Pittsburgh

Kathryn McPherson Gunning

Willow Bend Books
Westminster, MD
2003

WILLOW BEND BOOKS

AN IMPRINT OF HERITAGE BOOKS, INC.

Books, CDs, and more – Worldwide

For our listing of thousands of titles see our website
at
www.HeritageBooks.com

Published 2003 by
HERITAGE BOOKS, INC.
Publishing Division
1540 Pointer Ridge Place #E
Bowie, Maryland 20716

International Standard Book Number: **1-58549-885-8**

APPENDIX A

WILL TRANSCRIPTIONS

Will of Catharine ALLISON

In the name of God. Amen. I Catharine ALLISON of the Borough of Chambersburg, being in feeble health but of sound and disposing mind, memory and understanding, do make my last will and Testament as follows, that is to say: First I give and bequeath to my daughter Eveline Catharine, all my personal Estate. Secondly, I give and desire unto my three daughters Mary, Margaret, and Eveline Catharine my Lot of ground in Queen Street with a rough cast house thereon erected (where I now reside) to be held by them jointly during their joint lives and at the death of either of my said Daughters to go the other two during their joint lives and at the death of either of the said Surviving Sisters to go to the last Surviving of my said daughters during her life, and at her death it is my will that the same shall go to and be divided equally between my Son William ALLISON and my Grandson William Allison WHITESTONE (Son of my said daughter Mary) as tenants in Common, in fee Simple forever Provided that they both be living at the death of the last Surviving of my said three daughters but if only one of them (my said Son & Grandson) be living at the death of the last Surviving of my said daughters, then my will is that the Said house & lot go to him & his heirs, and if neither of them be living at the decease of the last Surviving of my said three daughters then my will is that the same go to my Son Alexander & his heirs. My will is further that the husbands of my two said daughters Mary & Margaret (if living at my decease) are to have no interest whatsoever in the devise above mentioned, the same being made & intended for their Separate use and if necessary to carry this intention into operation, I do appoint my Executrix hereinafter named a Trustee for my two last named daughters, to hold the estate above devised to them for their use. And I do hereby nominate and appoint my Said daughter Eveline Catharine to be the Executrix of this my last will & Testament Hereby revoking all former wills by me heretofore made. Witness my hand and seal this 23rd day of September A.D. 1840.

Sealed signed published & declared by the above named testator as & for her last will & Testament.

Catharine ALLISON

Tho. CARLISLE
Robert M. BARD

Will of Hannah ARCHER

In the name of God amen, I Hannah ARCHER of Washington County and State of Pennsylvania, being in a reasonable state of health and of sound and disposing mind, memory and understanding, do make and ordain this to be my last will and testament. First and principally, I commend my soul to God who gave it and my body to the Earth and as for such worldly property wherewith it has pleased God to intrust me, I dispose of the same as follows. I will that all my just debts and funeral expences be fully paid. I will that my wearing apparel be divided as follows, one share to my sister Charity KENN, one share to the daughters of my nephew John SHIPMAN, one share to the daughter of my sister Sarah WORKMAN decd. and one share to the daughter of my brother Elijah HUNT decd and one share to the daughters of each of my brothers William HUNT, Josiah HUNT, and Absalom HUNT. I give and bequeath unto my nephew John SHIPMAN, twenty dollars. The balance of my property to be sold, and the balance of the proceeds together with my money to be divided into seven principal shares and distributed as follows, viz., one share to my sister Charity KENN, one share among the children of my sister Sarah WORKMAN, decd. and one share among the children of Elijah HUNT decd. and one share to each of my brothers, William HUNT, Josiah HUNT, and Absalom HUNT, and one share to Thomas B. RINGLAND and lastly I hereby constitute and appoint my friend William LINDLY, Executor of this my last will and testament. In witness whereof I hereby request and authorize Wm. LINDLY, to affix my name and seal, to this my last will and testament, this tenth day of October in the year of our Lord, one thousand eight hundred and forty-eight.

Hannah ARCHER

Sealed, signed and delivered in presence of

Uzal DILLE
Phebe RINGLAND

Will of John BEECHER

In the Name of God Amen, I John *BIECHER* of Bern Township, Berks County, yeoman, being sick but of sound mind, memory, and understanding, considering the mortality of my body and, knowing it is appointed for all men once to die, do therefore make this my last will & testament in manner following. That is to say, first, it is my will and I do order that my beloved wife *Mary* shall have and keep in her possession during her natural life my chest, the best bed & bedstead amongst my beds, a tin plate stove with pipe, one table, four of the best chairs, one spinning wheel & reel, the best cow of my flock, all the yarn, linen and woolen, flax and linens, and all the woolen cloth which I may have at home or in the hands of the weavers, at and after my decease, one hundred weight of meat (if so much shall be left) if not all that remains in my possession at my decease, as also all the meal, rye, & wheat that shall be left together with four bags, and all my German prayer and hymn books and bibles, and as much kitchen furniture as she shall want for her use; and the remainder of my personal estate (except one other cow and one hog hereafter devised & bequeathed) shall be sold by my executors hereinafter named at public sale. Item, it is my will and I do order that my executors hereinafter named shall within six months after my decease shall at public sale sell all my m------- & tenement of land together with the yard thereon created, situate in Bern township aforesaid, bounded by lands of John BITNER, Adam ROCK, John ALTHOUSE, George SEHILD, & Magdelane ALWINE & others containing fifty-six acres be the same more or less, to wit, what is in the lines and limits thereof. Hereby empowering my executors hereinafter named to sign seal and acknowledge a deed to the purchasers or purchasers thereof, to his or their heirs and assigns for ever, as to vest such an estate in him or them as I now have & hold for the same. Item, it is my will and I do order that after first paying out of the moneys arising from the sale of my real and personal estate all my just debts & funeral expenses and reserving twenty-five pounds hereinafter bequeathed to my daughter Lidea, the remainder if any shall be paid unto my beloved wife *Maria* who shall have and keep the same for her own use and support during her natural life. Item, it is my will and I do order that the money which shall remain in the hands of my wife *Mary* after her decease, as well as the proceeds from the sale of the personal estate, hereinafter bequeathed to her after first paying & deducting all her just debts & funeral expenses out of the same the remainder shall be divided equally share and share alike between my six sons, to wit, Samuel, George, John, Jacob, William, and Benjamin. Item, I give and bequeath to my daughter Lidea one cow and one hog (hereinbefore reserved), the same which she now owns, and twenty-five pounds (heretofore reserved) in cash, to be her full share portion & dividend of all my real and personal estate which said twenty-five pounds shall remain in the hands of my executors until she arrives of age, who shall ----- and from time to time keep the same and at interest and good surety, the interest whereof my said daughter Lidea shall

receive yearly and every year as long as she shall be in her minority, and as soon as she shall arrive at the age of twenty-one years then my executors shall pay the aforesaid sum of twenty-five pounds unto her. Item, I give and bequeath unto my five daughters, viz. Elizabeth, intermarried with George *SEGNER*, Catharine, intermarried with Jonathan PAXSON, Margaret, intermarried with *MULLONER*, Magdelane, intermarried with Thomas RUSSEL, and Barbara, intermarried with Michael NEUSCHWENDER, the sum of five shillings each of them in full of their inheritance out of my estate both real and personal as I have considered them advanced in my lifetime, and lastly I do hereby nominate and appoint my son George BEECHER, and trusty friend John V. EPLER executors of this my last will and testament, hereby revoking all former wills by me made, ratifying and allowing this and no other to be my last will and testament, in witness whereof I have hereunto set my hand and seal the tenth day of August in the year of our Lord one thousand eight hundred and eighteen.

Signed, sealed, published, and declared by the testators as and so far his last will and testament in the presence of us and at his request and in the presence of each other subscribed our names hereto as witnesses

Michael SEIDEL
Adam KOCK

Registers office, Reading, Berks County, March 8th, 1819, then appeared Adam KOCH, and on the 15th of the same month appeared Michael SEIDEL, witnesses to the aforewritten will who were duly qualified according to law, did declare & say that they were present and did see and hear John *BEICHER* the testator sign, publish, pronounce, & declare the same writing as and for his last will and testament; and at the time of so doing thereof he the said testator was of sound mind, memory, and understanding to the best of their knowledge and as they verily believe and further, that the names Adam KOCH & Michael SEIDEL are of the deponents own handwriting there to subscribed as witnesses in the presence of each other and in the presence and at the request of the testator.

Sam *LEATHER*, D.R.

Berks County
I do hereby testify that the foregoing writing doth contain a true copy from the original will duly proven the 8th of March last past and remains in the registars office at Reading and for said county in testimony whereof I have hereunto set my hand and seal of said office this 17th day April domini 1819.

Dan'l RHOADS Jr., Registrar

Will of John BIRKHART

I, John BIRKHART, of Robeson Township, Berks County and State of Pennsylvania, do feel myself weak in regard to body, but, God be praised, of good memory and understanding, I therefore am resolved to make this my last will and testament, in order as follows, to wit: Firstly, it is my will and I do order that all my lawful debts, burial and other expenses be first paid out of my estate. Further is it my will and I do order, that my wife Margareth shall have her widow seat in my house and all my land and moveable property, during her widowhood; but she shall seek nothing of my estate. Further is it my will and I do order, that my son Frederick shall have in advance my Bible book and my son Adam my clock with the case, this I do bequeath unto them and their heirs to have after the demise of my wife.

Further, it is my will and I do order, that, after the demise of my wife, my herein after mentioned executors, shall sell at public *residue* all my land and what shall remain of my moveable property, so soon as they shall think proper and the money arriving therefrom, after accounting all expense and trouble, shall be inherited by my children in equal parts, as follows, to wit: my son Frederick one part, Adam, Jacob, and John each of them one part, and my daughter Eve one part and Barbara one part, so that non shall have an advantage over the other -- this I do bequeath unto them and their heirs for ever.

Further, it is my will that the parts of my daughter Barbara and of my daughter Catharine, what might have come to them, shall remain in the hands of my hereinafter named executors, so long as they do not deem it necessary, that said two daughters are in need of it, in case of sickness or other circumstances; but if my executors should deem it necessary, then they may let them have each of them her part, so as they shall think it expedient and proper.

Further, it is my will and I do order, that, in case of the demise of my daughter Margareth, something should be left of her portion in the hands of my executors, they shall pay the same immediately to her children in equal portions - this I do bequeath unto them and their heirs for ever. And in case something of the portion of my daughter Catherine should, after her death be in their hands, my after named executors shall pay the same to her daughter Margareth - this I do bequeath unto her and her heirs forever.

Further, it is my will that, in case my wife should marry, she shall leave my land immediately and all shall be sold as above provided.

Lastly, I do constitute and appoint as executors of this my last will and testament, in order to execute it, my two sons Frederick BIRKHART and Adam BIRKHART - and I do annul all wills and testaments previously made and acknowledge these presents as my last will and testament and have sealed and acknowledged and signed it with my own hand and seal this 28 day of December, 1822.

John BIRKHART

Signed and sealed and acknowledged by said John BIRKHART as his last will and testament, in presence of

George LUDWIG
John ZIEMER

Berks County
I, Peter *ALWAND* [sig.], Register for the Probate of wills and granting letters of administration in and for the county of Berks, do hereby certify, that the foregoing instrument of writing doth contain a true copy, the original whereof is in German, of the Testament and last will of John BIRKHART, deceased, which original was duly proven February the 8th A.D. 1823, and remains filed in the Register's office at Reading, in and for the County of Berks.

In witness whereof I have hereunto set my hand, and the seal of said office at Reading, April 19th A.D. 1823.

Peter *ALWAND*, Register

Will of Daniel BLACK

The last will and testament of Daniel BLACK of the township of Newport in the County of Luzerne. I, Daniel BLACK considering the uncertainty of this mortal life and being of sound mind and memory blessed be Almighty God for the same, do make and publish this my last will and testament in the manner and form following, viz., first I give and bequeath unto my three sons, to wit, John, James, and Charles BLACK two dollars each to be paid to each of the said legatees within six months after my decease. Also I give to James BLACK my grandson and son of Charles BLACK one large copper kettle. I give and bequesth to Margaret BLACK, my granddaughter and daughter of Charles BLACK, one big wheel, one spinning wheel, one bed and bedding, a set of silver tea spoons, and two brass candlesticks. I also give to my grandson Hiram BLACK, son of Charles BLACK, my small copper kettle, two copper ladles or skimmers, one iron shovel, fire tongs, one copper tea kettle, one flat iron. I also give to my grandson James BLACK my large Bible chest with all the property that I may be possessed of at my decease not mentioned above. I do hereby appoint Charles BLACK administrator of this my last will and testament, in witness whereof I have hereunto set my hand & seal this eleventh day of June A.D. 1825.
In presence of Samuel JAMESON, Daniel BLACK

Luzerne Co.,
I Isaac HARTZELL register for the probate of wills and granting letters of administration in and for the county of Luzerne do certify the foregoing will of Daniel BLACK late of Newport deceased to be a true and complete exemplification of the original remaining filed in the registers office of said county and recorded in will book A page 299 of the records of said county in witness whereof I have hereunto set my hand & seal of office at Wilkes-Barre the 24 January A.D. 1826.

Isaac HARTZELL [sig.]

Will of William BLAKENEY

In the name of God amen. I William BLAKENEY, late a captain in the United States Revolutionary Army, now resident in the City of Pittsburgh, being weak in body but of sound and disposing mind and memory do make and ordain and publish this my last will and testament as follows, viz., firstly I commend my soul to Almighty God who gave it, my body I commit to the earth whence it came to be buried in a decent Christian like manner at the discretion of my executor hereinafter named. Secondly, all my just debts I direct to be paid as soon as convenient after my decease. Thirdly, my friend James McELROY having paid a brotherly attention to me in my illness, having kept me in his house and procured for me nurses and other attendance, I hereby give and bequeath to the said James McELROY all the balance of pension which may be due to me from the United States at the time of my decease, also watch and wearing apparel, my two trunks and their contents, also all my estate and property whatsoever and of whatsoever kind hereby constituting him my whole and sole heir, my debts being first paid. Lastly, I do hereby nominate and appoint my friend Samuel BRYSON of the City of Pittsburgh to be sole executor of this my last will and testament. In witness whereof I have hereto set my hand and seal the twenty-third day of July in the year of our Lord one thousand eight hundred and twenty-one.

William B. BLAKENEY

Signed sealed and published by the testator as and for his last will and testament in presence of us who in his presence and at his request have signed our names as witnesses thereto.

James AGNEW [sig.],
John McGINESS [sig.],
James M. RIDDLE [sig.]

Will of John COOK

Know all men by these presents that I John COOK of Point Township in the County of Northumberland and State of Pennsylvania, being advanced in years but of sound mind and memory, do make this my last will and testament giving and bequeathing as follows to wit I give and devise to my frainds John COOK and Jane his wife or the survivor of them in consideration of their care attention to me when living all the estate real personal and mixed which I may possess after the payments of my funeral expenses and just debts to hold to them and their heirs forever, and I do appoint my fraind John BOYD of the Town of Northumberland executor of this my last will revoking by these presents all wills by me heretofore made, in witness whereof I have hereunto set my hand and seal the eighteenth day of December Anno Domini one thousand eight hundred and twenty one.

John COOK

Signed sealed and
delivered in presents of
Jacob COOK
Thos. H. IRWIN

Will of Methuselah DAVIS

Whereas I Methuselah DAVIS formerly of Chester County in the State of Pennsylvania, Now in the Lower Township in Cape May in the State of New Jersey, being advanced in age, and much indisposed in body but thank be to God of sound mind and memory and calling to mind the mortality of the body and for the satisfaction fo any dearest relations and friends, and in order to prevent all disputes as far as in me lies after my decease when it shall please God to call me out of this present world (I hope to a better) and to settle and dispose of my temporal affairs I do make this my last will and testament, and I do hereby Constitute and appoint my good friend Enoch EDMUNDS of the lower Township of Cape May to be my lawful executor to see this my last will duly executed after my decease in the manner following, to see my body decently interred and to pay all my funeral charges, all my just debts as soon as convenient after my decease.

I give and bequeath to my well beloved wife Abigail DAVIS all my household & kitchen furniture except such articles as is herein after mentioned, likewise all monies due and coming due in Chester County in the State of Pennsylvania.

I give and bequeath unto my niece Letticia Davis BYERS who I raised from a child and has been faithful unto me, first I give her my large Bible and large looking glass which was her mothers, likewise six silver teaspoons marked E.L.D. with two large tablespoons of silver marked D.L. Likewise my silver watch and one pair of flat or sad irons.

Signed sealed this twenty-fifth day of March in the year of our Lord one thousand eight hundred and twenty five. In the presence of

Ellis HUGHES
David REEVES

Methuselah DAVIS [seal]

Will of John EICHHOLTZ

In the name of God amen!
I John EICHHOLTZ of the City of Lancaster, knowing the uncertainty of life, and being of sound mind, but weakly in body, make this my last will and Testament, - whereby I appoint my Nephew Jacob EICHHOLTZ of the aforesaid City, my sole Executor, in order that he may collect all my outstanding monies, and therewith to pay my just debts, and if after they re thus discharg'd, to dispose of the balance in any manner he may think just. As witness whereof, I have set my hand and seal, this twenty eighth day of May 1821.

John EICHHOLTZ

Witness present at signing sealing and delivering

William FULTON
Luigi PERSICO

A true copy
W. WHITESIDE [sig.] for J[ohn] WHITESIDE, registrar

Will of Jane FERTENBAUGH

In the name of God Amen I Jane *FORTENBEH* of the township of Middle Paxton Township in the County of Dauphin being advanced in years, but of a sound memory and understanding and knowing well the uncertainty of life and being disposed to distribute what little worldly affairs and property it has pleased the Almighty to bestow on me, do make ordain and publish this to be my last will and testament. Principally and first. - I command my immortal soul into the hands of that God who gave it, and my body to the earth to be buried in a decent and Christian like manner at the discretion of my Executor, herein after named. - Secondly, It is my will and I direct by the authority given me in the will of my late Husband that the plantation whereon I now live Shall be divided by a line running from Peters mountain across to the little, or *Therce* mountain which Division line Shall be agreed upon by three disinterested persons to be chosen By Philip *FORTINBACH* or his representatives and by my Executor herein after named making each half as equal in number of acres as the nature and circumstance of the same will admit. - Thirdly, It is my will that John *BUTT* whom I have raised Shall have the eastern half of the plantation with the house and Improvements which I have made since the Death of my husband, together with all other Improvements which may fall to that part of the Plantation after the same shall be divided to hold the same to him self his heirs or assigns for ever. - Fourthly It is also my will and I direct that Philip *FORTINBACH* or his representatives pay unto John *BUT* or his heirs the sum of seventy eight dollars and twenty five cents being the one half of the sum in my ----- on the settlement of the estate of my last Husband this in consequence of my having paid the debts of his estate out of my private funds and not out of any monies which came to my hands from his Estate, By which means I paid his debts and prevented the selling of his real estate, this money having come to me after his death as a Gratuity from the Commonwealth of Pennsylvania in consequence of my being the widow of Captain Hawkins BOON whose service to his Country are well known. - Fifthly It is my will and I direct that Elenor KELLER whom I have raised from her Infancy Shall have my bed and Cow and all my clothes, except my Red cloke which is for John *BARTH*, said Elenor KELLER to have a pot her choice and my Bell metal tea kettle and also the Book in which her name is written also John *BUTT* to pay her twenty dollars in Money when she arrives at the age of twenty one also John *BUTT* to have the watch and Philip *FORTINBACH* to have the value of it in money. John *BUTT* to have my large Bible, all the Cloth which I have made since the death of my husband to be divided between John *BUTT* and Elenor KELLER. - Sixth I direct that my Executor after my Death Shall pay all my just debts, out of my monies which may come in to his hands and if there should be no cash on hand to pay the same that in that case he Shall dispose of as much personal property as is necessary to pay my debts which may be due and owing at the time of my death also that he

shall collect all my outstanding debts, he Shall also collect from Philip *FORTINBACH* the one half of the amount which his Father owed to Jacob STRICKER at this death the same being paid by me out of my own monies to save the Plantation Should I have sufficient monies at my death to pay my funeral expenses that the personal property which I kept at the death of my husband need not be sold, then the same Shall be divided agreeable to his will, and all the residue of my monies or property not specially distributed Shall go to John *BUTT* or his heirs. It is also my desire that my Executor act as guardian for Elenor KELLER during her minority. And lastly I nominate constitute and appoint my friend William COCHRAN to be Executor of this my last will, hereby revoking all other wills by me heretofore made and declaring this to be my last will and testament.

In witness whereof I have here unto set my hand and Seal this second day of May in the year of our lord one thousand eight hundred and thirty two.

Jane *FORTINBACH*

Signed sealed and pronounced by the said testatrix as her last will and testament in presence of

William MITCHELL.
Webster WYNN

Will of James GARDNER

24 May 1822

I James GARDNER being weak in Body but sound in mind and memory do bequeath & distribute of my little property In the following manner. In the first place my daughter Jean owns the following & it is not my property but her own earning as follows to 1 Dutch oven & lid one churn two blankets, two bed quilts, one new milk tub, one old trunk and one small chest all the kitchen furniture without exception one Ewe sheep & Further I do allow Thomas MOFFET for his professional services as a physician the sum of Ten Dollars in the hand of Thomas FLETCHER my agent to the War Department beginning the 4th March 1822 & I have a just account against James THOMAS of Seven Dollars and Eleven Cents the Items of which will appear on a piece of paper drawn of by Josiah LOWERY, James THOMAS Debt to James GARDNER July 3 1821 $16.59 Credit by Items $9.48 Dated January 16th 1822 Leaving a balance of Seven Dollars and Eleven Cents which I allow Josiah LOWERY to Collect from said Thomas for my funeral expenses as far as it will go. I have one mare executed at the suit of Jno. CRAWFORD for the amount of five Dollars and Costs. Josias LOWERY bound with me for the delivery of said mare, when the money is Due If there is any Balance after said Debt & Costs of the above Judgment with respect of said mare to be appropriated to pay my Just Debts. I have also one *Muley* Cow which I allow my Daughter Jean to have if my Lawful Debt can be paid without her. It is my will that after my Decease that all my Just debts are paid & that my daughter Jean shall hold & possess all the rest of my property.

James GARDNER

Witness
Josiah LOWERY
William LOWERY

Will of Jacob GEIGER

In the Name of God amen I Jacob GEIGER of Lebanon Township in the County of Dauphin, and in the State of Pennsylvania Yeoman being Sick and weak of Body, but of sound and well disposing mind memory, and understanding thanks be unto god for the same Do hereby make and ordain this to be my last Will and Testament, in manner following that is to say, First, It is my Will, that all my Just debts and funeral Expences be paid of and discharged out of my Estate as soon as may be done after my decease, - Item I give and bequeathe unto my beloved Wife Mary all my Estate whatsoever and wheresoever the same my be She paying thereout my Just Debts and funeral expences aforesaid And Lastly I Do hereby nominate and appoint my Said wife Mary Executrix of this my last Will and Testament, and I do hereby revoke all former Wills and Testaments, by me heretofore made ratifying allowing and confirming this and no other to be my last Will and Testament In Witness whereof I have hereunto Set my hand and Seal the fifteenth day of December in the year of our lord one thousand eight hundred and five.

Jacob GEIGER

Signed sealed published and pronounced by the above Testator Jacob GEIGER for his last Will and Testament in the Presence of us

Henry KILLIAM
Jno. GLONINGER

Will of Gurdon GIER/GEER

In the name of God amen I Gurdon GEER of lawful age being weak in body but of sound and perfect mind and memory do make and publish this my last will and testament in manner following. First I give and bequeath unto my wife Ruth GEER all the estate and personal property that I am possessed of at the time of my decease to have use and occupy the same during her natural life and after her decease the said Estate and personal property aforesaid is to descend to and be inherited by my son Benajah A. GEER and I hereby appoint and constitute my said son Benajah A. GEER my executor of this my last will and testament. I further give and bequeath to my son George GEER twenty dollars to my son Samuel GEER I give and bequeath the sum of twenty dollars and to my daughter Lucy WILLIAMS wife of Rock WILLIAMS twenty dollars which said legacies are to be paid by my executor to George GEER Samuel GEER and Lucy WILLIAMS in one year after the decease of my said wife Ruth GEER out of the estate and property aforesaid. I further give and bequeath unto my son Samuel GEER the large family Bible which I now own and possess and unto my grandson Gurdon GEER my silver watch. I also give and bequeath Ann WEST one set of silver teaspoons. The property that my said wife Ruth possessed at the time of my marriage with her I intend and authorize her to keep and dispose of as she shall see fit any thing in my will to the contrary notwithstanding. And lastly as to all the rest residue and remainder of my personal estate goods and chattels of what kind and nature whatsoever I give and bequeath the same unto Benajah A. GEER and I hereby evoke all former wills by me made. In witness whereof I have hereunto set my hand and seal this twenty third day of June in the year of our Lord one thousand eight hundred and twenty eight.

Gurdon GEER

Signed sealed published and declared by the above named Gurdon GEER to be his last will and testament in the presence of us who have hereunto subscribed our names as witnesses in the presence of the Testator

Alvah HAND
Seneca L. HAND

Will of Mary GOLDY

In the name of God amen I Mary GOLDY of the Borough of Williamsport, County of Lycoming & State of Pennsylvania widow being old & inform of body & of sound and disposing mind and memory do make and declare this to be my last will and Testament in manner following, that is to say I order all my just debts be paid, funeral expenses & charges of proving this will be in the first place fully paid & satisfied and after the payment thereof & every part thereof, I give bequeath and devise to my son in law Robert A. McMURRAY all my property real personal and mixed Except the sum of twenty dollars which is in the hands of James ELLIOT or Thomas LLOYD, which sum shall be equally divided between my three daughters viz. Aches THROP, Saray McMURRAY & Harriet ELLIOT, which distribution shall be made immediately after my death the Balance of my property of whatsoever kind or interest I do bequeath & devise to said R.A. McMURRAY as aforesaid and I do hereby nominate, constitute and appoint Robert A. McMURRAY of Williamsport Lycoming County, Pennsylvania Sole Executor of this my last will, revoking and avoiding all former wills and Testaments. In witness whereof I the said Testator Mary GOLDY have to this my last will and testament set my hand and seal this 30th September A.D. 1843.

Mary GOLDY

Signed sealed published & declared by the said Testator Mary GOLDY as and for her last will and Testament in presence of us who in her presence & at her request & in presence of each other have subscribed our hands as Witnesses thereto

E. COVERT
A.D. WILSON

Will of James GREENE

I, James GREENE of Brokenstraw Township, Warren County and Commonwealth of Pennsylvania, being of sound mind, In the name of God Amen. Do make this my Last Will and Testament - And first Give my Soul to God, and my Body to the Grave, and second that after my Doctors Bills and Funeral expenses are paid -

To my Daughter Abigail McKEE I give and bequeath my house and Lot in Youngsville during her life and afterward to James Gorton McKEE and his heirs forever.

I also give and bequeath to my daughter Abigail McKEE my beds, bedding and all my household furniture. I also have given my son James GREENE twenty Dollars which I think his portion.

I also give to each of my other children namely, Christopher GREENE, Nancy OLNEY, Alanson GREENE and Polly TUTTLE each of them five dollars in our year after my Decease.

I also give and bequeath to my son on law John McKEE my Tan Yard and Lot.

As Witness my hand and Seal this fifteenth day of March in the year of our Lord one Thousand eight hundred and forty two.

James GREENE

In presence of .

George BATES
James S. DAVIS

Will of Jonathan GUNNELL

In the name of God amen. I Jonathan GUNNEL of Hempfield township, in the County of Westmoreland, being of sound and disposing mind, memory and understanding - Thanks to Almighty God for the same - being mindful of my mentality do make and constitute this my last will and testament.

First and principally, I recommend my immortal spirit to God who gave it in hopes of a joyful resurrection and my body to the Earth, when it shall please God to separate my soul and body to be buried decently at the discretion of my executor. And as to such worldly estate wherewith it hath pleased God to bless me, I give and dispose thereof as follows. Item it is my will and I do bequeath unto my beloved wife Pamelia GUNEL all and every of my goods and chattels which are left at the time of my death, after the payment of my just debts and funeral expenses, during her natural life time or so long as she shall remain my widow, and if she should marry again after my deceased my will then is that she only have one good bed and the whole of the parlor and kitchen furniture which shall belong to me at the time of my decease. Further, it is my will that if my beloved wife Pamilia should marry or after her death, that my effects or the residue thereof not disposed of, shall be equally divided between my children to wit, Corben GUNEL, Beverly GUNEL, John GUNEL, and Kitty GUNEL. I do nominate and appoint my beloved wife Pamila GUNEL to be my sole Executrix of this my last will and testament. I publish and declare this and none other to be my last will and testament. In witness whereof I have here unto set my hand and seal the twentieth day of July in the year of our lord one thousand eight hundred and thirty one. 1831.

Jonathan GUNNELL

Signed and sealed in the presence of

George MECKLING
George ROBINSON

Will of William HARVEY

In the name of God Amen. The fifteenth day of February in the year of our Lord one thousand eight hundred and forty four I William HARVEY of the county of Butler Franklin Township State of Pennsylvania being of sound mind and memory but calling to mind the frail tenure of this life and that it is appointed that all must died, do make and ordain this my last will and testament in the mode and manner folloiwng, to wit first I recommend my soul to Almighty God who gave it and the disposal of my body I leave entirely to the discretion of my executor, wishing to be interred in a decent manner my property my Books and all that I have I allow to give to Mr. George KING and his wife except my large bible which I allow William MOORE to get all the money that is or may be coming to me from any person I allow George KING the executor of this my last will and testament to collect and after the funeral expense and all other lawful demands be paid if there be any balance left I allow him to get it, my spectacles I allow to Mrs. KING I do hereby appoint George KING executor of this my last will and testament hereby Revoking all former wills by me made and in testimony thereof I have set my hand and seal the day and year above written.

William HARVEY

Signed sealed and published and delivered by the above named William HARVEY to be his last will and testament in the presence of us and at his request and in his presence have subscribed our names as witnesses hereunto

Hugh STEVENSON
Rosannah MOORE

Will of Patrick HIGGINS

In the name of God Amen. I Patrick HIGGINS, being in sound mind and perfect memory, do hereby Acknowledge this Instrument to be my last Will and Testament, in the presence of Almighty God. First after my funeral expenses are paid, out of what moneys and Effects I do possess or may hereafter possess until I leave this world. Other balance, I leave and bequeath to my loving friend Hugh McDONNALD for his great fatherly care and attention and Expenses which he has been at during my illness and before and Also do hereby authorise Solomon G. KREPPS to pay over to Hugh McDONNALD what money he has or may have coming for my Services in his hands or may come into his hands Now or at any time hereafter. 3rdly I do and hereby appoint my dear and loving friend Hugh McDONNALD to be my sole Executor to this my last will and testament in the presence of God Amen done in the presence of this 18th day of August 1826.

Patrick HIGGINS

Test.
Jno. SHELDON
J.R. THORNTON
James SUITE

Will of Asher HUNTINGTON

In the name of God Amen I Asher HUNTINGTON of the Borough of Athens in the County of Bradford and State of Pennsylvania do make and publish this my last will and testament in manner and form following. That is to say First it is my will and I order and direct the payment of all my just debts, funeral expenses, and the expenses of settling my estate. Second I give and bequeath to my beloved wife Lydia HUNTINGTON all the real and personal estate of which I may die possessing for and during her natural life all household furniture including beds bedding and wearing apparel to be hers absolutely forever and after her decease I give and bequeath to my son Charles O. HUNTINGTON all the real and personal estate as above mentioned except the personal goods which is above given to my wife Lydia absolutely in her own right. And I do hereby appoint my son Charles O HUNTINGTON sole executor of this my last will and testament and hereby revoke all former wills y me at any time heretofore made. In witness whereof I have herewith set my hand and seal the 9th day of January A.D. 1857.

Asher HUNTINGTON seal

Signed sealed pronounced and declared by Asher HUNTINGTON the testator to be his last will and testament in the presence of us who at his request and in his presence and in the presences of each other have hereto subscribed our names as witnesses

H.L. SCOTT
James N. WELLS

Will of Frederick KEMMERER

I Frederic KEMMERER yet sound of mind and memory though feeble and weak of body and strength knowing that we are uncertain when the hour will strike that we have to leave this world therefore I make through the will of God this day my last will and testament to wit viz.

It is my sincere will in the name of God that my daughter Elisabeth the wife of Timothy *GEITNER* shall be and is hereby adopted my only sole and lawful heir of all I at present own on which can be considered my property personal and house furniture all and singular effects outstanding monies etc.

In order to have this my last will and testament after my departure when my body is deposited in my grave executed I hereby appoint constitute and adopt my son-in-law Timothy *GEITNER* as executor for that purpose. In testimony whereof I have here unto set my hand and seal this twenty fifth day of August Anno Domini one thousand eight hundred & forty one 1841.

Frederic KEMMERER

Witness present at signing
Charles SEIP
John F. HALBACK

Will of Andrew LIVELY

In the name of God, Amen.

I Andrew LIVELY of the City of Lancaster and State of Pennsylvania, late butcher, being weak in body but of sound and well disposing mind, memory and understanding, blessed be God for the same, Do make and publish this my last Will and Testament in manner and form following, to wit:

First it is my Will and I do order and direct that all my just debts and funeral expenses be paid and satisfied das soon as can be after my decease.

Item. I give and bequeath unto my beloved Wife Elizabeth during her natural life, or so long as she remains my widow, all that certain Dwelling house and Lot or piece of Ground thereto belonging, situate on the East side of Prince Street in the City of Lancaster aforesaid, with all the appurtenances thereto belonging, at present occupied by myself, and also all my personal property that may remain after the payment of my just debts and funeral expenses as aforesaid. All which my said real and personal estate, I do order and direct, shall be for the sole use, benefit and behoof of my said Wife Elizabeth during herlife or widowhood as aforesaid.

Item. It is my Will and I do order and direct that after the decease of my said Wife, or the expiration of her widowhood as aforesaid, the said Dwelling house and Lot or piece of Ground thereto belonging shall be sold by my hereinafter named executors, or the survivor of them, to the best advantage, at either public or private sale, and I hereby authorize and empower my said Executors, or the survivor of them, to give a good and lawful Deed or Deeds of conveyance for the same to the purchaser or purchasers thereof in fee simple, and the proceeds arising from such sale of my said real estate and the personal estate remaining after the decease of my said Wife, or the expiration of her widowhood as aforesaid, shall be equally divided to and amongst my seven Daughters, or their several heirs and assigns, in Share and Share alike.

And lastly I nominate, constitute and appoint my said Wife Elizabeth executrix, and my trusty friend Charles SHAEFFER executor of this my last Will and Testament, hereby revoking and making null and void all former Will or Wills by me heretofore made, and declaring this and no other to be my last Will and Testament.

In Witness whereof I have hereunto set my hand and seal this second day of June A. Domini 1839.

Andrew LIVELY

Signed, sealed, published, pronounced and declared by the Testator to be his last Will and Testament, in the presence of us, who in his presence and at his request have subscribed our names hereunto as witnesses.

The word "present" interlined before signing
Jacob ----, Jacob WEAVER, M. CARPENTER

Will of Robert LYON

Know all men by these presents that I Robert LYON of Point Township in the County of Northumberland and the State of Pennsylvania being weak in body but of sound mind and disposing memory for which I am thankful to the supreme disposer of all human events Do make ordain & confirm this to be my last Will and Testament and do hereby dispose at what worldly property I may died possessed of or Intitled to in the following manner, to wit -

I order and direct that all my funeral expenses and all my legal debts be paid.

Item. I give and bequeath unto my beloved wife Elizabeth all arrears of or what may be coming to me of my United States and state pension at the time of my death as well as all my estate real personal and mixed to her and her heirs forever this in consideration of her dutiful affection and attention to me during my life and I hope that my son Robert his family & her may live in same house a heretofore until some more suitably arrangement if any may be made by them, and I do hereby nominate & appoint my friend John BOYD of Northumberland Town executor of this my last Will and Testament. In Testimony whereof I have hereunto set my hand and seal the twelfth day of August Anno Domini one thousand eight hundred and twenty three.

Robert LYON

Signed Sealed and Delivered in the presence of

Isaac NEFF
John COOKE

Will of Samuel McCLAUGHAN

In the name of God Amen.

I Samuel McCLAUGHIN of Blacklick Township, Indiana County, Pennsylvania, being weak in body but sound in mind and memory do make and publish this my last will and testament in manner and form following that is to say first I do give and bequeath to my son James McCLAUGHEN the sum of one dollar and I do give and bequeath and hereby devise to my beloved grandchildren Silas HAMILTON and Rebecca Jane his wife and their heirs and assigns all that my messuage or tenement situate lying and being in the State of Pennsylvania obtained by me for services during the Revolution together with all the real estate that I now own or may hereafter be seized of within the State of Pennsylvania or elsewhere to hold to them the said Silas HAMILTON and Jane his wife their heirs or assigns forever and lastly as to all the rest residue and remainder of my personal estate goods or chattels I give and bequeath the said Silas HAMILTON and Rebecca Jane his wife and I do hereby appoint the said Silas HAMILTON my sole executor of this my last will and testament hereby revoking all former wills made by me.

In witness thereof I have hereunto set my hand and seal the 30th day of May in the year of our Lord one thousand eight hundred and twenty five.

J.M. BISHOP for Samuel McCLAUGHEN

Signed & sealed in presence of

J.M. BISHOP
Joseph LANGBERG

Will of Tabith McCLURE

I Tabitha McCLURE widow of William McCLURE of Jefferson Township Allegheny Co., State of Pennsylvania deceased do make and publish this my last will and testament hereby revoking and making void all former wills by me at any time heretofore made and first I desire that my body be decently interred with a respectable head and foot stone placed to my grave and as to such worldly estate as it hath pleased God to intrust me with I dispose of the same as follows.

First I direct that all my debts and funeral expenses be paid as soon after my decease as possible out of the first money that shall come into the hands of my executors.

I will and bequeath my ----- to Tabitha REED daughter of Walker REED. I will and bequeath my tables to Lydia WILSON wife of Thomas WILSON. I will and bequeath to Julia FLOWERS one bed and bedding if she returns, if not the bed and bedding I direct to be given to Hannah FLOWERS wife of Jacob FLOWERS. The balance of my property personal and mixed I will and bequeath to my daughter Mary WILSON and I do hereby make and ordain my esteemed friend James McGREW executor of this my last will and testament.

In witness whereof I Tabitha McCLURE the testatrix have to this my will set my hand and seal this eleventh day of October in the year of our Lord one thousand eight hundred and sixty-two.

Tabitha McCLURE

The above written instrument was signed sealed delivered and published by the above woman and she being blind the same was carefully and deliberately read to her in presence of us,

R.M. BLACKBURN
E.J. CURRY

Will of John MILLER 3rd

Know all men by these presents that I John MILER of the Borough of Wilkes-Barre in the county of Luzerne being weak in body but of sound mind do make and publish this my last Will and Testament as follows first my Funeral expenses and just debts to be paid.

Secondly I give and bequeath to my wife Peggy the House wherein I now live my Household furniture goods chattels and effects, whatsoever for and during her natural life and after her decease what may remain thereof, I give and bequeath to my six children to wit, John, Peggy intermarried with Isaac WICKIZER, Nancy intermarried with James DICKSON, Christiana, Catherena, Effy, equally to be divided between them and I hereby appoint my wife Peggy executrix of this my last Will and Testament hereby revoking all others. In Witness where of I have hereunto set my hand and seal this twenty second day of May AD 1815.

John MILLER

Luzerne Co.
 I Isaac HARTZELL Register for the Probate of Wills and granting letters of administrator in and for the County of Luzerne do certify the foregoing will of John MILLER late of Wilkes-Barre Deceased to be a True and complete exemplification of the original remaining filed in the Register's office of said county and Recorded in will Book A, page 291 of the Records of said County In Witness whereof I have hereunto set my hand and seal of office at Wilkes-Barre this 31 Day of December 1824.

 Isaac HARTZELL Register

Will of Solomon MOSS

In the name of God, Amen. I Solomon MOSS of Troy, in the County of Bradford and State of Pennsylvania, being weak in body, but of sound and perfect mind and memory, blessed be Almighty God for the same do make and publish this my last will and testament in manner and form following, I give and bequeath unto my eldest son Solomon MOSS Jr. all my pension money due from the fourth of March last which is to be continued during my life, whom I hereby appoint sole executor off this my last will and testament. In witness where of I have hereunto set my hand and seal the twelfth day of August, in the year of our Lord one thousand eight hundred and twenty two.

Solomon MOSS

Signed, sealed, published and declared by the above named Solomon MOSS to be his last will and testament in the presence of us who have hereunto subscribed our names as witnesses in the presesnce of the testator

Jeremiah COLE
Alanson TAYLOR
Walter YATES

Will of Joseph RAYNSFORD

In the name of God Amen

I Joseph RAYNSFORD of the Borough of Montrose in the County of Susquehanna and State of Pennsylvania, being sick and infirm in body but of sound and disposing mind, and being desirous of settling and disposing of all my estate and effects during my life time, that no difficulty or misconstruction may arise, or be given to my intentions for disposing thereof after my decease do make and declare this instrument of writing to be my last will and testament.

Having been dependent upon my only son Joshua W. RAYNSFORD for my maintenance and Support during a number of years, and the Congress of the United State at this last session having passed a law granting me a pension for eight dollars per month during my natural life, for services rendered my Country as a soldier of the Revolution, which annuity when received will constitute my chief estate, now in consideration of the Support and maintenance received form my said son, I do will and bequeath unto my said son Joshua W. RAYNSFORD all the money or monies which I may receive, or have in my possession, derived from my said pension or which my be due and owing to me from the Government of the United State under the Law of Congress aforesaid, at the time of my decease, Out of which if is my will that all my just debts and funeral charges be paid and I do hereby nominate and appoint my said son Joshua W. RAYNSFORD Executor, of this my last will and testament, revoking all former wills by me made.

In witness whereof I the said Joseph RAYNSFORD have hereunto set my hand and seal this seventeenth day of November A.D. 1830.

Joseph RAYNSFORD

Signed, sealed, published & declared by Joseph RAYNSFORD to be his last will & testament in the presence of us who at his request & in his presence have subscribed our names as witness thereto

T.F. THULER
Hariette AVERY
Asa DIMOCK Jr.

Will of Robert RICHIE

In the name of God Amen. I, Robert RICHIE of the Borough of Lewistown in the County of Mifflin & State of Pennsylvania, being far advanced in years, sick and weak in body but of sound mind, memory and understanding (praised be God for the same) & considering the certainty of death and the uncertainty of the time thereof, and to the end I may be the better prepared to leave this world whenever it shall please God to call me hence, do therefore make and declare this my last will and testament in manner following, this is to say -

First. I will that after my death my body be decently interred at the discretion of my daughter Martha McCLEAR who I hereby appoint, constitute & ordain nto be the sole executrix of this my last will & testament.

Secondly. I will that all my just debts, funeral charges & the necessary costs of Registering the will be first paid out of my estate.

Thirdly. It is my will that the pension money which shall be due to me at my decease by the United State & by the State of Pennsylvania be drawn by John B. BUCHER of Harrisburg and by him to be paid to my said daughter, to whim I will the same, together with all the other monies due to me as also all my personal property of whatsoever description or nature it may be.

In witness whereof I have hereunto set my hand & seal this fifth day of August in the year of our Lord, one thousand eight hundred and twenty five.

Robert RICHIE

Signed, sealed, published, & declared by Robert RICHIE in the presence of us as his last will.

John PIERCE
Henry FERER

Will of Henry ROWLAND

In the name of God Amen! I Henry ROWLAND Sr. being sick and in a low condition but of Perfect mind and Memory and calling to remembrance that it appointed unto all men to once die and after that the Judgment do make and ordain this my last Will and Testament.

And first I commend My Soul to God that gave it, and my body to be buried in decent Christian Burial and after my debts are paid the balance of all my property real and personal is to be left in the possession of my wife Mary for her use as long as she continues my widow and when her Time with my property is expired by death or marriage the Remainder is to be equally divided among my Children.

And I do hereby Constitute and appoint my two sons William and John to execute this my last will and testament after my decease. In testimony whereof I have hereunto set my hand and seal this eighth day of February in the year of our Lord one thousand eight hundred & twenty one.

Henry ROWLAND

Signed sealed and delivered in the presence of

Jonathan ROWLAND
David GORDON
Benjamin FOSTER

Will of Margaret SIMMONS

In the name of God Amen, I Margaret SIMMONS of Washington Penn. do make and publish this my last will and testament, in manner and form following, that is to say,

1st I order and direct my executor hereinafter mentioned, to pay all my just debts and funeral expenses as soon after my decease as may be convenient.

2nd I will and devise my tract of land of one hundred and sixty acres, situate in Cass County Iowa, being the Southwest quarter of Section 11 in township Seventy five and Range thirty four, to my daughter Mulvina L. ALLEN wife of John ALLEN, to the use of her and her heirs and assigns forever. I also will and bequeath to my said daughter Mulvina L. ALLEN all my personal estate.

Lastly, I nominate and appoint Joseph W. HENDERSON of Washington Pennsylvania my executor of this my last will and testament.

Margaret SIMMONS

Signed, sealed, published and declared to be her last will and testament in the presence of us, who have witnessed the same at her request, in her presence and in the presence of each other.

Jane McDERMOT
Wm. WYLIE

Dec. 18th 1863

Will of John SMITH 3rd

I John SMITH of Milford township Mifflin County and State of Pennsylvania, considering the uncertainty of this mortal life and being of sound mind and memory [blessed be the Almighty God for the same) do make and publish this my last will and testament. In the manner and form following, this is to say, first my will is that my granddaughter Sarah PENCE, have a Bedstead Bed and bedding, that now stands in the back room, and one year old Heifer. Item. I will to my granddaughter Catherine PENCE, a bedstead bed and bedding that now stands in the front room. Item. My will than is that my Executor shall have the remainder of my personal property appraised and sold as soon as convenient after my decease, and likewise my Real estate, as soon as a sale can be affected to advantage, and that all my just debtors that shall be by me owing at my death, together with my funeral expenses, and all charges touching the proving of, or otherwise concerning this my will, shall in the first place out of my real and personal estate be fully paid and satisfy'd and from and after payment thereof and subject thereto then my will is my son John Receive ten dollars, and the balance of Money arising from the sales of my real and personal estate be then equally divided amongst my three children, viz.: Catherine, Barbara, and John, share and share alike. And I make and ordain James PATTERSON, to be executor of this my last will and testament hereby revoking all former wills by me made.

In Witness whereof I have hereunto set my hand and seal the twelfth day of May in the year of our Lord one thousand eight hundred & twenty two.

Johannes SMITH

Signed sealed published and declared by the above named John SMITH to be his last will and testament in presence of us who at his request and in his presence have subscribed our names as witnesses thereto

Joseph KELLY
Soma JONES

Will of Enoch VARNUM

In the name of God Amen I Enoch *VERNUM* of Washington township Butler County and State of Pennsylvania, considering the uncertainty of this mortal life, and being of sound mind and memory blessed be Almighty God for the same, and being desirous to settle my worldly affairs while I have yet capacity so to do, do make and publish this my last will and testament, hereby revoking all former wills by me at any time heretofore made, and First and principally I commend my soul to God who gave it in hope of a joyful resurrection, and my body to the Earth (when it shall please God to separate my soul and body) to be buried decently and as to such worldly estate wherewith it hath pleased God to entrust me I give and dispose thereof as followeth. Second I give and bequeath unto my son Philip *VERNUM* the East end of my farm on which he now lives, bounded on the west by line run by Hugh McKEE county surveyor containing one hundred and fifty acres on condition that he pay all Judgments and costs thereof now in any way against me on the Prothonotary's Docket. Third. I give and bequeath unto my son Wm. *VERNUM* the west end of my farm on which he now lives Bounded on the East by a line run by Hugh McKEE dividing my farm, also all other Real estate Personal property, all debts coming to me and all money on hand, now or at my deceased on condition that he pay, all my debts my necessary funeral expenses and pay to my daughter Catharine MEALS one hundred Dollars in four equal annual payments commencing one year after my decease.

Fourth. I give and bequeath unto my daughter Catharine MEALS one hundred Dollars to be paid by Wm. *VERNUM* my son in four equal annual payments commencing one year after my decease.

Fifth and lastly I hereby appoint W.B. RIDDLE and James YOUNG of Washington Township Butler County Penna. my Sole Executors in the adjustment of all my temporal affairs. In testimony whereof I have hereunto set my hand and seal this twenty second day of January in the year of our Lord one thousand eight hundred and fifty two.

Enoch VARNUM

Signed sealed and delivered by the above named Enoch VARNUM to be his last will and testament in the presence of us who at his request have subscribed our names as witnesses thereto

John FOLWELL
A.J. HUTCHISON

Will of Isaac WALLS

In the Name of God Amen I Isaac WALLS being week of body but of sound Mind and Memory Do make this my last will and Testament in Manner and form as follows that is to say first Commit my soul to allmighty God who give it and My body to the Earth to be Decently Entered by my executor Herein after mentioned.

2nd and I do appoint Jesse FULTON of Patton Township and Centre county to be my Executor in full and thirdly after all my Debts and funeral expenses are paid I will and bequeath unto my Loving son Isaac WALLS all the Remainder if any in Witness whereof I Have Here unto set my Hand and seal this Twelfth Day of June AD one thousand Eight hundred twenty one.

Isaac WALLS

Witness present

Joseph POTTER
John FULTON

Will of John WOODS

The last will and testament of me John WOODS of Ross Township in the County of Allegheny and state of Pennsylvania. Item. I order and direct that all my just debts be paid also I order and direct that my Executors pay to my sister-in-law Fanny WOODS what may appear to be due her further I order and direct that my said executors pay to *Cisor* FISHER (a man of collour) what may appear to be right for service done me. Item. I will and bequeath to my eldest son James a lot of ground containing ten acres, adjoining Wm. CARSON on the east, Wm. DAVIS on the north and the rest of my land on the west, the place whereon he now resides. Item. I will and bequeath the rest of my estate real as well as personal to my beloved wife Sarah during her life or widowhood. Item. Immediately after the death of my wife Sarah it is my will that my estate real as well as personal be sold and the proceeds divided as my wife Sarah shall direct in her will but if she should marry or died without making a will I order and direct that my eldest son James will receive fifty dollars less than my other sons at the final settlement except the lot before mentioned which is to be his exclusive of this last divide, my other sons John, Joseph, Presley, Jeremiah & Peter shall each share alike. Item. If as aforesaid my wife should marry or die without making a will I order and direct that Fanny GRAY, Elizabeth MAYBERY, & Eleanor SPRAGUE shall each receive one hundred dollars also Rebecca STEVENSON and Sarah WOODS shall each receive one hundred and fifty dollars. Lastly I hereby constitute and ordain James & John WOODS my eldest and second sons to be the executors of this my last will and testament hereby revoking all former wills by me made. In testimony whereof I have hereunto set my hand and seal this ninth day of July A.D. One thousand eight hundred and nineteen.

John WOODS

Signed sealed and delivered in presence of

R. HILANDS
Wm. CHAPLIN

APPENDIX B

PENSION PAYMENT REGULATIONS AND FORMS

From Robert Mayo, M.D., Army and Navy Pension Laws and Bounty Land Laws of the United States, Including Sundry Resolutions of Congress, from 1776 to 1861: Executed at the Department of the Interior (Washington, DC: W.H. & O.H. Morrison, 1861), Appendix III Regulations and Forms, pp. 620-628.

VII.   Circulars to Pension Agents Respecting Their Disbursements

[1.]

[Instructions and forms prescribed by the Second Comptroller to be observed by pension agents for keeping and stating their accounts for settlement at the Treasury.*]

Treasury Department
Second Comptroller's Office, June 10, 1833

SIR

The following instructions and forms for keeping and stating accounts for settlement at the Treasury, are prescribed to pension agents agreeably to the provisions of the 9th section of "An act to provide for the prompt settlement of public accounts," approved March 3, 1817.

Recent acts of Congress, on the subject of revolutionary and other pensioners, rendered necessary a revision of the instructions and forms heretofore issued from this office on the subject; in doing which care has been taken to bring together the detached forms and instructions which have been prescribed at different times, as occasion required, arranged in the proper order, altered to conform to existing laws, and so modified as to simplify the vouchers, as far as a proper regard to the safety of the Treasury and the interests of the pensioners will admit.

They are intended to supersede all former instructions issued on the same subject, and are now officially communicated for your guide on the subject-matter of them, after the first day of September, 1833.

A prospective operation is given to these instructions, in order to afford the agents an opportunity to circulate the information and forms among all the pensioners prior to the time of their taking effect.

After the 1st day of September 1833, all vouchers must be made out to conform substantially to these instructions, or they will be rejected at the Treasury.

J.R. THORNTON,
Second Comptroller

[*The instructions and forms annexed to, and made part of, the above circular, were modified and extended by the Comptroller, on the 1st of September, 1846, as here given. The circular letter of Comptroller Thornton was then adopted and prefixed to the amended instructions. – Editor]

To the agent for paying United States'
   Pensions at -------------.

Instructions, &c.

The following order will be observed in the several documents composing the voucher, viz.:

I. When application is made for the payment of a pension, the first thing that seems necessary is, that the identity of the person, in whose behalf the pension is claimed, should be established. This must be done agreeably to the prescribed form, marked A; and for widows pensioned by the War Department, agreeably to form marked E.

II. Under the provisions of the acts of 6th April, 1838, and 23rd August, 1842, where a pension has remained unclaimed by any pensioner, for the term of fourteen months after the same became due and payable, it cannot be paid by the pension agent, but application therefor must be made to the Treasury of the United States through the Third Auditor, if the pension certificate issued from the War Department, and through the Fourth Auditor, if it issued from the Navy Department. The usual vouchers will suffice, with the exception that additional proof of the identity of the pensioner will be required, according to form marked B. Each pension agent, immediately on the expiration of fourteen months subsequent to each semi annual payment, will certify to the office of the Second Comptroller a correct list, containing the name, rank, rate of pension, amount due, and time of last payment of each pensioner remaining unpaid on the roll of his agency, whose pension has been due and payable for the term of fourteen months prior to the date of such certificate. When, however, a new pensioner is placed on the roll, or an old pension is renewed, the fourteen months commences, running from the semi annual payment next after the date of his, or her, pension certificate, and not from the commencement or renewal of the pension.

III. When an attorney shall make application for a pension, be the rank of the pensioner what it may, he must deposit with you a power of attorney in his favor, duly acknowledged, and dated on or subsequent to the day on which the pension claimed became due, and within ninety days of the time of his applying for payment, and also his own affidavit that said power was not given him by reason of any sale, transfer or mortgage of said pension; and the execution of the

power must be in the presence of at least one witness, other than the magistrate before whom it is acknowledged. These papers must be made out in strict conformity to the subjoined form, marked C.

IV. In all cases of payments upon a power of attorney, the justice of the peace or magistrate before whom it is executed, must have lodged with the agent the certificate of the clerk of some court of record, under seal of the court, that he is legally authorized to act as such; and also a paper bearing his proper signature, certified to be such by the clerk of some court of record.

V. It is advisable, and is so recommended, that pension agents procure and place in a book the signature and seals of clerks of the different courts within their agency, who may be authorized to certify as to the powers, the better to detect, by comparison of the signatures and seals, impositions that may be attempted.

VI. Under the provisions of the acts of 2d March, 1829, and 29th June, 1840, in case of the death of any pensioner, the arrears of pension due to him at the time of his death must be paid –
1st. "To the widow of the deceased pensioner, or to her attorney," proving herself to be such before a court of record.
2d. If there be no widow, then the executor or administrator on the estate of such pensioner, for the sole and exclusive benefit of the children, to be by him distributed among them in equal shares; and the law of 1849 declares that the arrears of pension "shall not be considered a part of the assets of said estate, nor liable to be applied to the payment of the debts of said estate in any case whatever."
3d. In case of the death of any pensioner who is a widow leaving children, the amount of pension due at the time of her death must be paid to the executor or administrator for the benefit of her children, as directed in the foregoing paragraph.
4. In case of the death of any pensioner, whether male or female, leaving children, the amount of pension may be paid to any one or each of them, as they may prefer, without the intervention of an administrator. If one of the children is selected to receive the mount due, he, or she, must produce a power of attorney from the others for that purpose, duly authenticated. The oath of identity for the widow, or child, of a deceased pensioner, must be according to form F; and when they appoint an attorney, the power of attorney must be according to form marked G.
5th. If there be no widow, child, or children, then the amount due such pensioner at the of his death must be paid to the legal representatives of the decedent.
6th. When an executor or administrator shall apply for the pension due to a deceased person, he must deposit with you a certificate of the clerk of the court,

judge of probate, register of wills, ordinary or surrogate, (as the case may be), stating that he is duly authorized to act in that capacity on the estate of the deceased pensioner, and, if a male, that it has been proved to his satisfaction that there is no widow of said pensioner living.

VII. In all cases of payments being made of moneys due a deceased pensioner, the original pension certificate must be surrendered, as evidence of the identity of the person to whom the pension claimed was due, or other substantial evidence of such identity must be produced in case such certificate cannot be obtained for surrendry; and that due search and inquiry have been made for the said certificate, and that it cannot be found. The date of said pensioner's death must be proved before a court of record.

VIII. A certificate of the facts proved must be obtained from the clerk of the court. It is not necessary for the clerk to give the evidence in detail, but only to state the facts that have been proved, and certify, under his seal of office, that the testimony adduced was satisfactory to the court, according to form marked H; and in case a pension certificate is legally withheld from a pensioner, he (or she, as the case may be,) must produce evidence of identity and the facts, agreeable to the form marked I.

IX. When a pensioner is placed under guardianship, the guardian applying for a pension must, in addition to the evidence of the pensioner's identity, deposit with you a certificate from the proper authority, that he is, at that time, acting in that capacity; and also satisfactory evidence that his ward was living at the date the pension claimed became due. The identity of the pensioner in such cases must be established under the form herewith, marked D.

X. For all payments made by you duplicate receipts must be taken, (agreeably to the subjoined form, marked K,) one of which you will forward, with your quarterly accounts, to the third Auditor of the Treasury for pensions under the War Department, and to the Fourth Auditor for pension under the Navy Department; and in all cases where a pensioner or attorney makes a mark, from inability to write his name, there must be a witness thereto, otherwise such receipt, or voucher, will not be admitted at the Treasury.*
* By the second section of "An act making appropriations for the payment of the revolutionary and other pensioners of the United States," approved February 22d, 1840, pension agents are authorized to administer all oaths required to be administered to pensioner, attorneys of pensioners, or others, in the course of the preparation of papers for the payment of pensions under any of the laws of Congress; and to charge and received the same compensation therefor as the laws of the State in which the agent is located allow to magistrates for similar services.

A.

State of   ,

          County,   §:

Be it known, that before me,   , a   , in and for the county aforesaid, duly authorized by law to administer oaths, personally appeared   and made oath, in due form of law, that he is the identical person named in an original certificate in his possession, of which (I certify) the following is a true copy:†

[Here insert a copy of the certificate of pension.]

that he now resides in   , and has resided there for the space of   years past; and that previous thereto he resided in   ; and that he has not been employed, or paid, in the army, navy, or marine service of the United States from the   day of   to   .

[Signed] A---------B----------.

Sworn and subscribed, this   day of   18   , before me.

C----------D----------, J.P.

† Where the pension has been increased since the certificate has been given, the magistrate will note the fact.

In case of a *revolutionary* pensioner, the part of the above form, which requires the pensioner to depose that "he has not been employed, or paid," &c., is not required. The law of April 30, 1844, forbids the payment of an invalid pension to any person, while in either of the military services, "unless the disability, for which the pension was granted be such as to have occasioned his employment in a lower grade."

B.

State of   ,

          County,   §:

I,   , a magistrate in the county above named, do hereby certify that I have the most satisfactory evidence, ‡ viz.: that   , who has this day appeared before me to take the oath of identity, is the identical person named in the pension certificate, which he has exhibited before me, number   , and bearing date at the War Office, the   day of   , 18   ; and signed by *Secretary of War*

Given under my hand, at   , on the day and year above written.

C----------D----------, J.P.

State of   ,
       County,   §:

      I,   , clerk of the   court, of the county and State aforesaid, do hereby certify that   is a justice of the peace, in and for said county, duly commissioned and qualified; that his commission was dated on the   of   , 18   , and will expire on the   day of   , 18   , and that his signature above written is genuine.

      Given under my hand and the seal of said county, this   day of   , 18   .

[L.S.]   C----------C----------, clerk.

‡ Here state what the evidence is; whether personal knowledge, or the affidavits of respectable persons, giving their names.

      Where the pensioner is personally known to the agent, and he will certify to his identity, the above form (B) may be dispensed with.

C.

      Know all men by these presents, That I,   , of   , (a) pensioner of the United States, do hereby constitute and appoint   my true and lawful attorney, for me, in my name, to receive from the agent of the United States for paying pensions in   , State of   , my pension from the   day of   , 18   , to the   day of   , 18   .

      Witness my hand and seal, this   day of   , 18   .

                            [Signed] A----------B----------.

      Sealed and delivered in the presence of

[L.S.]   C----------D----------, J.P.

State of   ,
       County,   §:

      Be it known, That on the   day of   , 18   , before the subscriber, a in and for said county, duly authorized by law to administer oaths, personally appeared   , above named, and acknowledged the foregoing power of attorney to be his act and deed. In testimony whereof I have hereunto set my hand, the day and year last above mentioned.

                            C----------D----------, J.P.

* State of   ,
       County,   §:

      Be it known, That on the   day of   , before me, a   , in and for said county, duly authorized by law to administer oaths, personally appeared   , the attorney named in the foregoing power of attorney, and made oath that he had no interest whatever in the money he is authorized to receive, by virtue of

the foregoing power of attorney, either by any pledge, mortgage, sale, assignment, or transfer, and that he does not know or believe that the same has been so disposed of to any person whatever.

Sworn and subscribed the day and year last above mentioned before me,

C---------D----------, J.P.

(*a*) In this blank insert the word invalid, or revolutionary, as the case may be.

*The above form of oath is necessary for the attorneys of widows pensioned under the laws of July 4, 1836, and July 7, 1838, and subsequent laws continuing their provisions. For other pensions, the old form of attorney's oath is sufficient; but as the above form is valid in all cases, to prevent mistakes, its general adoption is advised.

D.

State of   ,
         County,   §:

Be it known, That before me,   , a   , in and for said county, duly authorized by law to administer oaths, personally appeared   , guardian of   , and made oath in due form of law that the said   is still living, and is the identical person named in the original certificate in his possession, of which (I certify) the following is a true copy:

[*Here insert a copy of his pension certificate.*]

that he now resides in   , and has resided there for the space of   years past; and that previous thereto he resided in   .

---------- ----------, *guardian*

Sworn and subscribed this   day of   , 18 , before me.

C---------D----------, J.P.

E.

Form of an affidavit to be made by a widow placed on the pension rolls of the War Department.

State [or Territory] of   ,}
County of   }   §:

Be it known, That before me   , a   , duly authorized by law to administer oaths, in and for the county aforesaid, personally appeared   , and

made oath in due from of law, that she is the identical person named in an original certificate in her possession, of which (I certify) the following is a true copy:

[*Here insert a copy of her certificate of pension.*]

that she has not intermarried, but continues of the widow of the above mentioned   ; and, that she now resides in   , and has resided there for the space of   years past; and that previous thereto she resided in   ; of the truth of which statements I am fully satisfied.

[Signed.] A----------- B----------

Sworn to and subscribed to   day of   , 18   , before me.

C----------D----------, J.P.

[In cases where a widow was placed on the pension roll under the act of March 3d, 1843, and *had surrendered her certificate*, on the expiration of her pension, previously to the renewal of widows' pensions by the act of June 17, 1844, the following form may be substituted for the above. But as widows who were never placed on the pension list prior to the act of June, 1844, whose claims have subsequently been admitted, will be furnished with pension certificates from the War Department, *they* will be required to insert a copy of their certificates in the oath of identity, agreeably to the foregoing form.]

State of   ,   County -- §
    Be it known, That before me, a   in and for the county aforesaid, duly authorized by law to administer oaths, personally appeared   , and made oath, in due form of law, that she is the identical person who drew a pension under the act of 4th March, 1843, on account of the revolutionary service of her husband, the late   , at the rate of $ per annum; that she now makes this affidavit for the purpose of drawing a pension under the act of Congress passed on the 17th of June, 1844, entitled, "An act to continue the pension of certain widows," that she has not intermarried, but continues to be a widow; that she now resided in   , in the county of   , and State of   , and has resided there for the space of   years past; and that previous thereto she resided in

.

[Signed.] A----------- B----------

Sworn to and subscribed this   day of   , 18   , before me.

C----------D----------, J.P.

I certify that the above named affidavit is personally known to me, and that she is the same individual who drew a pension as stated by her in the foregoing affidavit.

C----------D----------, J.P.

F.

Oath of identity for the widow or child of a deceased pensioner.*

State of   ,   County -- §

Be it known, That before me,   , a   , in and for the county aforesaid, duly authorized by law to administer oaths, personally appeared   and made oath, in due form of law, that she is the widow (or son, or daughter, as the case may be,) of   , the identical person who was a pensioner, and is now dead, and   to whom a certificate of pension was issued, which is herewith surrendered.

That the deceased pensioner resided in   .

[Signed.] A----------- B----------

Sworn to and subscribed to   day of   , 18   , before me.

C----------D----------, J.P.

*The oath of identity for the executor or administrator of a deceased pensioner may be in the foregoing form substituting "executor" (or "administrator," as the case may be,) for "widow," &c.

G.

Power of attorney for the widow or child of a deceased pensioner.

Know all men by these presents, That I   , of   in the county of   , State of   , widow, (or child, as the case may be,) of   , who was a pensioner of the United States, do hereby constitute and appoint   my true and lawful attorney, for me, and in my name, to receive from the agent of the United States for paying pensions in   , State of   , the balance of said pension from the   day of   , 18   , to the   day of   , 18   , being the day of his death.

Witness my hand and seal this   day of   , 18   .

[Signed.] A----------- B----------

Sealed and delivered in presence of
[L.S.]

C---------D----------, J.P.

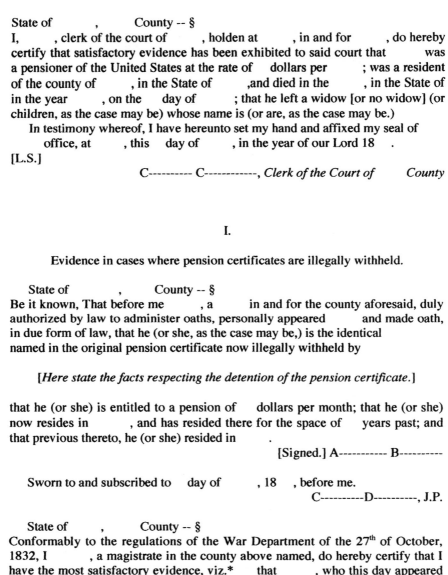

H.

Certificate of the court as to the death of the pensioner.

State of   ,   County -- §
I,   , clerk of the court of   , holden at   , in and for   , do hereby
certify that satisfactory evidence has been exhibited to said court that   was
a pensioner of the United States at the rate of   dollars per   ; was a resident
of the county of   , in the State of   ,and died in the   , in the State of
in the year   , on the   day of   ; that he left a widow [or no widow] (or
children, as the case may be) whose name is (or are, as the case may be.)
   In testimony whereof, I have hereunto set my hand and affixed my seal of
        office, at   , this   day of   , in the year of our Lord 18   .
[L.S.]
                C---------- C------------, *Clerk of the Court of*   County

I.

Evidence in cases where pension certificates are illegally withheld.

State of   ,   County -- §
Be it known, That before me   , a   in and for the county aforesaid, duly
authorized by law to administer oaths, personally appeared   and made oath,
in due form of law, that he (or she, as the case may be,) is the identical
named in the original pension certificate now illegally withheld by

   [*Here state the facts respecting the detention of the pension certificate.*]

that he (or she) is entitled to a pension of   dollars per month; that he (or she)
now resides in   , and has resided there for the space of   years past; and
that previous thereto, he (or she) resided in   .
                     [Signed.] A---------- B----------

Sworn to and subscribed to   day of   , 18   , before me.
                          C---------D----------, J.P.

State of   ,   County -- §
Conformably to the regulations of the War Department of the 27th of October,
1832, I   , a magistrate in the county above named, do hereby certify that I
have the most satisfactory evidence, viz.*   that   , who this day appeared
before me to take the oath of identity, is the identical pensioner he (or she)
declares himself (or herself) to be in the annexed affidavit; and I am also

satisfied that the statement made by him (or her) in relation to the pension certificate is true.

Given under my hand at   , the day and year above written.

C----------- D----------, J.P.

I,   , clerk of the court of   county, certify that   is a magistrate as above, and that the foregoing certificate, purporting to be his is genuine.

In testimony whereof, I have hereunto affixed my seal of office, and subscribed my name, this   day of   , in the year

[L.S.]

C---------- C----------, *Clerk of the Court of*   *County*

* Here state what the evidence is; whether personal knowledge, or the affidavits of respectable persons – giving their names.

If the pension agent acts as a magistrate in the case, the certificate of the clerk of the court is not required.

K.

Received of   , agent for paying pensions,   dollars   cents, being for   month's pension due to   from the   day of   , 18   , to the   day of   , 18   , for which I have signed duplicate receipts.

[Signed.] A---------- B----------

INDEX

ABBOT: Ebenezer, 1;
Lorenzo, JP, 244
ABBOTT: George W.M.,
294; John, 46
ABEL: John, 1
ABELL: Benjamin F., JP,
443
ABNER: Casper, 164
ACHESON: David, 374;
George, 456
ACKER: Christian, 1
ACKERMAN: Elizabeth
[KACHLEIN], 300
ACKLEY: Ahira, 1
ADAIR: Jonathan S., JP,
576
ADAM: Mary Catharine
[JAMISON], 289
ADAMS: A.V., 86;
Alexander, 597; Asa, 1;
Benjamin, 36, 76, 160,
316, 488, 545; Betsey, 2;
Deliverance, 1; Elizabeth,
2; Hannah, 1; Henry, 2;
Henry L., 68; Jacob, 1;
James, JP, 67, 124, 399,
592; Jedediah, 2; John, 2,
232, 279, 428, 543;
Joseph, 2, 43, 516; Mark,
1–2; Mary, 2; Mary
[PALMER], 431; Moses,
2; Olive, 1; Patrick, 16;
Samuel, 1; Sarah
[LIGHT], 336; Seth, 2;
Thomas, 1; William, 2, 43
ADDAMS: Abraham, JP,
315, 612; Catherine
[HUY], 281; Charles H.,
JP, 281; James H., 281;
Samuel, 281
ADDIS: William, 373, 542
AFFLICK: John, JP, 406
AGNEW: David, 53; James,
634; James C., 515; John,
33; Martin, 199; Richard
A., JP, 117; Samuel, 562
AIKEN: James C., 472;
John, Capt., 235; Joseph,
2, 346, 421; Thomas, 2

AIKENS: D.D., 62
AITKENS: William, 9
AKALEY: John, 3
AKE: David, 9; Joseph B.,
JP, 115
AKERIGHT: Absalom, 164
AKERS: Ralph, 266; Sarah
[HOLLENSHEAD], 266;
William, 3
AKINS: Anne Catharina
[HEMINGER], 253
AKRIGHT: Ellen, 164
ALBERTI: George F., 304
ALBERTSON: John, JP,
174
ALBREE: George, 155
ALBRIGHT: George, 332;
Jonathan, JP, 260, 274;
Philip, 170, 462, 517
ALDEN: Ann E., 3;
Bradford R., 3; David, 3;
Elizabeth, 3; Judah, Capt.,
107; Mary M., 3; Richard,
JP, 299; Roger, Brigade
Major, 3; Sally, 3; Susan,
3
ALDERMAN: Betsey
[WILLIAMS], 603;
Chauncey, 603; Homer,
603; Timothy Jr., JP, 324
ALESWORTH: John W., 9
ALEXANDER: Betsey
[WEBSTER], 588;
Elizabeth, 4; James, 242;
James A., JP, 129;
Jonathan, 30, 326; Joseph,
3; M.W., JP, 515; Mary
Ann [HARE], 242;
Michael, 242; N., 148;
Robert, 4; Sarah, 3;
William, 4; William G.,
102, 293; William, JP,
324
ALFORD: Benedict, 7;
Huldah, 7; John, 4
ALGER: Henry, JP, 420
ALIWINE: Lawrence, 7
ALLBRINGS: John, 496

ALLEGANY: Benjamin,
Capt., 444
ALLEN: Annanias, Capt.,
91; Asa, 41; Asher, 4;
Conrad, 6; David, 4, 518;
David S., 4; Elizabeth, 4;
George, 5; Isaac, JP, 325,
438; Jacob, 5; Jacob, Jr.,
5; Jacob, Sr., 5; James, 5,
167; Jane [KELLY], 307;
John, 5, 513, 659;
Jonathan G., 73; Lewis,
33, 52, 92, 120, 139, 142,
149, 182–83, 222, 224,
275, 321, 331, 336, 369,
417, 425, 440, 442, 450,
456, 459, 489, 494, 502,
512, 522, 524, 530, 555,
578, 586, 611, 618; Luke,
5; Mary, 5; Mathew,
Capt., 424; Mulvina L.
[SIMMONS], 513, 659;
Nehemiah, 4; Phineas, 4;
Polly, 4; Richard F., 435;
Robert, 45, 98, 141, 145,
236, 332, 409, 493, 509,
517, 563, 589; Samuel,
307; Susannah, 5;
Thomas W., 222; Titus, 6;
William, 5; William G.,
233; William R., JP, 299
ALLENDER: James, JP, 45
ALLGAIER: Catherine, 6;
George, 6; Jacob, 6;
Jonathan, 6, 227, 323,
460, 493; Joseph, 6;
Mary, 6; Sebastian, 6
ALLING: Ethan, 597
ALLIS: Moses, 6
ALLISON: A., 312; A.G.,
95, 125, 296, 406, 443,
526, 553, 605; A.J., 393;
A.O., 25; Alexander, 627;
Alexander S., 6;
Catharine, 6–7, 627;
Elizabeth [BRICKELL],
65; Elizabeth [SCOTT],
479; Eveline Catharine, 6,
627; H.G., 448;

(ALLISON, continued)

Isabella [MITCHELL], 399; James Jr., 62; James, JP, 6; John B., 7, 237; John M., 6; Jonathan, 6, 491; Margaret, 6, 627; Mary, 6–7, 627; Robert, 6–7, 73; Thomas, 7; William, 627; William *D.*, 6
ALLSHOUSE: David, 7; Henry, 7
ALLSWORTH: Benjamin, 458
ALLWINE: Lawrence, 7; Phebe, 7
ALLYN: Benajah A., 210
ALSHOUSE: David, 7
ALSWORTH: Andrew, 7; Elizabeth, 7; Mary, 7; William, 167
ALTEMUS: E.J., 246
ALTER: Henry H., 411; Jacob, 346; Solomon, 5, 24, 96, 145, 168, 215, 222, 252, 326, 402, 418, 425, 471, 590
ALTHOUSE: John, 629
ALVORD: Benedict, 7; Daniel, JP, 300; Esther [SEELY], 500
ALWAND: Peter, 632
ALWINE: Magdelane, 629
ALWORTH: James, 8; Polly [ROGERS], 480
AMBERSON: Capt., 375; J.B., 8; Mary, 8; W. Smith, 246; William, 8
AMENT: George, 8; Henry, 8; Henry, Jr., 8
AMES: Elisha, 8; Ephraim, 8
AMEY: Joseph, 8; Samuel, 8; William, 8
AMMENS: D., JP, 230
AMWEG: William S., 217
AMY: Alfred E., 21
ANDERS: John, 9; Sarah, 9
ANDERSON: Adam, 9; Amos, Capt., 508; Andrew, 9; Ann, 11; Anne D., 133; Augustine, 9; *Barnard*, 382; Benjamin, 10; Capt., 270; Charlotte, 9; David, JP,

103; Eleanor, 9; Eliza V., 10; Elizabeth, 9–10; Ellen, 10; Enoch L., 9; Enoch Lucius, 10; Enoch, 1st, Capt., 10; Enoch, 2nd, Capt., 10; Enoch, Capt., 9; Evaline, 10; George, 10; Hannah, 9; Harriet [DAVIS], 133; Isaac, 10; J.T., 217, 592; James, 10, 177, 230; John, 10; John M., 9; John, JP, 32; Joseph, 9, 162; Maria, 10; Mary, 9–10; *Matthias*, 11; Nancy, 9; Patrick, Capt., 243; Rachel [McKINLEY], 382; Rebecca, 10; Robert, 9, 137; Samuel, 11; Sarah, 9–10; Thomas, 9; Thomas D., 9; Thomas F., 9; Thomas, 1st, 11; Thomas, 2nd, 11; William, 9–11, 15, 514, 566; William G., 145; William V., 416
ANDES: Col., 523; Frederick, Col., 24
ANDRESS: Conrad B., 201; Elizabeth [FULMER], 201; Joseph, 201
ANDREW: J., 288, 587; Marey [DAY], 136; Sally, 12
ANDREWS: A.R., 400; Abraham, 12; Annis, 11; Arthur, 11; Arthur, Jr., 11; Chester, 12; D.B., 121; David, 12; Drayton, 298; Hannah [RIMMEY], 473; J., 176, 288, 387, 546; J.T., JP, 132; James, 12; Jeremiah, 402; Jonathan, 12, 300, 438, 451; Robert, 402; Sally, 12; William, JP, 429
ANDRUS: Clement, 12; Daniel, 443; George, JP, 112; Mirza, 12
ANDY: Daniel, 13; Mary [ANTRUM], 13
ANGEL: Daniel, 12; Henry, 12; John, 591
ANGST: Daniel, 13; Nicholas, 13
ANLE: Col., 488

ANTE: Philip, 13
ANTES: Col., 179, 528; Frederic, Col., 344; Jacob, 420
ANTHONY: J.B., 363
ANTREIM: John, 13; Margaretta, 13; William, 13
ANTRUM: Amos, 13; Catharine, 13; Daniel, 13; Elizabeth, 13; Hannah, 13; Jacob, 13; John, 13; Margaret, 13; Mary, 13; Samuel, 13; Sarah, 13; William, 13
APPELGATE: Daniel, 13
APPELTON: Richard, 411
APPLEBACH: Daniel, JP, 251; Paul, 251
APPLEGATE: Joseph, 13
APPLING: William, JP, 595
ARBAUGH: Henry, 374
ARBUCKLE: William, 9, 115, 126, 287
ARBUTHNOT: David, 298
ARCHBOLD: Edward, 119
ARCHER: George, 167; Hannah [HUNT], 13, 628; John, 13; Stephen, 14
ARCHIBALD: John, JP, 581, 601; William, 581
ARD: Sarah [OKESON], 425
ARDIS: John W., 26
ARMAND: Col., 33, 494
ARMBRUSTER: Catherine, 14; Mary, 14; Matthias, 14; Sophie, 14
ARMITAGE: Deborah Ann, 14; Jane K., 14; Sarah, 14; Shewbart, 14; Shubert, 14; Thomas Jefferson, 14
ARMOND: Col., 245
ARMOR: Margaret [ZIEGLER], 624
ARMOUR: Charles, 354
ARMS: Lucy [ROGERS], 480
ARMSDEN: Abraham, 14; Samuel, 14; Submitty, 14
ARMSTRONG: Allen, 231; Ebenezer, 14; Edward, 320;

(ARMSTRONG, continued)

Elizabeth [McCOY], 373; Francis, 20; George, 15; James, 56, 318, 320; James H., 15; James, Sr., 15; John, 80, 231, 355, 360; Milton, 1; Nancy, 14; S.M., JP, 6; Thomas, JP, 27, 52, 133
ARND: John, Capt., 80
ARNDT: Benjamin F., JP, 100; Jonathan, Capt., 513
ARNOLD: Abraham, 15; Abraham, Jr., 15; Andrew, 427; Capt., 600; Col., 188, 589; Eve, 15; Gen., 330; George, 15, 117; George E., 620; Henry, 15; John C., Dr., 175; Jonathan, 15, 519; Levi, 13, 602; William, 54, 170, 416, 438, 481
ARNOT: John, 461
ARNOUT: Hannah [DEWITT], 139
ARNSDEN: Thomas, JP, 514
ARTER: Michael, 330
ARTHUR: John, 15; Milton, 446
ARTIS: Chloe, 16; Col., 173; Isaac, 16
ARTMAN: Jesse, 172
ASH: George W., JP, 110, 487; Sarah, 107
ASHBURN: Nancy [LONGSTRETH], 345
ASHBURNER: Thomas, 134, 263, 341, 381, 397, 498, 611
ASHBY: Mary, 16; Nathan, Capt., 16
ASHCORN: Charles, 136
ASHCROFT: Charles D., 204
ASHFIELD: John, JP, 459
ASHLEY: Moses, Capt., 390; Zenas, 16
ASHMAN: George J., JP, 567
ASHMEAD: Jacob, Capt., 440; John W., 487, 533
ASHTON: Ann, 16; George, 16; Hannah, 16; John Jr., 304; Levi, 16;

Maria M. [KEEMLE], 304
ASKAM: Burton, 15
ASTLEY: Thomas, 79, 179, 586, 591
ATCHESON: John, 348
ATENBURG: G.H., 211–12
ATHERTON: Anson, JP, 45, 96
ATHSHIRE: Hannah [CORNELIUS], 115
ATKINS: Isaiah, 12; Josiah, 16
ATKINSON: Charles, 16; Lukens, JP, 220; Samuel C., 222; Thomas, JP, 129, 232, 316, 348, 604
ATLEE: Jonathan L., 336; Washington L., 336
ATTICK: Catharine [SUTTON], 550; Peter, 550
ATWATER: Amos, JP, 371; Stephen, 17
ATWOOD: Elijah, 17; Jonathan M., 145, 388
AUCHMUTY: Ann, 17; Hannah, 17; R., JP, 485; Robert, 17, 537; S. Perry, 485; Samuel, 17
AUGHINBAUGH: Peter, 159
AUKEN: Capt., 467
AULD: James, 17; John, JP, 310; William, JP, 618
AUSTIN: Aaron E., JP, 17; Amos, 447; Andrew A., 18; Bissell, 18; Cyrenus, 18; David, 17; Eliphalet, 17; George, JP, 1, 29, 130, 206, 262, 356; Laura, 18; Lewis, 17; N., 73; Nathaniel, 17; Polly, 18; Rachel, 18; Samuel, 18; Sibell, 17
AUSTINE: Andrew A., 18
AUTMAN: Stephen, 480
AVERILL: Abigail, 570; Elijah, 570
AVERY: Charles, JP, 47, 75, 109, 111, 131, 147, 224, 285, 342, 420, 453, 468, 535, 569; Christopher, 18; Cyrus, JP, 286; Ezekiel, 18; George, 18; George W.,

19; Hariette, 656; Hubbard, 147; Ira, JP, 130, 147, 170, 445, 558; Laura M. [EDWARDS], 165; Rosanna [BRUSH], 72
AWLL: Charles W., 104
AXE: Frederick, 18
AXTELL: Daniel, 591; Eliab, 472
AYERS: Jonathan, 300; Jonathan Jr., 418; Lt. Col., 496; Squire, JP, 129, 238
AYLESWORTH: Esther [GRAY], 221; Ira H., 221; Philip, 221; Polly [GRAY], 221
AYRE: Col., 495
AYRES: William, 181, 589

BABBIT: Elijah, 103
BABCOCK: Almon, JP, 365, 447; Amy, 18; Capt., 623; Clarinda, 18; Denison A., 18; Ezekiel G., 18; F., 450; Francis M., 18; G.B., 448; George, JP, 74; Isaac, 18; J.B.G., JP, 72, 448; Lucy, 18; Mary, 18; Nancy [REEVES], 465; Rachel [ROGERS], 479; Sally, 18; Valeria A., 72
BACHE: Richard, 458
BACHELDON: John, 487; Sarah R., 487
BACHELOR: Ruth [KELLOGG], 307
BACHER: Jacob, 19; Solomon, 19
BACHMAN: Christopher, 372; Jacob, Col., 393
BACHUS: George, 19
BACKER: Jacob, 19
BACKUS: John C., 527; Myron, JP, 200, 221
BACON: Andrew, 19; *Chozens,* 19; Hannah, 19; Josiah, 85; Nehemiah, 19
BADABOUGH: John M., 285
BADGER: J., JP, 26, 328, 498

BAGALEY: W., 20;
William, 35, 113, 162,
221, 232, 240, 535
BAGALY: William, 15,
279, 292, 439, 463
BAGARD: Samuel J., 313
BAGGS: James, 19; James,
Jr., 19; John, 19
BAGNALL: George Jr., 535
BAGSHAW: W., 217
BAHN: George, 21
BAILEY: Amos G., JP, 75,
286; Benjamin F., JP,
108, 196, 468; Capt., 590;
Daniel, JP, 92; Eliza Ann,
168; F.G., 58, 89, 469,
621; F.W., 105; Francis
G., 5, 267; Jonathan, JP,
180; Lydia R., 537;
Milton, 4, 333; Platt,
Capt., 472; Robert, 20;
Robert, JP, 140; Roswell,
20; Samuel, 19, 40, 75,
78, 83, 109, 209–10, 232,
275, 450, 455, 503, 517,
614, 617; Sylvester, 20;
William, 191, 373, 618;
William Robert, 537;
Zylpha, 20
BAILY: Ellis, 240; Milton,
240; Reuben, 240;
William, Major, 123
BAIN: George, 448, 561;
Hannah, 20; John, 20
BAINBRIDGE: Edward
W., 407
BAIRD: Francis, 20;
George, 44–45, 52, 136,
149, 255, 280, 296, 356,
411, 450, 489, 619; Henry
C., JP, 280; James P.,
540; Jane [HART], 20;
Margaret, 20; Nancy,
210; Robert, 20; Samuel,
129; William, 380
BAISLEY: John, 237
BAKER: Abner, 20; Ann
Emily, 21; Capt., 26, 409;
Christiana, 21; Edith
[SWAZE], 552; Edward,
JP, 112; Eli, Jr., 21;
Elizabeth, 21; Francis,
381; Frederick, 21;
George, 144; J. Rodman,
385; J.W., 20; Jacob, 21;
359; James, 21; Job, 83;

John, 21, 189; John C.,
384; Jonas, 215; Julia
[BRODHEAD], 66;
Lucius, 88; Michael, JP,
464; Phebe G.
[GOODELL], 215; Philip,
21; Robert, 171, 256;
Thomas, 164; William,
66, 221; William J., 26
BALAM: Eve [DUEY],
143; Michael, 143
BALCOM: Nathaniel, 22
BALDERSTON: Jacob,
618
BALDING: Elizabeth, 22;
Moses, 22
BALDRIDGE: Joseph, 381;
Samuel, 383; William T.,
383
BALDWIN: Abed, 200;
Anna, 22; Caroline, 22;
D., 37, 433; David, 553;
Dudley, 126, 203, 234,
277, 294, 451, 569; E.,
144; Elizabeth, 22; H.,
272; Isaac, JP, 279, 540;
Jabez, 22; Jared R., JP,
200; Jonathan, 22, 270;
Joseph, 199; Lucy, 22;
Mark, JP, 529, 606; Mary
A. [SHERER], 505;
Miles, 22; Moses, 22;
Nancy, 22; Peleg, 22;
Phebe, 22; Samuel, 22;
Seth, 23; Sidney, 338;
Stephen, 136; Submit, 22;
T.L., 346; Thomas, 22,
244; Walter W., 412
BALDY: Peter, 493;
Stephen, 151
BALL: Amos Washington,
299; Elizabeth M.
[McCORMICK], 372;
G.J., JP, 210; Henry, 144;
Lydia [CROWELL], 23;
Samuel, 372; Thomas,
Lt.Col., 23; William,
Capt., 545
BALLARD: Ann, 23; D.W.,
128; Elizabeth, 23; J.A.P.,
272; Lucretia, 23;
Margaret, 23; Martha, 23;
Mary, 23; Mary Ann, 23;
Myron, JP, 323; O.P., 68,
86, 114, 349, 572; Orrin
P., 22, 98; Rhoda, 23;

Stephen, 23; Was., 20;
William A., Capt., 114
BALLIARD: Col., 197
BALLIET: Col., 155
BALLINGER: Emanuel, 23
BALLIOT: Col., 359, 466
BALMER: Anna Mariah,
24; Jacob, 24
BALPH: Benjamin, 247
BANDWELL: Lt., 496
BANES: Mary [FESMIRE],
182
BANGER: Timothy, 197,
266, 528
BANGHART: Sarah, 384;
Thomas, 384
BANKES: Andrew, 24
BANKS: John, 304;
William, 237
BANKSON: Capt., 333,
409, 429
BANNATYNE: Amelia A.,
453
BANNER: Capt., 237
BANNON: Eli, JP, 433;
Jeremiah, 24; Jeremiah,
Jr., 24; Nancy, 24
BAPTISTE: John, 24;
Susannah, 24
BAR: John, 24
BARBER: Col., 326; David,
538; James, 24; L., 69;
Major, 103; Robert, 24,
292; S.B., JP, 24;
Thomas, 24; Zenus, 476
BARCHERT: Christian, 25
BARCKERT: Christian, 25
BARCLAY: A., JP, 319;
Andrew, JP, 497; Charles
R., 252; George G., 362;
J.T., 157; John, 228;
Jonathan S., 419; Joseph,
594; Stephen, 25
BARCROFT: Stacy, 267,
606; Stacy B., 29, 247,
458, 506
BARD: Richard, JP, 266;
Robert M., 432, 627
BARE: Catharine, 25;
Jacob, 25
BARGE: John, 305
BARGENHOFF: William,
25
BARGH: William, 136
BARKELOW: James, 25
BARKELY: Robert, 25

BARKER: Capt., 406; Harvey, 292; Joshua, JP, 412; Lewis, 88; Matthew, JP, 392
BARKHERT: Christian, 25
BARKLEY: Iddings, JP, 465
BARLET: Johannes, 30; John, 30; Paul, 26
BARLEY: Francis, JP, 597
BARLIN: Eli, 8
BARLOW: Joseph, 12; Lucius, 131; Thomas, JP, 308
BARNARD: Capt., 622; Elizabeth, 26; James C., 26; John, 26, 78; Joseph C., 26; Parker, 26; Robert W., 26; Susanna B., 26; William H., 355
BARNDOLLAR: Frederick, 26; Jacob, 136
BARNES: Abigail, 27; Ann, 27; Ann [DEYO], 143; Ashbe, 471; Barnet, 151; Betsey [SWAZE], 552; Britannia D., 499; Buell, JP, 339, 476, 546, 584; C., JP, 601; Charles, JP, 2, 349, 588; Charlton, 322; Chauncey, 78; Churchill, JP, 20, 22, 68, 390; Dolly, 26, 77–78; Eli, 78; Elias, 260; Elisha, 372; Eliza, 78; Ephraim, JP, 158; Ezra D., 97; *Gurden*, 26, 78; Hannah, 151; Hiram, 78; Jacob, 600; James, 26, 233; Joel, 26, 77; John, 26; John S., JP, 334, 430; Jonathan B., 586, 609; Laura, 78; Moses, 26; Polly, 78; R.D., 209; Roswell, 78; Sally [CHURCH], 97; Samuel, 27; Sarah [McCORMICK], 372; Sarah R., 27; Thomas, Capt., 451; William, 27; William H., 477, 480
BARNET: Jane [MURRY], 413; Robert, 27
BARNETT: Andrew, 27; George, JP, 71; Joseph, 27; William, 57, 151, 302, 353

BARNEY: B., JP, 38; Capt., 358; Harry, 31
BARNHARD: Daniel, 27; Naomi, 27
BARNHART: Catharine, 28; Elizabeth, 28; George P., 27; Henry, 28; Jacob, 28; John, 28; Maria, 28; Mary Sophia, 28; Naomi, 27; Sufiah, 28
BARNITZ: Charles A., 100; George, JP, 149, 182, 224, 265, 275, 331, 369, 425, 442, 450, 456, 459, 489, 586, 618; Samuel M., 567, 589
BARNS: Daniel H., 26; Harriet M., 76; Nancy S., 405; Richard, Col., 156
BARNSLEY: Jonathan, JP, 603–4
BARNUM: Eli, JP, 484; Stephen, 28; Zenus, 28
BARNWELL: Jane, 28; John, 28
BARR: Adam, 315; Amos, 394; Catharine, 28; Col., 123; David, 28; James, 28–29; Jane, 29; John, 24; John R., 474; John, JP, 178; Major, 38; Margaret, 578; Mary, 29; Robert, 29, 188; Samuel, 29, 51, 199, 474, 580; Susanna, 29; William, 29
BARRAL: Jacob, 29
BARREN: James, 29
BARRET: Capt., 329
BARRETT: Alonzo, 29; Amos, 29; Benjamin, 29; Charles, 29; George, 29; John, JP, 234; Jotham T., 29; Oliver, 29; Stephen, 29
BARRON: George, 217, 223, 348, 479, 494; James, 29; Robert, 30; Sophia, 30
BARROWCLIFF: William, 223
BARSTOW: Clarissa W. [WOODRUFF], 616; D.F., 82, 217, 303, 346, 392, 423, 616; David F., JP, 4, 183, 192–93; Oliver A., JP, 338; Seth T., 616

BARSTOWN: D.F., JP, 317, 334
BARTH: John, 638; Stephen, 30
BARTHOLOMEW: Benjamin, 30, 378; Capt., 39; Edward, 30; John, 30; Rabzamen, 330; Rachel, 30
BARTLESON: Nicholas, 293; Susannah, 3
BARTLETT: Ann M., 104; Calvin, 496; Christiana, 30; Ebenezer, 30; Isaac, 30; Jacob, 30; John, 30; Samuel, Capt., 390; Sybil, 30
BARTLEY: John, 31; William, 31
BARTLY: John, 436
BARTON: Benjamin, 80; Capt., 375; Col., 91; Cyrus, 152; Hannah E., 31; Henry, 31; Job, 31; John, 465, 510; Mary, 31
BARTRAM: George W., JP, 10
BARTRUM: John, JP, 466
BARVENAN: Susannah [WEAVER], 587
BARWICK: Sarah M., 44
BASFORD: J., 31; James, 31
BASS: Henry, 128; William, 534
BASSETT: Cyrus E., 407; Orville P., 96
BASSFORD: James, 31
BASTIAN: Jacob, 31
BATEMAN: John, 169
BATES: A. Jr., 454; Aaron Jr., 610, 613; *Benoni*, 31; Benony, 31; Capt., 78; Daniel, 31; David, 453; Ephraim, 31; George, 644; Luther P.,JP, 235; Walter, 325; William, 309
BATHRICK: Zebina, 444
BATHURST: Lawrence, 32; Rebecca, 32
BATSON: Ephraim, 387
BATTIN: John, JP, 16, 611; Samuel, 16, 611
BATTLE: Esther, 32; Justus, 32
BATTON: John, 32

BAUCHER: Jacob, 538
BAUER: Frederick, 32
BAUGH: Elizabeth, 32;
Henry, 32; Mary, 32;
Solomon, 32; Susan, 32
BAUM: Frederick, 32;
George S., 589; John, Sr.,
32; William J.C., Dr., 363
BAUMAN: Benjamin, 414
BAUMGADER: Henry, 33
BAUMGARDNER:
Godfrey, 251; Henry, 33;
Jacob, 287, 584
BAUMGARTEL: Leonard,
33
BAUS: David, JP, 428
BAUSHER: Philip, 33
BAUSMAN: Catharine, 33;
Charlotte, 33; Elizabeth,
33; Frederick, 33; Mary,
33; William, 33
BAVARD: James, 73
BAXTER: Col., 170
BAY: Robert, 33; Samuel,
305
BAYARD: George, 487
BAYLIE: George, 33; John,
33; Paul, 33; Robert, 33;
Samuel, 33; Sarah E., 33
BAYLOR: Col., 370;
George, 33; Walker,
Capt., 370
BAYMES: T., 212
BEABOUT: John, 34
BEACH: Charry, 34;
Cynthia E., 34; Daniel,
34; Elihu, 34; Ezekiel, 34;
Jay F., 34; Lebbeus, JP,
34, 298; Mercy, 34;
Reuben, 34; Reuben B.,
34
BEADER: Henry, JP, 305
BEAKMAN: Benjamin, 61
BEAL: Sharpless, 401
BEALE: Charles, 283;
Joseph, 515; Joshua, 386
BEALER: George, 34;
John, 620
BEALL: Elijah, JP, 453
BEALOR: George, 34
BEALS: Shepherd, JP, 286
BEAM: Lizzie, 495;
Thomas L., JP, 495
BEAN: Aaron N., JP, 177;
Charles Y., 34; David D.,
318; James, 34; James T.,

34; Jonathan, 17; Joshua
C., 34; Mary L., 34;
Samuel H., 34; Sarah, 34
BEANS: William, 35
BEAR: Andrew, Capt., 231
BEARD: Frederick, 35;
George, Capt., 38;
Magdalin, 35
BEARDSLEY: Albert, JP,
200; Harriett, 70; Levi, 70
BEATLY: James, 35
BEATTIE: John, JP, 35
BEATTY: Ann, 35; Charles
C., 35; Christiana, 35; F.,
JP, 620; James Sr., 35;
Jane, 36; John, 35, 617;
John 1st, 36; Mary, 35;
Reading, 35, 411;
Reading B., 35; Susan,
35; Thomas, 36; William
P., JP, 612
BEATY: Hugh, 36; John
2nd, 36; Mary, 36
BEAVER: Adam, 36;
Benjamin, 36; George,
37; Joseph, Col., 25, 402;
Peter, 55; Thomas, 9
BECHTEL: John, 236
BECHTOL: Samuel, 566
BECHTOLD: John, 142
BECK: Ann, 37; Eli S., 585;
Henrietta [WALTERS],
581; James, 421;
Susannah, 620; Thomas,
37
BECKER: Henry, 369, 513;
Michael, 400
BECKTELL: George, 37
BECKWITH: Benjamin,
37; Elijah, JP, 38, 439;
John, 7, 30, 389, 432;
Rice, 37; Rosanna, 37;
Samuel, 174; Susan
[EATINGER], 174;
William, 37
BEDEL: Robert, 550
BEDELL: David, 126; Julia
[CUMMING], 126
BEDFORD: Catharine, 452;
J.G., 336; Jonathan G.,
452
BEDKINS: Capt., 13
BEEBE: Barzilla, Capt., 18;
Capt., 577; David, 37;
Horace L., 437; Lemuel,
38; Reuben, 38

BEECHER: Barbara, 630;
Benjamin, 629; Catharine,
630; Elizabeth, 630;
George, 629–30; Jacob,
629; John, 38, 629; Lidea,
629; Magdalene, 630;
Margaret, 630; Mary,
629; Samuel, 629;
William, 629
BEEKARTH: John F., 38
BEEMAN: E.N., 168;
Ebenezer, 38; Nelson, 57;
Zina, 57
BEEMER: Wilson, 117
BEENIN: Capt., 345
BEENLEE: Elizabeth
[CAMPBELL], 85;
Joseph, 85
BEER: Addy, 38; James,
38; Robert, 38; Thomas,
38
BEERBOWER: John, JP,
278
BEERS: Zachariah, 39
BEESON: C.H., 581; Isaac,
75, 98, 107, 109, 135,
216, 255, 279, 335, 383,
485, 532, 550, 596, 611;
James M., 114; Richard,
JP, 475; W., 620;
William, 540
BEETAM: Jacob, 39
BEETLE: Col., 232
BEETMAN: Samuel, 310
BEETON: William, 39
BEETTON: William, 39
BEHM: Abner, 6; Abraham,
JP, 395
BEHNAY: Peter, 39
BEHNEY: Peter, 39
BEICHER: John, 630
BEIDELMAN: Abraham,
65
BEIDLER: Conrad, 6
BEIGART: Adam, 323
BEITCHMAN: Frederick
S., 221
BEITENMAN: John, JP,
326
BELAIR: Lewis D., JP, 436
BELAISE: Lewis D., JP,
292
BELCHER: John, 93; John,
Lt., 167; Sarah
[FULLER], 200; William,
200

BELDEN: Benjamin, 39;
Betsey [FANVER], 177;
George W., 114; Oliver,
39; Sylvia, 39
BELDING: E.P., Capt.,
364; Lemuel C., M.D., 57
BELKNAP: Abel, 268;
Calvin, 39
BELL: Asariah, 40; Capt.,
26, 574; Edward, 61;
George, 40; George N.,
290; J.B., JP, 419; James,
39–40, 200; James E.,
198, 466, 599; James R.,
40; Jane, 40; John, 40, 59,
252; John Jr., 40; Mary,
40; Patterson, Col., 11;
Robert, 39, 585; Samuel
C., 214, 404; Samuel W.,
305, 437, 523; Samuel,
JP, 61, 315; T., Capt., 29;
W.F., 313; W.M., 122,
380, 451, 507; William,
1–2, 34, 70, 76, 84, 106,
126, 147, 178, 203, 213,
238, 241, 253, 265, 307,
334, 398, 411–12, 420,
460, 569, 578, 591;
William D., JP, 119;
William M., 37, 78, 160,
170, 214, 268, 358, 373,
424, 431, 433, 519, 531;
William, Jr., 9, 21, 23, 37,
200
BELLAMY: Asa, 40;
Eunice, 40
BELLAS: Martha, 40
BELLESFELT: Peter, 41
BELLOR: Jacob, JP, 301
BELLOWS: Benjamin,
Col., 559; Curtis J., 439
BELT: Levin, 8
BELTZ: Eve [SOLT], 525
BELTZHOOVER: H., JP,
310; Jacob, 532
BELZ: Henry, JP, 281
BEMAN: Rufus, 19
BEMESS: Jonas, 41
BEMIS: John, 23
BEMISS: Jonas, 41
BEMUS: Daniel, 360
BENDER: Emericus, JP,
416; George L., 41;
Jacob, 416; John, 41;
John E., 41; Lewis, 41;
Margaret [FORD], 190;

Richard, 41; Samuel, 30;
Sarah, 538
BENEDICT: A., 211–12;
J.D., JP, 605; Mamre
[GILLET], 211; William,
JP, 66, 82
BENFORD: Cyrus, 77, 348;
James, 350
BENHAM: G.H., 37;
William D., 226;
Zedekiah, 41
BENJAMIN: Asa, 41;
Judah, 41; Polly, 41;
Reuben, 41; Susan, 41
BENNER: Hetty [PLANK],
447; P., Jr., 364
BENNET: Elias, 42; Hiram,
JP, 485; John, 42; Lydia,
42; Miles, 42; Rufus, 42;
Samuel, JP, 606; Sarah,
42; Solomon, JP, 261;
Zilia, 169
BENNETT: Amos, 42;
Capt., 470; David, 42;
Elias, 42; Esther
[McCLOUD], 370; H.C.,
438; Isaac, JP, 347; John,
42, 56, 494; Lucy, 42;
Lydia, 42; Olive, 42;
Pamelia, 42; Stephen, 42;
Wealthy L., 42; William,
42; William W., 514;
Ziba, 218, 607
BENSINGER: Daniel, 43
BENSON: Capt., 115;
Elizabeth, 254; Henry,
242; N.F., 5; Richard,
503; Simeon B., 271;
William, 204, 242, 335,
365
BENTLEY: Benjamin, 30;
Henry, 43; James, JP,
603; Sampson, 43
BENTLY: Hannah, 457;
James, 457
BENTON: Capt., 50, 582;
George P., 461; John,
234; Lydia, 43; Zadock,
43
BENTZ: Christian, JP, 324;
George Z., 249
BERDAN: John, JP, 479
BERGER: Christian, JP, 35,
257
BERGMEYER: Christiana,
43; Daniel, 43

BERGSTRESSER: Ann
[AUCHMUTY], 17
BERK: Capt., 372
BERKSHIRE: Ralph, JP,
14
BERLIN: Abraham, JP,
351; Isaac, 43; Israel, 43;
Jacob, 95; Mary, 43
BERNARD: John, 78
BERNER: Mary
[STALEY], 534
BERNHARD: Jacob, 27
BERNHART: Naomi, 27
BERRELL: Jeremiah, 287
BERRIMAN: R., 27
BERRY: Catharine, 44;
Daniel, 43; Dorcas, 43;
James, 44; Peter, 44;
William, 196, 377
BERSON: Isaac, 100
BERTOLETTE:
Benneville, 213, 246,
521, 547
BERTOTELL: M., 483
BERWICK: John, 44; Sarah
M., 44
BESS: Anning, 44; Edward,
44; Samuel, 44, 255
BEST: John, 44, 411;
William, 44, 268
BETHELL: Mary, 82;
Robert Jr., 82; William,
JP, 82
BETTERLY: Ann, 44;
William, 44
BETTES: Mary, 44;
Nathaniel, 44; Nathaniel
M.W., 44
BETTIS: Mary, 44;
Nathaniel, 44
BETTS: Silas, 498
BETZ: Elizabeth, 181;
Ezekiel, 99; Henry, 13,
38, 132, 175, 181, 193,
197, 252, 265, 270–71,
323, 334, 353, 416–17,
460, 483, 623; Peter, 45;
Samuel, 251; William,
234, 279, 288, 417
BEUCK: Jonathan, JP, 187
BEVANS: M., 452
BEVIER: Simon, 45
BEVINGTON: Thomas, 45
BICKEL: Catharine, 45;
Jacob, 45; John Jr., 45,
277; John M., 341;

(BICKEL, continued)

Jonathan, 45, 149, 315; Samuel E., 45
BICKING: George, 151; George H., 466, 475; Robert, 72
BICKNELL: Robert T., 323, 334
BIDDEN: Capt., 260
BIDDLE: Capt., 8, 226, 480; Charles, 368; Charles J., 203, 302; Eliza J., 45; George, 45; Jesse, 45; Martha, 45; Mary L., 45; Robert, 603
BIDLACK: Benjamin, 45
BIDWELL: J.C., 604; John C., 268
BIEBER: George, 32; William S., JP, 173; William, JP, 322
BIECHER: Barbara, 630; Benjamin, 629; Catharine, 630; Elizabeth, 630; George, 629–30; Jacob, 629; John, 629–30; Lidea, 629; Magdalene, 630; Margaret, 630; Mary, 629; Samuel, 629; William, 629
BIERCE: Columbus, 46; Hannah B., 46; Lucinda, 46; Lucius V., 2, 46; Lucretia, 46; Marcus A., 46; William, 46; William W., 46
BIETZ: Eleanor, 48; Michael, 48
BIGELOW: James H., 46
BIGHAM: John, JP, 307
BIGNELL: Thomas G., 492
BILDERBACK: Charles, 462
BILL: Abiel, 46; Earl, JP, 89; Peleg, 46
BILLGER: George, 543
BILLINGS: Benjamin, JP, 154; David, 445; Otis, 166
BILLS: Elizabeth, 46; Huldah, 129; William, 46
BILMAN: Dewalt, 46
BINDER: William, 358
BINGHAM: Joseph, 400; Ozias, 46; Roxa, 46;

Sarah, 46; Thomas, 46, 325; *Tryphena*, 46
BINNS: M.C., 34
BINSWANGER: Isidore, 306
BIRCH: Christina, 47; Herman, JP, 79, 121, 432, 483; John, 47, 178, 451; Mary, 47; Rebecca, 47; Sarah, 47; Thomas, 47
BIRCHARD: Mary [FAWROT], 179
***BIRCHFIELD*:** Thomas, 47
BIRD: Andrew, 47; Mark, Col., 621
BIRKHART: Adam, 38, 631; Barbara, 631; Catharine, 631; Eve, 631; Frederick, 38, 631; Jacob, 631; John, 631–32; John F., 38; Margareth, 631
BIRNE: *Lucius V.*, 204
BIRRIMAN: R., 176
BIRTH: Archibald, 47; Sarah, 47
BISBEE: Affa, 47; Betsy, 47; Hannah, 47; James, 47; Jane, 47; John, 47; Leah, 47; Levi, 47; Lydia, 47; Martin, 47; Noah, 47; Sally, 47; Seth, 47
BISBING: Jacob, 102
BISEL: Levi, 5, 96, 590
BISHOFF: Capt., 528; Major, 452
BISHOP: Calvin S., 453; J.M., 652; Joel, 48; John, 14; Joseph B., 76; Phebe, 48; Polly [WOODCOCK], 615; Thomas, JP, 453
BISON: Charles, 48
BISSEL: Capt., 88
BISSELL: Peter M., JP, 17; Samuel N., 555
BISSHAM: John, 375; Samuel, 59, 78, 113, 129, 160, 200, 328, 372, 533–34, 572, 594
BISSON: Charles, 48; John, 48; John R., 500; Susan [SCHATZ], 500
BITNER: John, 629
BITTENBENDER: Jacob, JP, 94

BITTERLY: Anne, 48; William, 48
BITTING: Capt., 343; Col., 179, 528; Joseph, 48; Lewis, Capt., 48
BITTINGER: Capt., 180
BITTLE: George, 516; Samuel, 48
BITYER: John, 188
***BITZ*:** Eleanor, 48; Michael, 48
BIVINS: Hannah, 48; John, 48
BIXBY: Benjamin, 49
BIXLER: Abraham, JP, 437
BIXLEY: J.P., 40
BLACK: Adam, Capt., 50; B.F., JP, 125, 553, 605; Benjamin F., JP, 316; Charles, 49, 633; Charles S., JP, 97; Daniel, 49, 633; Elizabeth, 49–50; George, 49, 517; George, Sr., 49; Henry, 49; Hiram, 633; Hugh, 50; James, 49–50, 633; Jane, 49–50; Jesse, 397; John, 49, 633; John Gabler, 125; Jonathan, 49; Lydia, 49; Margaret, 49, 633; Margaret [OKESON], 425; Mary, 50; Mary [OKESON], 425; Nancy, 49; Rebecca [VanKLEEK], 498; Robert, 87, 94; Samuel, 49, 523; Sarah, 50; Thomas, 49–50; William, 50
BLACKBURN: Moses, 50; R.M., 370, 653; Thomas, JP, 611; William M., JP, 345
BLACKESLEE: James, 50
BLACKFORD: Aaron, 476; Jacob, 50; Margaret, 50; Price, JP, 273; Rice, JP, 476
BLACKMAN: Elijah, Capt., 580; Elisha, 50; Franklin, JP, 154
BLACKMERE: Isaac, 51
BLACKMORE: Timothy, 51
BLACKSTACK: Jonathan McD., 27

BLACKSTOCK: I., 137;
J.D., 576; J.M.D., 277,
552; Jonathan D., 432
BLAESSER: Peter, 263
BLAIN: James, 51; William
A., JP, 75; William,
Capt., 51
BLAINE: A.W., 529;
Ephraim, 51; James, JP,
294, 456, 617; Sarah E.,
51
BLAINES: James, JP, 136
BLAIR: Alexander, 51, 61;
Andrew, 25; Benjamin,
51; David, 51; Eleanor,
51; John, 419; Lucy
[MEEKER], 388; Maria
[KING], 313; Mary, 51;
Mary [MYERS], 415;
Thomas, 51, 480;
William, 51, 238
BLAKE: William, 51
BLAKELEY: Capt., 39
BLAKENEY: William B.,
634; William, Capt., 51
BLAKESLEY: *Keathy*
[MAKEPEACE], 355;
William, 355
BLAKSLEE: Lucius, JP,
474
BLANCHARD: Abner, 52;
Andrew, 52; Anna, 52;
David B., JP, 169; Phebe,
52
BLANK: Peter, 52
BLASDELL: Andrew, 52;
John, 52; Lancy, 52
BLAWFULL: John, Capt.,
235
BLEAKLEY: George, 52
BLEAKNEY: William,
190; Wilson, 168
BLEAN: John, JP, 157, 395
BLEECHER: Anna Maria,
52; Yost, 52
BLIN: T.D., 12
BLINKER: Henry, 52
BLISH: John G., 413; N.H.,
JP, 413
BLISS: Capt., 182; Daniel,
53; Hannah, 507; Massey,
53
BLODGET: Prescott, 549
BLOOM: Daniel, 53
BLOOR: James H., JP, 79

BLUE: Frederick, 53; Isaac,
150; Isaac
[DONALDSON], Mrs.,
150; Michael, 53; Oliver
H.P., 150
BLUMER: William H., 139
BLUNDIN: John, 53;
Letitia, 53
BLY: David, 210
BLYE: Polly
[CUMMINGS], 127
BLYTHE: Ann W., 53;
Calvin, JP, 205; David,
35, 53; David B., 53;
Elizabeth, 53; James, 53;
Mary, 54; Robert R., 53
BOARDMAN: Capt., 606;
H.A., 51
BOAS: John, 213; William,
213
BOCK: George, 54
BOCKIUS: Catherine, 19;
George, 19; John, 19;
Joseph, 19
BODELL: Jonathan, 43
BODEN: Anderson, JP,
112; Andrew, JP, 162;
Jonathan, 112, 425, 435
BODEY: Joseph, 56
BODINE: Frederick, 54;
Thomas, 54
BODLEY: A.D.W., JP, 5;
Thomas, 54
BODWELL: John, 54; John
Jr., 54
BOEMAN: Leonard N., 250
BOEN: Jane, 606
BOGARD: Elizabeth, 205;
John, JP, 205
BOGARDUS: Thomas O.,
72
BOGGS: David, 54;
Francis, JP, 388; George,
5, 77; James, 57, 97, 242,
284, 295, 342, 481, 514,
579, 608; Knox, 88, 131,
153; William, 271, 276;
William L., 105
BOHN: Valentine, JP, 614
BOICE: Jacob, 616
BOILEAU: John, 418;
Nathaniel B., 151;
Samuel, 128
BOILS: Capt., 612
BOKER: Charles S., 308

BOLLEN: Ann, 54; John,
54
BOLLES: John, 41
BOLLINGER: Emanuel,
30; Jacob, JP, 143
BOLLMAN: Henry L., 239,
531
BOLSINGER: William, JP,
540
BOMBERGER: John, 336,
452; Polly [POWELL],
452
BOMGARDNER: George,
54
BOND: William, Capt., 5
BONEWITZ: Benjamin,
13; John, 13
BONHAM: Abram N., 55;
Joseph, 315; Prudence,
55; Zedekiah, 41, 55
BONNELL: Ann M., 380;
Ithamer, 380; John, 55,
467
BONNER: Capt., 465;
Charles F., 55; E.
Eurydice, 55; Elizabeth,
55; Isabella, 55; James,
55; Jane, 55; John, 55;
Robert, 55; William F.,
55
BONNET: Jacob, JP, 328;
John, 319
BONNHORST: S. Frank,
579
BONSALL: Benjamin, 55;
Cynthia S., 324; Henry
L., 399; Jesse, 55; Samuel
C., 324
BOOKER: Abraham, 55;
Frances, 55
BOON: Hawkins, Capt.,
181, 638; John, 55;
Moses, 56
BOONE: Capt., 370; John,
Capt., 355; Joseph, 138;
Ralph, 56; William, 451
BOOTH: Elihu, JP, 468;
Hilen, 3770; John M.,
126; Margaret
[CUMMING], 126; Sally
[McCLOUD], 370
BOOZ: Jacob, 56
BORDEN: Ansel, 56;
Roswell, 56; Selden, 56
BORDER: George, 339
BORDMAN: Rebecca, 106

BORGER: Yost, 56
BORING: Thomas, 426
BORLAND: Isaac, 274
BORROW: John, 56; Mary, 56; Mary Ann, 56; Nathaniel, 56; Samuel T., 56; Sarah, 56; Susan, 56
BORRY: George, 57; John, 57
BORTNER: Jacob, 320
BORTREE: William, 3
BOSLEY: H.C., 3
BOSS: Daniel C., 57; Margaret, 57
BOSSERT: William, 80
BOSTICK: Isaac, Capt., 229; Jonathan R., 584
BOSTWICK: A.H., 57; Charlotte, 254; Ebenezer, 57; G.T., JP, 192; Hiram D., 57; John, 57, 486; Nathan, 57; Reuben, Capt., 72
BOSWELL: James J., 490
BOSWORTH: Benjamin, 57; Marcus, 492; Salmon, 614; William B., 476
BOTTUM: William, JP, 82
BOULAND: Mark, 36
BOUND: Joseph, JP, 321, 381, 448, 533, 594
BOUS: William, Rev., 347
BOUSTEAD: Maria [SHUTTELL], 512
BOUVIER: Jonathan, 570, 593
BOVAN: Philip, 57
BOVARD: H., 9, 352
BOWEN: Capt., 208; Catharine [SINGLEY], 515; Daniel, 57–58; David H., 568; Hannah, 16; Henry, 515; John, 90, 100; Martin, JP, 265, 488; Mary R., 58; Samuel, 58
BOWER: Charles, 155; Ellis, 58; Franklin, 58; Henry, 58; Jacob, 58, 83, 252, 395; Jeremiah, 58; John Jacob, 58; Rebecca, 58; William, 58
BOWERS: George 2nd, 58; Polly P. [GAYLARD], 206; Sebastian, 59; Susan [GENTZERMAN], 208

BOWHANNON: George, 598
BOWLAND: Thomas, 59
BOWMAN: Catharine, 59; Charolett, 59; Christian, 59; Elijah, 59; Elizabeth, 59; Godfrey, JP, 69; Jacob, 59, 569; Joanna, 59; John, 59; Joshua, 59; Keziah, 59; Nicholas, 59; Philip, 59; Rachael, 59; Rebecca, 59; S.M., 84; Sally, 59; William, 59
BOWNE: Elizabeth, 72; William, 72
BOYCE: Abraham, 59–60; Abram, 59–60; Hannah, 59–60; Jacob, 59–60; John, 59–60; Margaret, 59–60; Mary, 59–60; Richard, JP, 280; Robert, 59–60; Sarah, 59–60
BOYD: Alexander, 35; Ann [BEATTY], 35; Charles C., 337; Copeland, 590; Edward C., JP, 284; Eliza, 590; Ellen, 590; Horace, 590; J., 412; J.J., 425; James, 60; John, 2, 50, 60, 79, 111, 190, 218, 312, 314, 330, 351, 353, 356, 380, 396, 403, 426, 433, 536, 579, 590, 635, 651; Joseph, 36, 67, 73–74, 76, 159, 343, 349, 361, 409, 415, 426, 449, 530, 540; Joseph T., 300; Letitia [HORSFIELD], 590; Reading B., 35; Rebecca, 60; Reed, 590; Robert, 60, 619
BOYDSTON: Boaz, JP, 25
BOYEE: Ansel, 38
BOYER: Calvin, 567; Christian, 61; Elizabeth, 61; Frederick, 60; George, 81; Henry, 61; Isaac, 27; J., 263; Jacob K., 180; Jonas S., JP, 65; Joseph, 60–61; Julia, 61; Maria Elizabeth, 60; Mary, 81; Mary [TURNER], 567; Samuel, 61; Sophia, 61
BOYERS: Anne Maria W., 569

BOYLAN: Aaron, 61; Elizabeth, 61; Sarah, 61
BOYLAND: James, Capt., 465
BOYLE: Capt., 163; Charles, 61; Daniel, 61; James, 61; John, 61; Michael, 622; Robert, 61, 596
BOYLES: William, Capt., 395
BOYLSTON: Boaz, JP, 10
BOYNTON: Elbridge G., 582; John, JP, 146; Lewis D., JP, 389, 591
BOYS: John, 174, 216; Robert, 535
BOZELL: Daniel, 382; Elizabeth [McKINLEY], 382
BOZZARD: Andrew, 400
BRACKENRIDGE: David, JP, 81
BRACKETT: Capt., 277; Edward H., 118; Elya [ELY], 170
BRADBURY: David W., 294; Lydia [JOHNSON], 294
BRADFORD: Capt., 325; Charles S., 3; Col., 483; James, 62; James H., 283; Samuel, 282; Ziporah, 62
BRADLEY: Capt., 193, 387, 407; Catharine [WILLIAMS], 604; Col., 18, 345, 427, 577; Daniel, 243; Gomer, 364; Joshua, 109; Parnet, 62; S.S., JP, 115, 266; Thaddeus, 62
BRADSHAW: Robert, 62; Robert Jr., 62; Salmon, 526
BRADY: Capt., 73, 365; H.Y., 371; Hannah [AUCHMUTY], 17; Hugh Y., 90, 133, 153, 250; J., 235; James, 11, 90, 97, 197, 271, 289; James Jr., 271; Jasper E., 7; Margaret, 62; William P., 62; William, Capt., 474
BRAINARD: Daniel, 62

BRAINERD: Daniel, 62; Enos, JP, 59; Margaret, 59
BRALEY: Gideon, 62
BRANCH: Abijah H., JP, 211; Hilliam, JP, 552; J. Starkweather, 2; Walter, 523; William W., JP, 170
BRANDT: Elsey [COX], 118
BRANNON: Margaret [WHITE], 596
BRANTHEVAN: Adam, 62; Daniel, 62; John, 62; Magdalena, 62; Peter, 62
BRANTHHEVER: Adam, 63
BRANTHIFER: Adam, 63
BRANTHOFER: Adam, 63
BRANTON: John, 125
BRASSBRIDGE: George W., 63; John, 63; Phebe, 63
BRATION: Napoleon B., 220
BRATTEN: James, JP, 227
BRATTON: Bartholomew, 63
BRAUN: *Johannes,* 229
BRAUTIGAN: Daniel, JP, 341
BRAWLEY: James, JP, 302; Mary, 302
BRAY: Daniel, 551; Elizabeth A., 54; J.W., 305; James, 54; John, 54; John W., 485; Mary [BLYTHE?], 54; William K., 171, 303
BRAYMER: J., 211
BRECHAL: Catharine, 63; Martin, 63
BRECKER: Peter, 63
BREDEN: James, 522
BREDIN: James, 202, 406, 592; James M., 555; John, 125, 591; Maurice, JP, 81, 125, 223, 251, 281, 460, 485, 539
BREED: Charles W., 63; George, 18, 352, 365, 447; Joseph, 63; Mercy, 63; William, 404
BREES: Catherine, 65; Falla [JENKINS], 290; James, 290; Samuel, 65

BREESE: William, JP, 37
BREIDENSTEIN: Cornelius, 220
BREINER: Samuel, 318
BREISCH: John, 341
BRENEMAN: A.N., 473; George F., 33
BRENEZE: Catharine, 63
BRENNON: Charlotte, 64; John, 64
BRETCH: Elizabeth, 64; Henry A., 64
BRETZ: John, 143
BREWER: Elisha, Capt., 64; Fanny, 64; John, 64; Martha, 64; Mary, 64; Nancy, 64; Polly, 493
BREWSTER: A.W., 427, 547, 579; Abigail, 64; Anna, 64; Capt., 595; Daniel, 64; Elizabeth R. [HUBLEY], 441; George R., 161; James, 64; L.E., 441; Polly [RAYNSFORD], 461
BREY: Christopher, 65
BRIANT: Jonathan, JP, 67, 244
BRICE: George W., JP, 10, 85, 178, 457; George, JP, 98, 394; James, 69
BRICK: H., 89; Herman, JP, 99
BRICKELL: Elizabeth, 65; George, 65; John, 65; Lydia, 65; Samuel, 65; Susan, 65; William, 65
BRICKER: Daniel, 53
BRIES: Catherine, 65; Samuel, 65
BRIESH: Mary [McELROY], 377
BRIGDON: William, JP, 39
BRIGGS: John, 617; Joseph, 65; Mary, 65; Norton, 272, 415; Otis, 557
BRIGHAM: John, JP, 279
BRIM: Henry, 65; Mary, 65
BRINDLE: Eleanor [WHITE], 596; Susannah [WHITE], 596
BRINK: Benjamin, 65; Daniel, 65; James, 65; Jonathan, JP, 457

BRINKER: Jacob, 538; M., 472
BRINKERHOFF: J., 369
BRINTON: Hannah [HOWELL], 273
BRISBAN: John, 65
BRISTOL: Chlora M. [KEELER], 304
BRITT: Capt., 494
BRITTAN: Daniel, 66
BRITTON: Charles, 27; Daniel, 66; John, Capt., 482; Joseph, 66; Samuel, JP, 62
BROADHEAD: Affy, 66; Col., 410, 429; *Gerret,* 66
BROBIT: Matthias, Capt., 197
BROBST: Catherine, 66; Christian G., 301, 582; John, 66; Joseph, JP, 172, 301, 582; Michael, 301; S.K., 132
BROCK: Capt., 20; John, 162, 165, 170, 242, 587
BRODHEAD: A.J., 573; Affy, 66; Amanda, 66; Charles, 172, 404, 482; Daniel, 66; Daniel M., 391; Ellen, 66; Garret, 66, 335, 573; H.R., 457; Henry R., 51, 116; John, 105; John H., 138; Julia, 66; Mira, 66; R., 80; R. Jr., 110, 359, 551
BRONS: Nicholas, JP, 192
BROOK: David, 66; Watty, 66
BROOKE: Charles W., 622; Elijah, 559; George, 66; Moses D., JP, 249; Nathaniel, JP, 278; Owen, 66; Robert, 48; Robert H., 310; Robert M., 308; S.H., 70; Thomas W., 138
BROOKENS: Catharine [LUKER], 349; Katharine, 349; William, 349
BROOKES: Thomas, JP, 296
BROOKINS: Jane, 246; William, JP, 246
BROOKS: Capt., 523; Charles, 66; Col., 342; Drucilla [WHITE], 596;

(BROOKS, continued)

Eleazer, Col., 364; Eliza
[INSKEEP], 283;
Hezekiah, JP, 67; Hiram,
560; J.W., JP, 398, 435;
James, 67; John, 58, 65,
67, 108, 172, 409, 523;
John R., 176; John W.,
JP, 460; Jonas, JP, 558;
Joseph J., 59; Lydia, 67;
Malinda, 66; Samuel,
283; William, 603
BROOM: Isaac, JP, 55;
Jacob, 332
BROOMFIELD:
Alexander, JP, 563
BROOMHALL: M.B., 486
BROONLEE: Joseph,
Capt., 231
BROTHERS: Francis, 379
BROWEN: Jacob, 67
BROWER: Benjamin, 67;
Charles, 356; Christian,
344; Jacob, 67; Mary, 67
BROWN: -----, 523; A., 4,
8, 46, 57, 118, 342, 353,
421; A.B., JP, 34; A.G.,
JP, 46; Adin, 68;
Alexander, 67, 71, 88,
112, 175, 179, 242, 284,
291, 481, 492, 514, 522,
609; Alexander H., 67;
Alexander Jr., 522;
Andrew, 68; Avery, 68;
Barbara, 67; Barker, 479;
Benjamin, 67; Benneville,
281; Betty [FLAUGH],
186; Caleb, 71; Capt., 80,
87, 495; Catharine, 68;
Charles, 71; Charles R.,
303; Christian, 461, 536;
Christiana, 67; Col., 51,
197; Daniel, 68, 186;
David, 68; E.A., 235–36,
278, 312, 441, 554;
Eleanor, 604; Elizabeth,
69; Ellenor [IDLE], 281;
Enos, 68; Ezekiel, JP,
296; George W., 584;
Hannah, 70; Henry W.,
595; Isaac, 618; J., 139; J.
Henry, 278; J.F., 112;
J.M., 188; Jacob, 68, 70;
James, 68, 71, 151, 342;
James 1st, 68; James 2nd,

69; James 3rd, 69; James
E., JP, 61, 184, 313, 613;
James M., 577; James W.,
84, 182, 284, 297, 426,
458; Jane, 71; Jane
[BARR], 29; Jeremiah,
69; Johannes, 566; John,
4, 67–69, 71, 78, 229,
494; John C., 15; John
Peter, 408; Joseph, 327;
Katharine, 68; L.K., JP,
17; Levi, 70; Lucy, 70;
M.F., 338; Margaret, 67;
Maria, 70; Marvin H.,
518; Mary, 71, 618; Mary
[PECK], 439; Miriam, 69;
Nancy, 71, 281; Nancy
[HUTCHINS], 281; O.P.,
JP, 43, 70, 197, 564, 568;
Oliver, 70; Oliver P., JP,
536; Ozias, JP, 444; Paul
S., 606; Phebe, 604; Pitt,
JP, 70; Polly, 68; *Rex*, 69;
Robert, 68, 284, 405, 467;
Robert Alexander, 67;
Rosanna, 68; Ruth, 69;
S.H., JP, 277; Sabina, 70;
Samuel, 69–70, 156, 469;
Samuel 3rd, 70; Samuel
P., 369; Sarah, 71;
Sarepta, 71; Sarepta
[REEVES], 465; Silas,
273; Silence, 71; Simon,
604; Susan, 67; Thomas,
71, 78, 358, 473; W.A.,
465; *W.D.*, 69; William,
67–68, 71, 78; William
2nd, 71; William R., 400;
Z.G., 519
BROWNE: James M., 97,
263, 438, 486; James W.,
143; William, 72
BROWNELL: Peggy
[JACKSON], 286; Peter,
286
BROWNFIELD:
Alexander, JP, 212, 240;
Ewing, 50, 454
BROWNING: Capt., 485
BROWNLEE: Archibald,
400; James, JP, 280, 399
BROWNMILLER: Barbara
[NOLF], 422
BROWNSON: Isaac, 72;
Nathan, 284

BRUCE: Henry, 280; Jacob,
622; William, 392
BRUMBAUGH: George,
202
BRUNDAGE: James, 435;
Robert, 177
BRUNER: Catherine, 235;
Charles J., 222, 590; Isaac
Jr., 526; John, 235; Mary
[GRAY], 222; Peter, 72
BRUNSON: Levi, 72
BRUSH: Jonas, 72; Lewis,
72; Pamela, 72; Rosanna,
72; Tamar, 72
BRYAN: Adam, 382; Guy
A., 121; James, 73;
Joseph, 73, 534; Russel
C., JP, 35; Samuel, 73
BRYANT: D.F., 242;
Joseph, 76, 242, 405, 534;
Mordecai Y., JP, 162;
Thomas, JP, 118; Tiberius
Jefferson, JP, 492;
William, 615
BRYSON: Andrew, 73;
Ann, 73; Samuel, 51, 634
BUCHANAN: Alexander,
73–74; Andrew, 388;
David B., 409; George,
205, 395, 454; James, 73,
397; Jane, 73; John,
73–74; McKean, 577;
Robert, 74; Sarah
[PYLES], 456; William,
379
BUCHANNAN: James, 73
BUCHER: Conrad, JP, 119;
George H., 172, 283, 332;
George, Capt., 212;
Jacob, JP, 81, 172, 188,
247, 283, 314, 332, 471;
John B., 657; John C., 45,
172, 223, 303, 321, 471;
Jonathan, 108, 247, 314;
Lewis, 107
BUCHTER: Mathias, 74
BUCK: Ebenezer, 74;
Francis N., 169; Henry,
74; Ichabod, 74; John,
612; John H., Capt., 19;
Jonathan, 74; Leonard, 75
BUCKELY: Chauncey, JP,
336
BUCKHER: George, 75
BUD: J., Capt., 412
BUDA: Charles J., JP, 273

BUDD: Bristol, 75, 490; W.A., 366
BUEHLER: A.D., 397; D.A., JP, 376, 397; David A., JP, 293, 329; William, 79, 181, 210, 529, 534, 545, 576
BUEL: *Arphaxad,* 75; Mary, 75; Nathan, 75
BUELL: Christian, 101; John H., Capt., 23; John M., 552; Nathan, 75
BUFFINGTON: John, 111, 455; Joseph, 135; Samuel, JP, 384
BUGHMAN: Reuben, 586
BUGLE: David, 249
BUKER: Alpha, JP, 583
BULER: Henry, Capt., 329
BULGER: Rhinard R., 425
BULKLEY: Chauncey, JP, 156, 233
BULL: Col., 185, 259, 393; David M., 616; G.H., JP, 167; Levi, 23; Lucretia [BALLARD], 23; Lydia [CROWELL], 23; Thomas, 23, 466
BULLARD: Elijah, 75; Hezekiah, 75; Isaac, 75; Otis, 75
BULLOCK: D., 443; Darius, 99, 113, 194, 206, 434, 528; Ira C., 206, 333, 434, 499; Jesse E., JP, 225; John, 75; T.C., 194
BUMGARNER: Jesse, JP, 259, 609
BUMPUS: Frederick, 75; Reuben, 76
BUNGE: J., JP, 14
BUNHART: Henry, 501
BUNKER: Jesse, JP, 437
BUNN: Solomon N., 34, 122
BUNNEL: James, 348; John, Col., 25
BUNNELL: David, 1; James, Capt., 250
BUNTING: John, 586
BURBRIDGE: J.W., 402, 448, 483; James W., 202, 232, 307, 309, 362; Thomas, 430
BURCHFIELD: Thomas, 47

BURD: Col., 604; George, 197
BURDEN: Nathaniel, 76
BURDICK: Gideon, 76
BURDUE: John, 76; Mary, 76; Nathaniel, 76; Nathaniel Jr., 76; Rebecca, 76
BURG: William, JP, 104, 205
BURGER: Samuel, 308
BURGET: Isaiah, 13
BURGHOLER: Michael, 536
BURGIS: Mary, 352
BURK: Catharine, 77; Elizabeth, 77; Gaius, 76; Joseph, 76; Nathaniel, 297; Patrick, 76; Polly, 77; Sylvanus, 76; Thomas, 76–77, 590; William, 76
BURKARD: Frederick, 77
BURKART: Valentine, 29, 215, 333, 366, 396, 436–37
BURKE: Amos, 141; Axa, 76; Elizabeth, 76; Patrick, 76; Sylvanus, 76; Thomas, 77
BURKEHART: Jacob, 77
BURKHART: Charles, 77; Peter, 47, 330, 446
BURKS: Thomas, 579
BURLEY: Ebenezer, 77
BURLINGAME: Adaline, 92; Asa, 501; Sarah, 501; William, 92
BURN: Thomas, 77
BURNAP: Capt., 576
BURNES: Dolly, 77; Joel, 77
BURNETT: Edmund, 78; Henry, 203; Mary, 100; William, 275; Ziba, 192
BURNEY: John, 152
BURNHAM: Isaac, 78; Isaac Jr., 78; Jedediah Jr., 365; John, 78
BURNHART: Anne, 78; John, 78
BURNIE: John, 78
BURNS: A., JP, 169; Charles, 100, 402; Eve, 78; John, 293, 413, 579,

590; Samuel, 78; Sarah, 79; Stephen D., 79
BURR: Henrietta [WALBRIDGE], 578; J.N., 135; James, 265; Pliny, 318, 578
BURREL: Col., 601; M.M., JP, 397; Zachariah, 79
BURRELL: Myron, 215; Zachariah, 79
BURRIL: Aaron, 79; Martha, 79
BURRILL: Jedediah, 79; Margaret, 79
BURROUGHS: Eden, 79; Jacob, JP, 7, 269, 449, 599; Sabin [TILDEN], 562
BURROWS: Christann, 162; Eden, 79; Eliza, 79; G., JP, 68, 439; Hubbard, 79; Joseph, 79; Lomber, 47, 171; Rebecca, 79
BURSON: L.M., 521
BURT: Aaron, 79; Nathaniel, 400, 427
BURTEN: Elijah, Dr., 412
BURTON: Benjamin, 80; Edmund, 488; Joseph, JP, 533, 586; Merrick, 74; O.G., 154; William, JP, 2
BURWELL: Elizabeth, 80; Martha, 80; Zachariah, 80
BUSCH: Felix, 143
BUSH: Abram, 322; Amy [KALLAM], 301; Benjamin V., JP, 322; Daniel, 80; Elvina, 397; Eve, 80; George, Capt., 24; Henrietta [SIDMAN], 512; Henry, 80; William, 158
BUSHFIELD: Samuel, 64
BUSHNELL: John W., 300; Sidney S., 421
BUSKIRK: T. Van, 467
BUSS: Jonas, JP, 427
BUSSARD: Jacob, 80
BUSTARD: Alexander, 80; George *Mearshall,* 80; James, 80; M.A., 80; Margaret Ann, 80
BUTCHER: Mary [GOHN], 214
BUTLER: -----, 30; Ann, 81; Bartley, 103;

(BUTLER, continued)

Capt., 30, 449, 470, 609;
Chester, 69; Col., 27, 39,
208, 260, 372, 605, 623;
Hiram, 105; *J.S.*, 113;
James, 386, 421, 594;
Jefferson, 261; Joseph,
457; Lydia, 81; Martha
Ann, 81; Nancy, 81;
Nicholas, 464; Patrick,
81; Perry C., 236; Phebe,
81; Polly [REEGER],
464; Richard, Col., 475;
Samuel, 9; Samuel G., 81;
Steuben, 81; William, 81;
William 1st, 81; Z., Col.,
217, 579; Zebulon, Col.,
42, 81, 410
BUTT: John, 638
BUTTON: Alvin, 152;
Lodenia [DOUD], 152
BUYERS: George, 81
BUZARD: T. Engle, 173
BUZBY: Benjamin C., 290
BYE: Amos, JP, 376, 378;
Deborah, 378
BYERLY: A.J., 86; Adam,
JP, 240
BYERS: Letticia Davis, 636
BYLE: Mary [ROTH], 482
BYRER: Frederick, 335
BYRNE: Margaret, 147
BYSELL: Frederick, JP,
233

CACKLER: Christian Jr.,
81
CADMUS: Jasper, 481
CADWALADER: Col., 218
CADWALLADER: Rees,
552; S., 299
CADY: Anna [SEELY],
500; Lemuel, 488
CAHILL: Richard, JP, 289
CAIN: Dennis, 82; Thomas
C., 324
CAIRNS: William, 350
CALAHAN: Dennis, 171
CALDWELL: James, 414,
445; John, 69, 98, 440,
572; Mary, 82; Robert,
82; Ruth [BROWN], 69;
S.W., 249; Thomas, 473
CALEY: Samuel, 559

CALHOUN: A., 73, 361;
Andrew H., 170; John,
Col., 252; Johnston, 133;
Robert C., 374; Samuel,
82
CALKIN: Lyman L., 333
CALKINS: Darius, 82;
Moses, 82
CALL: John, JP, 79
CALLA: Alexander M., 57;
E.M., 50
CALLAN: Ellen, 82; John,
430; Rebecca, 82;
William, 77
CALLANDER: John, 82
CALLEN: James, 82
CALLENDER: Samuel, 83
CALVER: Solomon, 83
CAMERON: Alexander,
83; Daniel, 530;
Elizabeth, 83
CAMM: William, 53, 222,
253
CAMP: Casper, 83; J., 516;
J.C., JP, 488; John, 516;
Margaret, 516
CAMPBELL: A., 360;
Albert, 280; Alexander,
83; Ann, 84–85; Anne,
85; B., 410; Benjamin,
11, 31, 95, 117, 254, 326,
345, 360, 387, 391, 393,
406, 443, 522, 550, 568,
596, 600, 611; Benjamin
Jr., 268, 498; Capt., 36,
261; *Cassandana*, 84;
Cassandra, 84; Catharine,
85; Catharine
[MERSHIMER], 360;
Charity, 85; Charles, 84,
360; Christopher, 84–85;
David, 205; Elizabeth,
85–86; George, 269;
George J., 17; H., 106;
J.R., 318; James, 84, 164,
539; James A., 84; Jane,
85, 266; Jeane, 83;
Jonathan, 84–85, 160,
197, 205, 296, 326, 345,
371, 399, 409–10, 598,
600; Joseph, 85; Juliana
W., 84; Lawrence, 418;
Lucy L., 572; Margaret,
85; Martha, 85; Mary, 85;
Mary [LITTLE], 340;
McDonal, 84; *McDonald,*

84; N.K., 160; Nathaniel,
JP, 568; Phebe, 85; R.,
184; R.K., 102, 326, 391,
600; Rachel, 85; Richard,
85; Robert, 85, 266, 319;
Robert 1st, 85; Robert
3rd, 85; Rufus H., 403;
S.N., 504; S.Y., 605;
Sample, 248, 362, 571,
611, 616; Sampson, 196;
Samuel, 85, 351; Sarah,
85, 611; Susan, 86;
Thomas, 86, 456, 618;
William, 86, 159, 193,
219, 332, 485, 539;
William R., JP, 292
CAMPFIELD: Col., 265
CANAN: Moses, JP, 462,
612
CANBY: Joshua C., JP, 53,
496
CANDLESS: John M., JP,
84
CANDOR: Jonathan H., 73
CANEDY: Alexander, 68;
Katharine [BROWN], 68
CANELY: William J, 86
CANFIELD: Andrew, 86;
Austin, JP, 568; Charles
R., 86; Col., 193, 594;
Elijah, 86; Eunice, 86; H.,
312; Henry J., JP, 577;
Herman, JP, 216, 429;
Hilen, JP, 166, 449, 487,
622; Israel, 86; Moses B.,
86; Oliver, 86; Samuel,
Col., 182; W.H., 473;
William H., 14, 370, 444
CANNON: Fergus, JP, 330,
380, 410; Patrick, 180;
Tamar [COVERT], 180
CAPP: Charles, 143; John
C., 278, 409
CARBAUGH: John, 393
CARBERRY: Francis, 87;
Sarah, 87
CARBURY: Sarah, 87
CARD: Varnum J., JP, 234
CAREFOOT: Barbara, 87;
William, 87
CAREY: E., JP, 90;
Eleazer, 28; Eleazer, JP,
42; Francis, Dr., 71;
Henry C., 183; Mathew,
414; Sarah [DAY], 136

CARHUFF: Elizabeth [DECKER], 138; William, 138
CARIS: Frederick 2nd, 174; Frederick Jr., JP, 174; John, 174; Mary [EATINGER], 174
CARLILE: Mary, 87; William, JP, 159
CARLIN: David, JP, 158; Ruth [CARLIN], 200
CARLISLE: Mary, 87; Thomas, 627; William, 87; William Jr., 496
CARLY: John, 412
CARMAN: Andrew, 87; Martin H., 87; William, 390
CARMOODY: John, 87
CARNAHAN: Alexander, JP, 29, 253, 374; James, Capt., 94; Joseph, JP, 444; William, 253
CARNER: Anthony, 116; Catharine, 116; John, 116; Julia/Julean, 116; William, 116, 323
CARNES: Edward, 87; Elizabeth, 87; George, 87; Godfrey, 87; Jane, 87; John, 87; Margaret, 87; *Rhenhanah*, 87; Robert, 87; Samuel, 87; William, 87
CARNOCHAN: W.M., JP, 454
CARNOCHUN: William, JP, 86
CAROLL: David, 88
CAROTHERS: James, 233; Jesse, 107, 116, 158, 210, 282, 349, 364, 419, 437, 555, 569; John, 87, 420; Robert, 298; Thomas, 87; William S., 340, 587; William, JP, 585; Williamsen, JP, 471
CARPENTER: Asa, 88; Balser, 441; Capt., 70; D., 30; Daniel, 88, 444; Eber, 88; Ezra, JP, 70; Harvey, 88; Henry, JP, 391; J. Murry, 135; Jacob, 515; Jane A., 441; Jeremiah M., 135; Joseph, 515; M., 72, 650; M., JP, 28; Mary

[SKIMER], 515; Michael, 333, 366, 436, 446, 482, 488; Nancy/Ann [SKIMER], 515; Orson, 88; Rosana, 88
CARREL: David, 88
CARRENGER: Joseph, 88
CARRIER: Phebe [FAWROT], 179
CARRIGAN: James K., 371; Peter, 88
CARRINGER: Martin, 88; Molly, 88
CARROLL: Dennis, 88; Edward, JP, 93
CARROW: Henry, Capt., 242
CARSON: Benjamin, 88; George, 4; P., 576; Rebecca, 11; Rosannah [WHITE], 596; Thomas, JP, 353, 361, 449; William, 88, 107, 265, 663
CARSWELL: Anna [BLANCHARD], 52; Daniel, 52; David, 89; Euphemia Ann, 91; Martha, 89; Samuel, 91
CARTER: Col., 358; Debora, 89; Elbert V., JP, 34; Elizabeth [MASSEY], 364; Erastus, 601; John, 89; Jonah, 89; Jonas, 89; Joseph, 608; Margaret, 89; R.W., JP, 261; Sophia [FRENCH], 521; Stephen, 89; Tempa, 89; Thomas, 89; Thomas B., JP, 427; Ziporah [BRADFORD], 62
CARTY: Ellen, 89; John, 89–90; Mary, 90; Michael, 90; Millie, 90; Phoebe, 90; Thomas, 90
CARUTHERS: Jesse, 272
CARVER: Daniel, 202; George, JP, 140; J.B., 299
CARVIN: William, 92
CARY: John, 15, 90, 114, 155, 162, 411; William, 15, 114, 162
CASADAY: William L., 575
CASBER: Jonathan, 90; Margaret, 90

CASE: Ariel, 502; James H., 443; John, 484; Olive [ROWLAND], 484; Otis P., 502; Persis [SEWARD], 502; William F., JP, 599; William T., 78; William, JP, 26
CASEBEAR: Jonathan, 90; Margaret, 90
CASEBEER: Agnes, 90; David, 90
CASEBIER: Agnes, 90; David, 90
CASEY: John, 90; R.I., JP, 137
CASH: *Elhauncey*, 210
CASHMAN: Isaac, 90
CASMAN: Julia [DOWDERMAN], 154; William, 466
CASS: Aaron, Capt., 453
CASSAT: R.S., 389; Robert S., 295
CASSEL: Jacob, JP, 255
CASSIDY: Nicholas, 90
CASSILLY: Michael P., 379
CASSIM: Luke, JP, 356
CASTER: Hannah, 91; Isaac, 91
CASTILE: Samuel, 91
CASTNER: Samuel, 355
CASTOR: Hannah [DYER], 162; Isaac, 91; Jacob, 91; Samuel, 162, 483
CASWELL: Daniel, 496; Euphemia Ann, 91; Oliver, 431; Samuel, 91
CATHCART: Alexander, 587
CATHERS: Robert, 385
CATHIN: Eli, Capt., 91
CATLETT: A.G., 342
CATLIN: Eli, 91; George, 91; Putnam, 42, 72, 91, 559
CATTELL: A.G., 501
CAVANAUGH: Edward, 91
CAVANEE: Joseph, 91
CAVENOUGH: John, 92; Mary, 92; Patrick, 92
CAVIET: Capt., 594
CAVIN: William, 92

CAWTHUS: Jesse, 99
CHACE: N.K., 468
CHADWICK: Elihu, 92;
Jeremiah, JP, 127, 527;
Rebekah, 92; Richard,
127; William, 92
CHAFFEE: N.L., 398
CHALFANT: Henry, 298;
John, JP, 208
CHALSTON: Jonathan,
174
CHAMBERLAIN:
Abagail, 93; Albert, JP,
285; Ann, 92; Col., 84;
Isaac, 157; James, 92;
Jane, 92; John, 92;
Joseph, 92; Margery, 92;
Moses, 93; Nancy, 92;
O.D., 115; Philena
[KELLOGG], 307; Polly
[COOK?], 93; Samuel,
93; Samuel S., 93; Stout,
93; Washington, 92;
William, 93
CHAMBERLIN: A., JP,
78, 179, 286, 477, 554,
558; A.S., 209, 616;
Albert, JP, 75, 134, 169,
615; Asenath
[KELLOGG], 307; D.,
498; Ebenezer, JP, 460;
Ives, 488; Orpha
[SCOVILLE], 498;
Samuel, 93
CHAMBERS: Alexander,
465; Col., 130, 571;
Hannah, 93; James, 93,
299–300, 567, 577; John,
93–94; John D., 372;
Robert, 93–94; William,
93–94; William Sr., 93
CHAMPING: Elizabeth
[ADAMS], 2
CHAMPNEY: B., 101;
Benjamin, 185
CHANCE: Jeremiah C., 527
CHANDLER: Charles, JP,
366; Daniel, JP, 493;
Josiah, 94
CHANEY: Charles, JP, 407
CHAPIN: Capt., 445, 496;
J.P., 90; Selah Jr., 415
CHAPLIN: Harriet
[CRAIG], 118; William,
663

CHAPMAN: Abigail D.,
364; B., 2; B.B., 315, 388,
431, 439, 484; Betsy
[BISBEE], 47; Capt., 69;
Catharine [SHAFFER],
503; Constant, 94; David,
94–95; Edwin, JP, 30,
364; Elizabeth, 95;
Francis, 561; George Sr.,
94; H.C., 94; Isaac A., 94;
James, Capt., 452; Jane,
95; Joseph, 94; Levi, JP,
345; Margaret, 95; Mary,
95; Nathaniel A., JP, 19;
Robert, 95; Samuel, 502;
Seth, JP, 2; Theodore C.,
435; William, 95;
William T., JP, 260, 373
CHAPPEL: Ezra, 88;
Rosana [CARPENTER],
88
CHARLES: Eliza
[McGLAUGHLIN], 331;
James, 331
CHARLTON: Phebe
[HOLLAND], 266
CHARNLEY: W.S., 572
CHARTERS: Susana, 552;
William, 552
CHARTON: James, 343
CHASE: E.E., 477; E.H.,
534; Edward E., 286;
Edward H., JP, 109; J.,
202; Joseph L., 468;
Lester, JP, 198; Samuel,
95; Seth, 614; *Syene*
[WOOD], 614
CHATHAM: Capt., 173;
John, Capt., 465
CHATMAN: Capt., 594
CHEESEMAN: Benjamin,
95; H., 95; Sarah A., 95
CHENEWORTH: Richard,
441; Tamor [HUBLEY],
441
CHENEY: Gilbert, 225;
Richard, 95
CHERINGTON: Ezekiel,
JP, 151
CHERRY: Abigail, 95;
George, 310; Hannah, 95;
Henry, 95; James, 95;
John, 95; William, 95
CHESMAN: Benjamin, 95

CHESNEY: Samuel, JP, 11,
161, 258, 357, 428, 566,
604
CHESNUT: Benjamin, 95;
Samuel, 301
CHESSMAN: Benjamin, 95
CHESTER: Erastus, JP,
158; Joseph L., 12
CHEW: Benjamin, 356
CHEYNEY: Richard, 95
CHICK: Emily
[HERTZOG], 355; John,
355
CHIDESTER: Henry, 603
CHILD: Cromwell, 96;
William, JP, 33
CHILDS: Benjamin, 178,
549; Charles, JP, 570;
Harvey, 259
CHITTENDON: Belinda
[WHEELER], 595
CHOCKLEY: Thomas, 96
CHRISE: Jacob, 319
CHRIST: Henry, Capt., 237
CHRISTIAN: Valentine, 96
CHRISTIE: Capt., 390,
587; James, Capt., 157;
Mirand, 584
CHRISTMAN: Elizabeth,
96; Felix, 96; George, 279
CHRISTY: Daniel, JP, 135,
295; Robert, 107, 300,
532; Rt., 155; W.L., 35;
William, JP, 87
CHUBBACK: Aaron, 146
CHUBBOCK: Bissell, 96;
Eben, 260; *Lucina,* 96;
Nathaniel, 260
CHUBBUCK: Ebenezer, 96
CHURCH: A.C., 96, 581;
Abigail, 96–97; Addison
C., JP, 142; Capt., 46,
343, 463; Ebenezer, 97;
Eleazer, 97; Erastus, 165;
Eunice, 97; G., JP, 152;
Gaylord, JP, 175; Gideon,
96; John R., JP, 212;
Mary "Polly," 97;
Philemon, 97; Prudence
[EDWARDS], 165; Sally,
97; Samuel, 30, 38, 76,
79, 99, 104, 112, 114,
125, 144, 156, 221, 233,
241, 243–44, 252, 259,
273, 286–87, 381, 386,
410, 426, 448, 455, 487,

(CHURCH, Samuel, continued)

501, 506, 513–14, 522, 532, 580–81, 590, 600, 618; Thomas, Capt., 37; William, 96; William J., 97

CHURCHE: Philemon, 97
CHURCHFIELD: John, 97
CILLEY: Col., 508
CLAFFLIN: Fanny, 574
CLAIBORNE: Catharine T. [ROSS], 482
CLAMEN: Mary, 100; Peter, 100
CLANBAUGH: Abraham, 97; Catherine, 97; Elizabeth, 97; Jacob, 97; Margaret, 97; Martin, 97
CLAPSADDLE: James, 82
CLARK: A., JP, 182; Abraham R., 274; Amelia, 98; Ashbel, JP, 200, 533; Barbara [KEYS], 311; C.H., 150; Catharine [WERTZ], 592; Catherine A., 98; Charles, JP, 353; Clement, 99; David, 40, 78; David J., 412; *Eleanor,* 99, 221; Elijah, 99; Elizabeth [LUDWICK], 349; Elizabeth [WALTERS], 581; Ephraim Jr., 204; *Eugena,* 99; *Eugenia,* 99; F.H., 574; Francis, 97; Francis Jr., 97; George S., 582; George W., 100; Henry, 120; Hugh, 124; Isabella [MORRIS], 406; Jacob N., 98; James, 98, 186, 386, 545; Jane C., 98; Job, 98; John, 98, 100; John 3rd, Capt., 100; John 4th, 98; John B., 12; John C., 99; John G., JP, 446; *Jononas* W., 221; Lemuel, 99; Lewis, 604; *Lofnies,* 99; *Loron,* 112; Margaret [BLACK], 49; Mary, 99; Mary [MARSHALL], 360; Milton, 297; Nancy, 99; Philo, 215; S.M., 164; S.S., 293; Samuel, 99,

458; Sarah, 98; Seth, 99; Tabitha, 98; Thomas, 99; Timothy, JP, 599; W.W., 461; Walter, Lt., 36; Whitney, JP, 473; William, 388, 409, 566, 616; William E., 99
CLARKE: Adna, 99; Clement, 99; Elizabeth, 100; F.J., 174; James, 619; John, 100, 300, 542; John 3rd, Capt., 100; Samuel, 613; William B., 325; William L., 594; William, JP, 325, 562; Zelotes, 100
CLARKSON: Jacob, 392
CLAUBAUGH: Martin, 100
CLAVENGER: Amos, 102; Catharine, 102; Isaiah, 102
CLAWELL: Catherine [DIETER], 139
CLAWSON: Garrett, 100; Keziah, 100
CLAY: John, 395; Margaret [MILLER], 395; Stephen F., 555
CLAYDER: Capt., 179
CLAYMAN: Mary, 100; Peter, 100
CLAYPOLL: Capt., 551
CLAYTON: Elizabeth, 100; Noah, 100
CLEARFIELD: M., 212
CLEAVENGER: Jonathan, 387; Samuel, 121
CLEAVER: Hiram, 10; Jonathan, JP, 328; P.P., 222
CLELAND: William, 419
CLEMENCE: Peter, 100
CLEMENS: Henry, 101
CLEMENT: Derick, 101; Ebenezer, JP, 248; Jarvis, 125; Lambert, 101
CLEMONS: Patrick, 101
CLENDENIN: Daniel, 101; David, 101; Eliza, 101; James, 101; James P., JP, 101; John, 101; Margaret, 101; Mary, 101; Samuel, 101; Sarah, 101
CLENDENNING: David, 131

CLENENDEN: Peter, 409
CLEVEDENCE: John, 101; Mary, 101
CLEVELAND: Elisha, 99; James D., JP, 472; Mercy, 101; Samuel, 101; Tracy, 102
CLEVENGER: Catharine, 102; Isaiah, 102
CLIFFORD: Capt., 474
CLIFT: Capt., 534
CLINE: A.J., 592; Daniel, JP, 329; Henry, 329; John, 102; William, 102
CLINGAN: Capt., 477
CLINGEN: Capt., 553
CLINK: Henry B., 8
CLOKEY: John S., JP, 85
CLOSE: Catherine [NOLF], 422; Daniel, 422
CLOSSEN: Zachariah, 102
CLOTZ: Col., 455
CLOUSON: Betsey [ROWLAND], 484
CLOVE: Edward, 517; Hannah [SMITH], 517
CLOVER: Levi, 562; Levi G., 27
CLUGGAGE: Major, 49; Thomas, Capt., 538
CLUMP: Jonathan W., 120
CLUNG: Henry, 317
CLYDE: James, JP, 394
COATES: Joseph P.H., 333
COATS: *Jno. Jr.,* JP, 195
COBEAN: James Jr., JP, 374
COBSON: Samuel, 472
COBURN: Ann, 102; Capt., 102; John, 102; Nathaniel, 102; Phineas, 102; Samuel, 102
COBY: Capt., 328
COCHRAN: *Balney,* 103; Blaney, 103; Edward, 103; George, 41, 151, 215; George C., JP, 246; Hannah, 103; John F., JP, 108; Jonathan, 103, 237, 245; Mary, 103; Robert, 103, 199, 343, 444, 497; Samuel, 103; Stephen H., 311; William, 181, 639
COCKER: Catharine [LYN], 351

COCKLIN: John W., 587;
Margaret [McKINZIE],
383
COCKSHOOT: Luke, 374
CODDING: John, JP, 595
COE: Ebenezer, 103, 289;
Haward, 99; Joseph, 103;
Peter, 103; Seymour W.,
218; Stephen, 103;
Thomas, 103
COEN: James, 104
COFFIN: Albert M., 611;
Charles, 413; J.G., 221,
415
COFFINBURG: George,
104
COFFMAN: William, 172
COFFROTH: Conrad, 104,
441; Magdalene, 104
COGGINS: Thomas H.,
257
COIT: Joseph, 82
COLBERG: George W.,
532
COLBORN: Robert, 104;
Silvester, 104
COLBY: William J., 261
COLDWATER: Margaret,
104; Philip, 104
COLE: Alethea, 105;
Alworth, 105; Amplias,
105; Andrew, 105;
Barnabas, 105, 571;
Daniel, 105; Eli, 175;
Elihu, 105; Gideon, 105;
Hannah, 105; Henry, 105;
Herman N., 224;
Jeremiah, 408, 655; John
W., 105; L.B., JP, 105,
461; Lydia, 106; Phebe,
105; Priscilla, 105;
Rachel, 106; Royal, 105;
Samuel, 106; Sarah, 105,
237, 571; Sarah [BIRCH],
47; Simon, 247; Solomon,
106; Tobias, 106
COLEMAN: Jacob, 106;
John, 106; Nancy, 106;
Nathaniel, 106; Nathaniel
Jr., 106; Noah, JP, 311;
Peter, 124; Rachael, 106;
Thomas, 106
COLEY: Capt., 594
COLLAR: Harvey W., JP,
41, 197; S.P., JP, 198

COLLIER: Daniel L., 511;
Jonathan, 107, 565
COLLINS: Abraham, 110,
343; Charles, 107–8;
E.B., 50; Ebenezer 2nd,
107; Elizabeth, 107–8;
Elize B., 126; Florenda,
218; George, 107;
Hannah, 107; Isaac, 107;
James, 107; James, JP,
218; Jehu, JP, 450;
Jonathan, 21, 107, 362,
565, 604; Mary, 107;
Nancy, 107; Rachel, 107;
Sarah, 107; Thomas, 107;
Timothy, 107–8; William,
107–8
COLLUM: John, 426
COLLVER: Catharine
[COVERT], 180; Phineas,
180
COLMER: William, 163
COLT: Henry, 49
COLTRANE: Samuel, 220
COLVIN: Calvin, 108;
Cyrus, 108; Joseph, 108;
Levina, 108; Mercy, 108;
Peter, 108; Philip, 108;
Prudence, 108; Rhoda,
108
COLWELL: Capt., 357;
John, 69; Ruth
[BROWN], 69; Stephen,
580
COLYER: John, 107
COMAN: Joseph, 108
COMBS: R.M., 104
COMINGS: James, JP, 256
COMINS: Alexander, 108
COMLY: Samuel, 327
COMMAYER: Fanny, 536
COMSTOCK: Capt., 37;
Jacob, JP, 475
CONAWAY: Elizabeth,
109; Samuel, 109
CONDIT: David, JP, 472
CONE: A.P., 224; Calvin,
34
CONGDON: Henry, 109
CONGLETON: Moses, 348
CONINE: Delila, 109; Jane,
109; Jeremiah, 109; Otha
G., 109; Richard, 109;
William, 109

CONKLEN: Elke
[VanANKEN], 571;
Margaretta, 462
CONLY: Mary, 109;
Nicholas, 109
CONN: Andrew, JP, 272
CONNAWAY: Andrew,
109; John, 109
CONNELL: Christopher,
109; George, 484; Henry
M., 16, 194; John, 205
CONNELLY: Hugh, JP,
290; Isaac, 207; John, JP,
137
CONNER: Dosiah, 110;
Isaac, 361; James, 109;
John, 110
CONNOR: Catharine
[FONT], 110; George Sr.,
110; James, 109
CONOVER: Lewis T., 605
CONRAD: Anthony, 347,
598; Edward, 115; Henry
W., 13; James, 88; James
M., 186; William P., 567
CONVERSE: Daniel G.,
89; L.P., 617; Porter, 295
CONWAY: Charles, 110;
David, 110; John, 110
CONYNGHAM: John N.,
JP, 180
COOK: Abraham, 110–11;
Archibald, 377; Capt.,
260, 466; Darius, 110–11;
E., 379; Ebenezer, 111;
Edward, Col., 241;
Electa, 112; Eliza, 111;
Elizabeth, 110–11;
Erastus V., 110–11; G.B.,
486; George, 111; Henry,
111; Horace, 111; Jacob,
635; Jacob W., 344;
James B., 487; James, JP,
486; Jane, 635; Jasper C.,
111; Jemima, 111; Joel,
111, 170, 182, 195; John,
111, 635; Johnson, 128;
Joseph, 49, 112, 161, 326,
336, 436; Joshua, 112,
179, 325; L., 548; Levi,
111; Lucinda
[STURGES], 548; Mary
Ann, 110; N.S., JP, 31;
Noah, 112; Polly, 93;
R.L.M., 317; Rufus R.,
JP, 211–12; Samuel, 152;

(COOK, continued)

Sarah, 111–12; Thomas, 373, 384; *Uri,* 111; William, 81, 112; William H., JP, 27; William, Col., 474; Worthy, 111
COOKE: Charles L., 112; Chauncey, 112; E., 89; Giles B., JP, 29; Jane, 111; Jay, 430; John, 111, 651; P., 89; William, 111
COOL: Daniel, 15
COOLBAUGH: John, 481, 500; W.F., 291
COOLEY: Esther, 112; Luther, 112; Luther Jr., 112; Sally, 335
COOLMAN: George Jr., JP, 562; William, Jr., JP, 18
COON: J.T., 591; Jesse, 301; Mary, 231; Temperance [KALLAM], 301
COONEY: James, 112
COOPER: Abner, 113; Asa, Capt., 492; Capt., 483; Charles, 113; Charles J., 270; Col.s, 190; George, 113; James M., 391; John, 76, 79, 113, 303; Joseph, 113; Margaret, 113; Mary, 113; Samuel, 113; Thomas, 276, 376; William, 275, 460
COOSART: Valentine, 113
COOVER: John B., JP, 587; John, JP, 531
COPE: Caleb, 394; Herman, 372; J.J., 233
COPELAND: Eleazer, Dr., 372
COPENHAFFER: Catharine, 113; Michael, 113
COPES: George, 543; Hannah [STONE], 543; William, 114
COPP: George, 495
COPPENHAFFER: Catharine, 113; Michael, 113
COPPENHEFFER: Henry, 113

CORBIN: David, 207; Elijah, JP, 207; John, 114
CORBUS: John, JP, 447
CORD: S.T., 19, 74–75, 111, 169, 468, 471, 615
CORDLEY: Lyman, 64
CORE: Henry, 114; Isaac, 114; Sarah, 114
COREY: David, 63, 399, 456, 590, 613; Ebenezer, 114; Elnathan, 114; Joanna, 114; Sally, 114; Sybil, 114
CORK: William, 114
CORL: Leonard, 115
CORLEY: George, 115
CORN: Catharine, 115; Daniel, 115; Elizabeth, 115; George, 115; William, 115
CORNELIUS: Betsy, 115; Hannah, 115; Henry, 115; Mary, 115; Peter, 115
CORNELL: William, 115
CORNER: Anthony, 116; Catharine, 116; John, 116; Julia, 116; William, 116
CORNWALL: William A., 531
CORNWELL: Job, 116; Josiah, 428; Sarah, 116; William, 116
CORREY: James, 158, 166, 244, 357, 405, 492, 522, 599
CORRY: Alexander, 201
CORSE: Melo [TIFFANY], 561
CORTRIGHT: Thomas, 195
CORTZ: David, 448
CORWIN: Benjamin, 127; Diana, 127; Edward, 127; Eliza, 127; Esther, 127; Ghordus, 127; John, 127; Joseph, 585; Nancy, 127; Olive, 127; Thomas, 476
CORY: Elnathan, 114; Gabriel, 116; Sarah, 116
CORYELL: Sarah [BORROW], 56; Tunison, 56
COSE: Mariba [LINE], 338

COSSITT: Epaphnoditus, Dr., 514; Henry D.L., 221; James, Dr., 514
COTSMOYER: Barbara [COX], 117; Catharine, 117; Eliza, 117; George, 117; Samuel, 117; Sarah, 117
COTTON: Benjamin, 116; Dolly, 116; John, 116; Lucy, 116; Theophilus, 116
COTTRELL: John F., 110, 343
COUCH: Ebenezer, Capt., 183
COUDEN: Andrew, 444
COULSON: Jesse, 485; William, JP, 370
COULSTON: Sarah [BEAN], 34
COULTER: *Isabela,* 116; J.P., 167; Nathaniel, 116; William, JP, 371
COUNLY: Mercer Jr., 88
COUNT: Tunis, 180
COURT: John, 116; Joseph, 117
COURTNEY: Capt., 385, 592
COVANHOVAN: John, JP, 52, 91, 179, 294, 303, 474, 620
COVENHOVEN: Robert, 117
COVENS: Isaac, Capt., 59
COVENTRY: J., 209
COVER: A.J., JP, 393
COVERT: Catharine, 180; E., 215, 575, 643; Elisha, JP, 437; Hannah C., 180; Hiram, 180; John, 180; Polly, 180; Rachel, 180; Richard, 180; Tamar, 180; Tunis, 180; William H., 180
COWAN: Amos, 108; Andrew, Capt., 92; Edgar, 117; Elizabeth [ANDERSON], 10; Florence "Fanny," 108; Joseph, 108; William, 117
COWDEN: Capt., 244; John H., 331
COWDERY: Lyman, 242

COWELL: Henry R., 108; Isaac, 117
COWEN: Hannah [COLLINS], 107; William, 117
COWLES: Johnson, JP, 96
COWLEY: Sarah [MASSEY], 364
COX: Alexander, 117; Barbara, 117; Charles, 117–18; David, 285; E., 340; Elsey, 118; Jacob, 117; James, 12; John, 117; John W., 117; Joseph, 117; Mary, 117; Mary Ann [FRAZER], 195; Nancy, 117; Paul, 117; Thomas, 118; Tunis, 118; W., 340; William, 117–18; William Jr., JP, 118; Zachariah, 604
COXE: A.S., 292; James E., 328
COYLE: Barnabas, 385; Isabella, 118; Manassah, 118; Robert, 118
CRABS: Henry, JP, 58
CRAEL: James, 118; John, 118
CRAFFORD: Elijah, 118; Elizabeth, 118; Joseph, 118
CRAIG: Amelia, 118; Capt., 164, 187, 247, 251, 327; Col., 36, 157, 381, 392; Harriet, 118; Henry K., 118; Isaac, Major, 118; *Issabella*, 119; James, 119, 594; John, 118–19, 580; John C., 307; John Jr., 119; John N., 118; Lydia [BRICKELL], 65; Martha, 119; Mary, 119; Matilda, 118; Neville B., 118; Oldham G., 118; Samuel, 119; Samuel Jr., 36; Samuel, Capt., 56; Thomas, 119, 248, 264, 465; William, 85, 119, 121, 399; William P., 308
CRAIN: Adam, 119; Hannah, 526; Roger, 119; Sarah, 119
CRAINE: J.W., 119
CRAM: John, 119

CRAMER: A.L., JP, 57; Andrew, 119; Christian, 120; Elizabeth, 120; Enos, 233; Helfer, 120; Henry, 120, 331; Jacob, 120; James, 156; John, 120; Julian, 120; Lawrence, 331; Lorence, 120; Margaret, 120; Polly [LEHMAN], 331; Sophia, 120
CRAMOND: Henry, 35
CRANDAL: Ariel, 146; Edward, 41
CRANE: A.R., 256; Col., 238; Elihu, 120; Freeland A., JP, 559; Jacob, Capt., 77; Joel, JP, 591; John, 126, 467; Mary, 126; Mary [THOMPSON], 560
CRANMER: Ashbel L., 217; Electa [FOWLER], 192; Josiah M., 192; Morris, 446
CRAPO: Celia, 120; Jonathan, 120
CRAVATH: Roxa [BINGHAM], 46
CRAVEN: Ebenezer, 557; Elijah R., 218; *Ishi*, 115, 598; Jane, 120; John, 120, 168; Julia Ann [TEVIS], 557
CRAWFORD: A.W., 73; Alexander, 78; Allen, 300; Andrew, 120; David, 121, 362; Edward, 73, 498; Eleazer, 121; Elizabeth, 121; George T., JP, 371; James, 203, 380, 540; John, 90, 121, 154, 467, 640; Joseph, 174; Julia [LANE], 324; Mary, 120; Peter, 121; Polly, 121; Robert, 121; Thomas Hartley, 258; Val, Col., 93; William, JP, 82, 102
CRAY: William M., 21
CRAYCROFT: B.B., 105
CREAMER: Ann, 218; Joseph, 387
CREARY: Samuel, JP, 283, 324
CREASY: Samuel, JP, 209

CREEKBAUM: Philip, 121
CREEVER: Elizabeth [NOLF], 422
CREIGH: John T., 563; Thomas, 540
CREIGHBAUM: Philip, 121
CRESS: John, 315; Juliana [KIRK], 315
CRESSMAN: Daniel, 124; Elizabeth, 124
CRESSON: Eliott, 419
CRESSWELL: John, 536; Robert, 429
CRESWELL: Samuel, JP, 185
CRIDER: David, 121
CRISE: Andrew, 122; Catharine, 122; George, 122
CRISMAN: Jacob, 481
CRISSEY: Elizabeth, 33
CRISSINGER: Simon, 474
CRISSMEN: Enoch, 299
CRIST: Capt., 81
CRITCHFIELD: Asa, 125; David, 125; Jacob, 122; James, 122; Jesse, 122; John, 122, 125; Joseph, 122; Lemuel, 125; Lorenzo, 125; Martha, 122; Phoeba, 122; Polly, 122; Rachel, 125; Sally, 122; Susanna, 122; William, 122
CRITCHLOW: James Jr., 125
CROCKER: *Byer*, 122; Dyer, 122; Jedediah, 122; Silvanus, 122
CROFFORD: Stephen, 122, 555
CROFT: Joseph, 122; Juliann, 122
CROGHAN: William, Capt., 520
CROLL: Margaret, 199; Zebulon, 199
CROMIUS: Stephen, Capt., 246
CROMWELL: James F., 35; James S., 624
CRONINGER: Joseph, 122
CRONK: Garret, 123; Susannah, 123

CRONMILLER: Martin, 123
CROOK: George, Rev., 247
CROOKS: John, 497; Mary [SCOTT], 497; Robert, 317
CROPSEY: William A., 399
CROSBIN: James, 328
CROSBY: Capt., 344; Catharine A., 10; David, 123; David T., 123; Eliza, 123; Hannah, 123; James, 123; Nathaniel P., 123; Rachel, 123; William H., 123
CROSIER: David, JP, 547
CROSKEY: Henry, 76, 574
CROSLEY: James, 328
CROSS: Daniel, 123; George D., JP, 84; James, 123, 563; John, JP, 598; Samuel, JP, 494
CROSSLEY: James, 328
CROSSMAN: Daniel, 124
CROSSOM: John, 124
CROSTHWAITE: Barbara [WAGNER], 577
CROSWHITE: Barbara [WAGNER], 577
CROTHERS: William S., 213
CROUSE: Jonathan J., JP, 36, 253
CROUT: Mathias, 124
CROW: David, JP, 92; George, 124; Hannah [McGLAUGHLIN], 331; Samuel, Col., 130; William, 331
CROWELL: Elisha, JP, 439, 545; Lydia, 23; W.N., 545
CROWER: Elizabeth, 124; Rudolph, 124
CROWL: Capt., 264, 511; Jacob, Capt., 276
CROWLEY: Miles, 124
CROWSE: John J., JP, 13
CROXTON: Abraham, 124
CRUM: Adam, 119; Cornelius, 119; John, 119; Mary, 119
CRUMBINE: Peter, 125
CRUMLOW: Caleb, 125; Catlip, 125

CRUSE: John, 125
CRUSEN: Elizabeth A. [McELROY], 377
CRUTCHFIELD: John, 125
CRUTCHLOW: James, 125; Mary, 125
CUCKLE: Sarah [FOULKROD], 192
CULBERTSON: Col., 131; Robert, JP, 59
CULLOUGH: Patrick W., 104
CULP: Jacob, 313, 330
CULVER: Abraham, 126; Caty, 372; John, 372; Mary, 126; Milicent [ROBERTS], 476; Solomon, 83; Timothy, 126
CUMMING: Eliza, 126; John, 126; John C., 126; Julia, 126; Margaret, 126; Mary, 126; Nancy, 126
CUMMINGS: Alexander, 512; David, 126; Hannah, 127; Hannah M., 126; Jacob, 127; James, 400; Jonathan, 127, 555; Mary, 127; Nathan, 126; Olive, 127; Polly, 127; Ruth, 127; Tyler, 127; William, 108
CUMMINS: Isaac, 146, 192, 598; James, 276; James C., 575; John, 22; John D., 133; Robert, 379; William B., 366
CUNE: Joseph W., JP, 148
CUNNINGHAM: Archibald, 383; Cathrine [RIBERT], 469; Col., 4, 624; Cyrus, JP, 361; Hugh, 469; J.T., JP, 58, 445; Jesse, 575; John, 122, 399; John M., 71; John W., 327; Jonathan F., 87; Joseph, 126; Margaret, 126; Mary [HARBISON], 239; Patty [HANKS], 238; William, 80
CURRAN: Samuel, JP, 486, 492
CURREY: Col., 259

CURRIER: David, 38; Samuel, 127
CURRIN: Benjamin, 127; Diana, 127; Edward, 127; Eliza, 127; Esther, 127; John, 127; Nancy, 127; Olive, 127
CURRY: Catharine, 127; Col., 266; Daniel, 239; E.J., 653; Ebenezer D., 370; Elizabeth [WERTZ], 592; James, 127; John, 131, 164, 310, 423; Robert, JP, 93; Samuel, 127; T.B., 356; William, JP, 560
CURTIS: A.S., 447; C., 48, 119, 453; Carter, 52, 203, 451, 506–7; Gilbert, 151; Henry, 128; Isaac, 128; J.F., 42; Joel B., 46; John, 388; Marmeduke, 128; Martin, 564; Mary Ann [HORTON/HOUGHTON], 270; Nelson, 270; Willard, 603
CURTISS: J.C., 111, 238, 455; Nehemiah, 128; Persis, 498; Persis [SCOVILLE], 498; Peter, Capt., 529
CUSACK: John, 407
CUSTAR: Isaac, 91
CUSTARD: Conrad, 128; Jacob, 128
CUSTER: Jacob, 243; Jonathan, 129
CUTHBERT: Allen, 252, 593; Emily [RUSH], 486
CUTLER: George N., 242
CUTWATER: Col., 249
CYPHERT: George, 176, 425

D'AVRAINVILLE: A., 593
DAGER: Lewis, 475; Lydia [ROBERTS], 475
DAGGETT: Huldah [BILLS], 129; Jacob, 128; John, 129
DAILEY: Daniel, 129; David, 129; G.B., JP, 182; George, 129; Johannes, 129; John, 129;

(DAILEY, continued)

Maria, 129; Maria E., 129; Rebecca, 129
DAILLEY: Dennis, 129
DAILY: James, 224; William, 91
DAITON: Col., 103
DAITT: Justus, 129
DALE: E.B., 8; Ellen [BOYD], 590; James J., 306, 408, 525; Leah L., 212, 436; Michael G., 229, 338; Nicholas, 546; Samuel F., 323, 621; Samuel, JP, 21, 24, 37, 48, 153, 188, 212, 229, 269, 306, 308, 310, 323, 337–38, 359, 372, 394, 399, 408, 414, 423, 455, 473, 476, 525, 546, 552, 621; William W., 338
DALRYMPLE: David, 129; Thomas, 129
DALY: George, 308; John, 129
DALZELL: James, 529, 540; Robert, 59, 90, 266, 374
DALZEN: James, 185
DAMAN: Abraham, 130; H., 38
DAME: Timothy, JP, 118
DAMON: Dexter, JP, 76
DANA: Daniel, 130; E.L., 31
DANADILL: George, 130
DAND: E.L., 97; John, 130
DANDLE: Capt., 565
DANFIELD: Catherine, 130; John, 130; John H., 130
DANFORD: Asa, Capt., 564
DANFORTH: Capt., 357
DANGLOP: N., JP, 150
DANIELS: Frederick, JP, 5; Henry, 624; John V., JP, 23, 480
DANIELSON: James A., 22
DANLEY: Martin A., 372
DANN: Philip, 130
DANNAKER: Christian Henry William, 141

DANNER: George S., 508; J.B., JP, 231; Joel B., JP, 219, 447, 624; Sarah, 508
DANSDILL: George, 130
DARBEE: Moses, 131
DARBY: Dorothy, 130; Moses, 130–31
DARE: John, 572
DARLING: Derrick P., JP, 367; Joshua W., 427; Theron, JP, 70, 111
DARLINGTON: Brinton, 273; Edward, 344; Jesse, 354; John, 131
DARRAH: Capt., 247; Charles W., 542
DARROW: John, 131; Lyman, 579; Martha, 131; William, 535
DART: A., JP, 74; Alfred, 543; Cyrus, 131; Hannah, 131; Hart, 131; Irene, 131; Justus, 131
DARTT: Cyrus, 129; Hannah, 129; Justin, 131; Justus, 129; Solon S., 129
DARVIS: Levi, 131
DASHER: David, 469
DATAMER: John, 131
DAUB: Henry, JP, 319
DAUD: Elizabeth, 130; Isaac, 131; John, 130
DAUGHERTY: Mary, 132; Patrick, 132; Peggy [HARTMAN], 246; William T., 256
DAUGHTEN: Capt., 483
DAVENPORT: John, 132
DAVID: Jacob, 253
DAVIDHEISER: Elizabeth, 132; Henry, 132; Solomon, 132
DAVIDHISER: Elizabeth, 132; Henry, 132
DAVIDSON: C/Katherine, 132; Capt., 333; David, 132; E.C., 132; James, 132; John, 181, 562; William, 132, 241
DAVIES: Edward, 201; John, 143, 166, 303, 415
DAVIS: Abigail, 636; Ann, 133; Arman, 422; Cadw. E., 297; Capt., 259, 480, 607; Catharine, 135; Charles, 502; Daniel, 113,

133; David, JP, 421; Elizabeth, 135; Emry, JP, 390; George, 133; Hannah, 133; Harriet, 133; Henry, 133, 135, 220, 295; Henry R., 202; Hezekiah, 133; Hugh, 471, 580; Isaac, 134; Isaiah, Capt., 528; Izabella, 135; James A., 414; James Baron, JP, 278; James S., 644; Jane [JOHNSTON], 295; John, 113, 133, 135, 243, 539, 623; John 2nd, 134; John D., 177, 298, 403, 434, 459, 492, 548, 583; John F., JP, 225, 229, 344; John P., 78, 313, 346, 352; John S., 135; John W., 7, 554; Joseph, 134; Josiah, 134; Julia, 133; Levi, 134, 147, 228; Lewellyn, 134; Margaret, 135; Maria, 133; Martha, 134; Mary, 132–33; Methuselah, 134, 636; Moses, 134; Nancy, 135; Nathaniel, 133; *Nethuselah*, 134; Philip, 135; Rachel, 134; Rachel Ann [TERPENNING], 554; Rachel H., 135; Samuel, 53, 133, 135; Samuel L., 499, 528; Sarah, 132–33, 135, 198; Sarah [BOYCE], 59–60; Stewart, JP, 83, 108, 207; Susan [JACKSON], 286; Susanna, 134; Thomas, 135, 186; William, 133–35, 358, 663; William S., JP, 7
DAVISON: Patrick M., 376; Samuel, 370
DAVITT: J.W., 260
DAWES: Francis Y., 436; Henry, 37, 507; Samuel, JP, 269
DAWICK: William, 245
DAWLING: G., JP, 151
DAWSON: Augustin M., 87, 280; Elizabeth [WILKINSON], 602; J., 13; Robert D., 352; William, 406

DAY: Abraham, 136;
Artemas, 136;
(DAY, continued)

Benjamin, 136; Bethany,
136; Daniel, 136; E.H.,
588; Ezekiel, 136; H.L.,
113; James, 136; John,
136; John Beatty, 136;
Laura C., 191; Leah
[BISBEE], 47; Luther,
136; Marey, 136; Moses,
136; Nehemiah, 136;
Sarah, 136; Wareham, JP,
404, 480; William, 136
DAYTON: Col., 211
DEAL: Daniel, 253;
George, 136; Jacob, 288
DEAM: Jane, 136; Samuel,
136
DEAMER: Philip, 136
DEAN: Aaron, 137;
Benjamin, 137; C.M.,
397; David, 595;
Elizabeth [TEVIS], 557;
G.W., 596; Jane, 137;
John, 137, 557; Joseph
W., JP, 137; Katharine,
595; Martha, 137; Mary,
137; Samuel, 137;
Samuel, Capt., 206;
Sarah, 137; Thomas, 396
DEANE: Samuel, 137
DEARDORF: Daniel, 395;
Eve [MILLER], 395
DEARDORFF: William,
385
DEARMOND: Michael,
137
DEARY: James, Capt., 555
DEATS: Jane [YOUNG],
622; John, 137
DEBREE: John B., 251
DECKEL: Capt., 623
DECKER: Abraham, 138,
144; Benjamin, 138;
Cornelius, 138; Elizabeth,
138; Hannah Ann, 138;
Isaac, 138; Jacob, 417;
James, JP, 105; John,
496; John Jr., 138; Leah,
138; Simon J., 138;
Thomas, 138
DEDIER: John, 138; John
Sr., 138

DEEBLER: Abraham, 138;
Mary, 138
DEEMER: Peter, 138
DEEN: Benjamin, 137;
James, 137
DEETZ: Peter, 52; Phebe
[BLANCHARD], 52
DEFFENBAUGH: Eve
Mary [HUBLEY], 441;
Henry, Dr., 441
DEFORD: David, 381; J.H.,
90, 557
DEGAL: Lewis, 368
DEHAAS: Charles, 190
DEHART: A., 14; Jane K.
[ARMITAGE], 14;
Samuel, 138
DEHAVEN: A.H., 528;
Jonathan, 138; Peter, 542
DEHM: William, 138
DEHOFF: Samuel, 235
DEHUFF: Jacob, JP, 183
DEILEY: Daniel, 139;
Philip, 139
DEILI: Daniel, 139
DEILY: George, 139; Maria
E., 129
DEIS: John, 139
DEITER: Ann Maria, 139;
Catherine, 139; Conrad,
139; George, 139; John,
139; Magdalena, 139;
Susanna, 139
DEITRICH: Conrad, 417
DELANCEY: John, JP, 216
DELANEY: Michael, 110
DELANO: Kesiah
[WINSLOW], 610
DELEMORE: Robert, 169
DELONG: David, 359;
Jesse, 139; John, 139;
Rachel, 139
DELWBITT: Elizabeth,
139; Paul, 139
DEMARIANVILLE:
Charles, 140
DEMING: Buel, JP, 236;
Chauncey, 137; Correl,
140, 273; Jonathan, 314;
R.H., 106; Solomon, 140;
Sylvester, JP, 331;
William S., 38
DEMMON: Col., 411
DEMMONS: Catharine
[KLYNE], 317
DEMPSEY: Dennis, 140

DEMUTH: John G., JP, 133
DENBY: Charles T., 595;
Consider T., 130
DENIG: Levi, JP, 426;
Lewis, JP, 130, 224, 540
DENIKE: Catharine, 140;
Davis, 140; John, 140;
Samuel, 140
DENIS: Lewis, JP, 37
DENLINGER: Christian,
JP, 481
DENMAN: Aaron, 129,
190, 218, 312–14, 316,
330, 346, 386, 497, 545,
560; M.B., 50, 380, 564;
Matthias B., 302, 348,
604
DENMANS: Reuben, 58
DENNING: Mary, 140;
William, 140
DENNIS: Andrew, JP, 342;
J.J., JP, 204
DENNISON: Andrew, 140;
Ann, 140
DENNISTON: Joseph, 141;
William, 141
DENNY: James, 141; John,
289
DENSMORE: Asa, JP,
211–12, 297
DENT: George, JP, 606;
T.J., 606
DENTON: David, Capt.,
168
DENTSLER: Christian, 141
DENTZLER: Christian,
141
DENZLER: George, 141
DEPEYSTER: George B.,
JP, 81, 580; Joel B., 207
DEPUY: Aaron, 141;
Abraham, 141; Isaac,
141; Jacob, 193
DERBY: Consider T., 130;
Dorothy, 130
DERICKSON: David, JP,
426; Joseph, 171, 200
DERR: Christian, 141;
Daniel, 157; David W.,
173; Elizabeth, 141–42;
Israel, JP, 332; John, 142;
John F., 117; Margaret
[ROTH], 482; Mathias,
141–42, 151
DERRICK: A.H., 370
DERSHAM: Ludwig, 142

DESROSIERS: Léopold, JP, 486
DETHMORE: Elizabeth, 142; William, 142
DETOR: Simon, JP, 465
DETRICH: George, 147; Susanna, 147
DETRICK: David, 478; Jacob, 229, 517; John, 368
DEUTZLER: Christian, 142; Elizabeth, 142; Eve, 142; George, 142; Lydia, 142; Margaret, 142
DEVALL: Mary [CHAPMAN], 95
DEVANPORT: Oliver, 496
DEVEBAUGH: Adam, 361
DEVEN: James A., 500
DEVENEY: John, 142
DEVENNY: Charles D., JP, 40; Lafayette, 317
DEVIN: Thomas, 611
DEVONS: Leonard, 142
DEVOY: Peter, 143
DEWALT: Michael, 143
DEWARD: W.L., 536
DEWCES: William P., Dr., 10
DEWEY: C., 591; Eli, 258; Emanuel, 143; John Woodward, 143; Justin, 495; Levi, 495; Mary, 495; Mary [SCOTT], 495; Oliver, 143; Rodolphus, JP, 267
DEWITT: Betsy, 140; Elijah, 441; Elizabeth, 139; George, 139; Hannah, 139; James, 139; Julia A., 140; Morgan, 139; Paul, 139; Polly, 140; Susannah, 139
DEWOLF: Alice [PELTON], 441
DEYO: Ann, 143; Elias, 143; Elias Jr., 143; Emmy, 143; Mary, 143
DIAS: George, 143
DIBBLE: Capt., 106
DICE: George, 143
DICK: David, 297, 348, 377; George, 331; J. Moore, 146; J.R., 297; James R., 360; Moore, 182; W.W., JP, 3

DICKASON: Samuel, 144
DICKENS: James, 144
DICKENSON: Sarah, 491
DICKER: Abraham, 144
DICKERSON: John, 349
DICKESON: Peter, Capt., 103
DICKEY: Charles, 144; I., 66; Isaiah, 6, 11, 13, 17, 26, 41, 69, 148, 184, 198, 206, 226, 228, 232, 234, 258, 261, 289, 311, 324, 382, 390, 397, 454, 476, 479, 554, 584, 588, 603, 606, 610, 613; James, 144; John, 144; Lydia, 144; Moses, 144; Peter, 144; Robert, 39, 126, 130, 262, 595; Robert Jr., 258, 422
DICKIE: William H., JP, 237
DICKINSON: Capt., 354; Friend, 145; George H., 527; Mary "Polly" [CHURCH], 97; O.C., 479; Samuel W., 145; Sarah K., 491; Waitstill, 145; William, JP, 403, 434
DICKSON: Benjamin, 145; James, 145, 654; James N., 201, 242, 337; Nancy [MILLER], 654; Rachael, 145; T.H., 33, 282, 553; William, 148
DIEDRICK: Reuben, 551
DIEHL: Jacob, 145; William, 54
DIETER: Ann Maria, 139; Catherine, 139; Conrad, 139; George, 139; John, 139; Magdalena, 139; Michael, 139; Simon, 139, 351; Susanna, 139; William, 139
DIETRICH: Elizabeth [GENTZERMAN], 208; Henry P., 33, 624
DIFFENBACH: C.P.J., 33
DIFFENDERFER: David, 145; John, 145; Mary "Polly," 145; Michael, 145
DIHM: William, 138

DIKE: Adin, 145; Benjamin, 146; Calvin, 146; Susannah, 146; William, 145
DILL: David, 146; James, 136
DILLE: Uzal, 471, 628
DILLER: Amos, 87; Roland, JP, 87, 145, 173, 236
DILLINGER: Jacob, 308, 471; John, 476; Margaret, 398
DILLON: Capt., 157
DILWORTH: George, 319
DIMACK: Davis, JP, 42
DIMICK: Amasa, 146; Matilda, 146; Sally, 146
DIMMICK: Dan, 593; E.C., 270; Edward, 146; Isaac, 290, 299; M.M., 116, 138, 270, 391, 402, 535; Milton, 593; Moore, 146; Moors, 146; Oliver S., JP, 551; W.H., 263
DIMOCH: Shuball, JP, 531
DIMOCK: Asa, 38, 146, 258, 396, 440, 497, 598; Asa Jr., 452, 656; David, 146–47; Davis, 146–47, 167, 258, 598; J.H., 146; John H., 147; Sarah, 146
DIMON: Ann, 559; Charles, JP, 1, 72, 559; Delawgor, 41
DINGMAN: Daniel W., 358, 481, 598
DINIMICK: Edward, 146
DINSLY: William F., JP, 122
DINSMOOR: Rebecca [ANDERSON], 10
DIRHAM: James, 200
DIRL: Jacob, 145
DISE: John, 139
DISENBERG: Peter, 418
DISHONG: William F., 266
DISMANT: John, JP, 622
DITCHER: Robert, 147
DITRICK: George, 147
DITTO: Francis, 147; John, 147
DIVELY: Michael, JP, 509
DIVINS: William, JP, 231
DIVVERS: J.F., 231

DIXON: Hugh, 147; Jacob, 147; John, 147; Margaret, 147; Marshall, 147; Mary, 147; Nancy, 147; Patrick, 147; Rachel, 147; Sarah, 147; Walter, 148; William, 148

DIXSON: Joseph J., 273

DOACH: Robert, 148

DOAK: Mary [ANDERSON], 10; Moses, 148; Robert, 148

DOAN: Job, JP, 412

DOBBIN: James, 148; Robert, 148

DOBBINS: Catharine, 148; James, 148; Jane, 148; John, JP, 22; Jonathan B., 521; Robert, 148

DOCK: Elizabeth, 156; Jacob, 156; Mary, 156; Philip, 156; William, 156

DODDRIDGE: Jacob, 148

DODGE: Mehitable, 148; Shadrach, 148

DODSON: John, JP, 189, 242, 253, 540; Michael, 148

DOEBLER: Abraham, 149; Rudolph K., JP, 319, 480; Solomon, 462

DOLBY: Joseph, 134, 318, 475; Mark, 352

DOLIN: Michael, 149

DOLL: Christian, 158; Henry, 149; Jesse, 158; John, 149; Martin, 149; Peggy, 149

DOLLINGER: John, 149

DONAGAN: J.W., JP, 26; James, 224, 234, 301, 316, 482, 588

DONAGH: John, 614

DONALD: James, 149; William, 149

DONALDSON: James, 40; John, 149; P., 478; Susanna, 150; William, 150, 423

DONEGAN: James, JP, 25

DONEHOO: James, JP, 373, 442

DONKEYMOYER: Frederick, 40–41; Martha [BELLAS], 40–41

DONKOMOYER: Frederick, 40–41; Martha [BELLAS], 40–41

DONLEY: James, 47, 82, 427, 430

DONLY: Hugh, 150; John, 150

DONMAYER: Lewis, JP, 250

DONNAN: H., 70

DONNELL: Lany, 252; Nathaniel, 150; William, 150

DONNELLY: William, JP, 357, 562

DONNER: J., 367

DONNEY: Richard, 353

DONOGHUE: Albinus, 150; Alphonsus, 150; Cornelius, 150; Frances Cornelia, 150; Julian, 150; May Emelia, 150; Susan, 150

DONOHO: James, 150

DOOEY: Peter, 143

DOOGAN: George, 157

DOOLITTLE: David, 150; James, 97; John T., JP, 54

DORATEY: John, Capt., 15

DOREN: John, 335

DORIN: R.S., 595

DORLAND: Lambert, 151

DORMAN: H., 42, 96, 106, 194, 349, 434, 467, 564; Howell, 2, 306; William, 29

DORMYER: Solomon, 238

DORNAN: H., 547, 555

DORNBACK: John, 151

DORNBAUCH: John, 151

DORNBOUGH: John, 151

DORNEY: Philip, 334

DORONEY: John, JP, 624

DORR: Benjamin, 23; Matthias, 151

DORRIS: Wiliam, 312

DORROW: James, 173

DORSEY: Larkin H., 194

DORWART: Henry, 229; Jonas, 310; Samuel, 372

DOTTER: Samuel Solomon, 151

DOTTERER: Capt., 523, 528

DOTY: Asa, 151; David, 324; Gillis, 151; Haldy,

475; Jerusha, 475; Jonathan Sr., 151; Juliet, 475; Laurana, 151; Nathaniel, 151–52; Zebulon, 152, 291

DOUD: Jesse, 152; Jesse G., 152; John, 130; *Lodenia,* 152; Lucia, 152; Marcia, 152; Rebecca, 152; Thomas Shepherd, 152

DOUGAL: James L., Dr., 103; T.B., 408

DOUGHERTY: A.E., 207; Andrew, 152; Capt., 468; Col., 38; James, 152; John, 152; Mary, 153; Roger, 153; Sarah, 153; William, 153; William Jonathan, 153

DOUGHTY: Christopher, 153

DOUGLAS: John, JP, 240, 530; Woodroe, JP, 7

DOUGLASS: Andrew, 153; Col., 277; Eliza, 153; Elizabeth, 154; Ephraim, 153; James, 262; John, 153, 328, 496; Joseph G., 273; Robert, 154

DOULEY: James, 223

DOUTHILL: R.H., 184

DOVER: John, 154

DOWDERMAN: Catharine, 154; Jacob, 154; Julia, 154; Sabina, 154; Sarah, 154

DOWELL: Charles W., JP, 141

DOWLIN: Paul, 102

DOWLING: John, 184

DOWNEY: John, JP, 73, 275; R.W., 443

DOWNING: George W., 507

DOWTHET: Mary [WILKINSON], 602

DOYLE: Edward, 154; Elisha, JP, 59, 110, 178, 181, 202, 216, 295, 425, 435; William L., 196

DRAKE: Benjamin, 154; C.S., 532; Charity, 154; Charles B., 31; Col., 236; F.D., 154; James, 154; Martha [DEAN], 137; Orsamus L., JP, 325, 532;

(DRAKE, continued)

Rachel [CRITCHFIELD], 125; William, 155; Zachariah, 137
DRALLY: John, 155; Margaret, 155
DRAPER: A., 155; Jonathan, 155
DRAUGHT: Richard, 155
DRAY: Luke, Capt., 342
DRAYER: George, JP, 50
DREAHER: George, 155
DREAHR: George, 155
DREKER: Godfried, 155
DRENNAN: James A., 155; Martha, 155; Thomas, 155
DRESSER: Samuel, 319
DREW: Ira, Capt., 87
DREXEL: A.I., 304; F.M., 242, 504, 526; Francis M., 144; J.W., 409; James W., 209, 356
DREXLER: Jacob, 318
DRINKER: Richard, JP, 548
DRISCOLL: Denis, 525
DRISSEL: David, 251
DRUENING: William, 156
DRUM: Christopher, 156; Jacob, JP, 44; Philip, 156; Simon, 7, 52, 236, 329, 506; Thomas L., 27; W., 26; William, 7–8, 10, 54, 120, 138, 148, 156, 186, 284, 302, 329–30, 346, 354, 367, 369, 374, 465, 472, 504, 506, 542
DRUMHELLER: Jacob, 586
DRURY: Leonard, 156
DUANE: William, 282, 342; William Jr., 283
DUBBS: Catharine [DUEY], 143; Jacob, 143
DUBOIS: Col., 89; Henry, Capt., 419; Martha [PATTERSON], 435; Samuel F., 436; William E., 140, 436
DUBREE: Charles, 195
DUCK: Daniel, 156; Elizabeth, 156–57; Henry, 156; Jacob, 156;

John, 156; Mary "Polly," 156; Philip, 156–57
DUCKETT: Abraham, 606
DUCKMAN: William, 158
DUDLEY: Gilman, 144, 600; Isaac, 157
DUEY: Catharine, 143; Elizabeth, 143; Emanuel, 143; Eve, 143; Frederick, 143; John, 143; Peter, 143; Simon, 143; Susan, 143
DUFF: D., JP, 163; Henry, 157; James, 157; John, 375
DUFFIELD: James, 157; Mary, 157; William, 483
DUFFY: Capt., 392; John, JP, 81, 239; Peter, JP, 160
DUGAN: Catharine, 157; Daniel, 157; George, 157; John, 158; Margaret, 158
DULIN: Anne, 158; George S., 158; Jane, 158; John, 158; John H., 158; Margaret, 158; Mary, 158; Sarah, 158
DULL: Christian, 158; Joseph, JP, 364
DUMARS: John, 81, 237
DUMER: Eli, 346
DUMPHEY: James, 158
DUMUN: Horrell, 130
DUMUTH: Samuel, 542
DUNBAR: George, JP, 114, 167, 194, 364, 416
DUNCAN: Alexander, 159; Emily, 51; George, 159; James, 159, 187; James J., 159; John, 159; John N., 159; Joseph, 159, 540; Margaret, 159; Matthew, 25; Rebecca, 159; Temperence, 159; William F., 180; William, Gen., 159
DUNGAN: Elizabeth, 269; Isaac, 162; James, 162; Jesse H., 526; John, JP, 265, 322; Mary [DYER], 162; Phoebe [DYER], 162; Thomas, 162, 550
DUNGLISON: *Robler*, 161
DUNHAM: Abraham, 160, 349; Adelia, 160; David, 130, 160; Edwin, 160;

Samuel, 160; Sylvester, 160
DUNKLEBERGER: Peter, 160
DUNLAP: Andrew, 279; Lot S., 545; Mary [SOLLIDAY], 525; Peter O., 348; William, 160
DUNN: Andrew, 160; H.D., 137; Isaac, 160; James L., 212; James W., JP, 3; John, 39, 160; John H., 556; Philip, 130; Samuel, 610; Washington, JP, 607; William, 113
DUNNELL: Stephen, 160
DUNNING: Dennis, 161; Robert D., 565
DUNOTT: H.H., 310
DUNSCOMB: Orren H., JP, 419
DUNWELL: Deborah, 160; S.A., 160; Stephen, 160
DUNYAN: John, 138
DUPEY: Catherine, 161; Isaac, 161
DUPONCEAU: Peter S., 161
DURAM: Edward, 177
DURAND: Andrew, 161
DURBOROW: Samuel, JP, 288
DURGEY: Col., 19; John, Col., 455; Robert, Capt., 441
DURGY: Col., 617
DURHAM: B.R., 572; Jane [SMITH], 520; Joseph T., 520
DURKEE: Col., 90, 461; Ebe, 161; Joel, 161; John, Col., 161; Solomon, 161
DURLING: Andrew, JP, 482
DUSENBERRY: William, 161
DUSHAM: Joseph T., JP, 199
DUSKY: John, 162
DUTCHER: Henry, 162
DUTOT: Ferdinand, JP, 322, 596; Frederick, JP, 535
DUTTON: Henry, JP, 587; Jonathan M., 193; Solomon, JP, 76, 143, 461

DWIGHT: Charles, JP, 466
DYCE: Thomas, Capt., 161
DYE: William, 568
DYER: Christina, 162;
Edwin, 222; Hannah, 162;
Herman, 147; Joseph,
162; Mary, 162; Phoebe,
162; Thomas, JP, 50, 189,
192, 223, 452; Walter,
162
DYRE: Joseph, 162
DYSART: James, JP, 431

EAGLE: Daniel, 164;
Dominick, 21, 569
EAGLES: Maria E., 322
EAKER: G.W., 376
EALER: Abraham, 269
EAMES: *Granot,* 502;
Sylvia [SEWARD], 502
EARL: Susan J., 299
EARLE: Emily, 162;
Henry, 121, 162; Joseph
O., 162; Mary W., 162;
Sarah, 162; William, 162
EARLY: Capt., 130; John,
325
EARNEST: Elizabeth, 162;
George, 162
EASTERWOOD: J.D., JP,
145, 232
EASTMAN: Deliverance,
163; James, 163
EASTON: Justus, JP, 26,
198; Richard, 163;
William S., 434
EATINGER: Betsey, 173;
Catharine, 173; George,
173; Gotlieb, 173; Henry,
174; Jacob, 174; James,
173; John, 173;
Margarett, 173; Mary,
174; Mary Ann, 173–74;
Rachel, 174; Samuel S.,
173; Sarah, 174; Susan,
174
EATON: Aaron, 163;
Robert, 163
EATTON: Jannet, 163;
Joseph Sr., 163
EBARHARD: David, 7
EBB: Emanuel, 163
EBBS: Emanuel, 163; W.,
568; W. William, 541;
William, 61, 309, 361,

364, 427, 449, 470, 515,
578, 588
EBERLE: Charles L., JP,
80, 251, 359, 466;
Elizabeth, 163; Henry,
163
EBERLY: John, JP, 479
EBERMAN: George A.,
450; Matthias, 37
EBERT: Betsey
[WARNER], 584; Jacob,
397; Joseph, 584
EBLING: Emma L., 163;
William, 163
EBNER: Casper, 164
EBY: David, JP, 415
ECK: Anthony, 553
ECKART: John 2nd, 164
ECKEL: John, 214, 441
ECKELS: William, 108
ECKERT: David, 25, 188,
340; Marks B., JP, 358
ECKHART: John, 164;
Sarah, 164
ECKMAN: James, 496,
607; Mary [WILSON],
607
ECKNIGHT: Isaac, 164
ECKOLS: John, 164
ECKRIGHT: Isaac, 164
ECKROADT: Solomon,
283
ECKROTE: Velle
[IRELAND], 283
EDDINGTON: James C.,
616
EDEL: Sarah [McELROY],
377
EDER: Joshua, 437
EDGAR: David, 164, 611;
Susan [SCHENCK], 493
EDGARTON: Edward,
164; Jesse, 164
EDGCOMB: Roger, 164
EDGE: John, 165; Nancy,
165
EDGECOMB: Luzerne,
164
EDGELY: Elizabeth
[KELLER], 305
EDGINGTON: Thomas,
JP, 455
EDINGER: Abraham, 520;
John, 174, 520
EDMOND: Samuel, 209

EDMUNDS: Enoch, 134,
636
EDSON: Abed, 207; Jonas,
313; Nehemiah, 70
EDWARDS: Capt., 259;
David, 477; Dorcas, 165;
Edward, 36; Emanuel,
165; Enoch, 165; Frances,
165; Gardner, 165;
Henry, 165; Hosa, 165;
J.L., 34–35, 37, 45, 83,
94, 263; Jonathan, 165;
Joshua, 165; Laura E.,
165; Mary, 165; Perry,
165; Phebe, 165;
Prudence, 165; Rhoda,
165; Ruth, 165; Samuel,
10, 354; Sivia, 165;
Susan, 165; Susan E., 165
EDWIN: Sarah [DIXON],
147
EGBERT: Thomas, JP, 135
EGE: George, JP, 479
EGGLESTON: Eliab, 166;
Fanny [WHITE], 597;
Lucy, 166; Moses, 597;
Timothy, 166
EGLESTON: Lucy, 166;
Timothy, 166
EGLIN: Benjamin, JP, 457
EGNER: Charles, 24, 56
EGOLF: Henry, 166;
Michael, 166
EHLER: Elizabeth
[SHELLEY], 506; Jacob,
506; John, 8
EHRENZELLER: Jacob,
166
EICHBAUM: William,
165, 438, 610
EICHELBERGER: Capt.,
180, 515
EICHHOLTZ: Jacob, 164,
637; John, 164, 637
EICKHOLS: John, 164
EICKLEBERGER:
Elizabeth, 166; George,
166
EIMER: Eva Elizabeth
[SCHNEIDER], 494
EIRICH: David E., JP, 27;
David W., JP, 569
EISEMAN: Michael, 284;
Peter, 284
EISENBISE: Henry, JP,
472, 495

EISENHOUR: Philip, 284
ELDER: Ann, 167; Cyrus, 291; John, 166–67; Mary, 166; William, JP, 593
ELDMAN: Isaac, 528
ELDRED: Capt., 431; John, 167; N.P., JP, 156; Nathaniel B., 207, 226, 233; Richard, JP, 138, 391; Zephaniah, 167
ELDREDGE: Orlando A., 167
ELDRIDGE: Fanny, 167; James, 167; Lucretia, 167; Lydia, 167; Mary, 167; Robert, 167; Sally, 167
ELEY: William, 167; William Jr., 167
ELLINWOOD: *J.N.*, 21
ELLIOT: Harriet [GOLDY], 215, 643; James, 643; John, 160, 167–68; Robert, 167
ELLIOTT: David, Rev., 49; James, 35, 167–68, 258, 510; Jonathan, 38, 136, 167–68, 311, 465, 529; Joseph, 168; Lewis, 281, 465; Ralph, 97; Rebecca, 168; S.W., 168; William, 168, 220
ELLIS: C.H., 169; Charles, 186, 261, 340, 400, 484, 573, 578; David, JP, 400; Henry, 168, 461; J.P., 120; *J.W. Alder*, 186; James, JP, 138; John, 168; Jonathan T., 169; Joseph, 168; Lois, 168; Nathan, 558; Pamelia [BENNETT], 42; Rebecca, 169; *Rebekah*, 169; Stephen, 169; Thomas, JP, 253
ELLSWORTH: D.F., JP, 12; John, 169
ELLY: Michael, 169
ELMER: Susan [EDWARDS], 165
ELMORE: Major, 447; Robert, 169
ELMS: Col., 594
ELSWORTH: David, 169
ELTON: Thomas, 169
ELWELL: Elijah, 342

ELY: Catharine [CAMPBELL], 85; Elisha, Capt., 94; Elya, 170; Gabriel, 170; John Jr., 170, 382; Jonathan, 170; Mary, 382
EMBICH: F., 138, 149, 257; Frederick, 188, 319; Israel, JP, 149
EMBLY: Capt., 275
EMERICK: Daniel, 163; Elizabeth, 170; John, 170; Philip, 170
EMERY: George, JP, 555; Jacob H., 170; John, 170; Josiah, 285; Margaret, 170; Philip, 170
EMMERSON: Sarah, 170; Stephen, 170
EMMERT: George W., 125; Horatio W., 263
EMMIS: Joshua, 170
EMMITT: John, JP, 222, 233
EMMONS: D.W., 587
EMRIE: Jehu A., JP, 478
ENDLY: Henry, 559
ENGAL: George, 170
ENGEL: George, 170; George Jr., 170; Solomon, JP, 276, 542
ENGELHAUPT: Barbara, 171; Hannah, 171; John, 171; Solomon, 171
ENGLE: Jacob, 171
ENGLER: John, 171; Leonard, 171
ENGLISH: James, 171; Jane, 171; John, 171; Oriann, 407; William, 171
ENMINGER: Henry, 171
ENNES: Alexander, JP, 281
ENNIS: Deborah, 91
ENOCH: Homer, 400; Thomas, 297
ENOS: Col., 72, 480; Roger, Col., 12, 529; Roswell, JP, 297
ENSIGN: Joel, 270
ENSMINGER: Henry, 172
ENSWORTH: Allen, JP, 442; Anson L., 105
ENTERLINE: Michael, JP, 465

ENTREKEN: James, JP, 387
EPLY: John, 172
EPPLER: John V., 38, 630
EPPLEY: Elizabeth, 172; Jacob, 172
ERB: Anna [SANDERSON], 491; Benjamin, 491; Elizabeth, 172; Jacob, 172; Polly, 172
ERDMAN: Andrew, 172; Susannah, 172
ERUS: David, 611
ERVIN: John, 563
ERWIN: Col., 225; Daniel, 456; Elizabeth, 173; Henry, 173; Joseph, Capt., 262; Margaret, 173; Maria, 172; Mary, 173; William, 173; William L., 173
ESCHLEMAN: Abraham, 173
ESHELMAN: Henry, 469
ESHLEMAN: Benjamin, 248
ESPY: Capt., 124; George, 173; James S., 201, 237; James, JP, 173, 314
ESSER: Anna Maria, 173; Charles W., 173; Jacob, 173
ESTEL: Artimesia [ROGERS], 480
ESTEP: Joseph, 367
ESTERLY: Daniel, 526
ESTLE: E., 605
ETTER: Dorothy [KAUTZ], 302
ETTINGER: Jacob, 173–74; Mary Ann, 173–74
EUWER: Daniel, 360
EVANS: Abel, 174; Almira [PARRISH], 434; B., JP, 254; E., Col., 11; Eleazer, JP, 65, 610; Evan, 59–60, 174, 212; Ezekiel, JP, 353; F.G., 287; George A., 72; Jane, 106; Jeremiah W., JP, 293; Joel, 526; John, 106, 174; Joshua, 297; Josiah W., JP, 378; Lott, 213, 467; Lott Jr., 243; Louis, 269;

(EVANS, continued)

Mary, 247; Mary A., 294; *Mordecai*, 174; Randal, 297; Robert T., 297; Samuel, 11, 40, 72, 227; Susannah, 174; Thomas, 160; Walter G., 215, 235, 256, 305, 352; William, 434; William B., 174

EVELAND: Daniel, 174; Peter, 175

EVERENGER: Polly [SUMMERS], 549

EVERETT: Homer, 31, 62, 468; Mary, 175; Oliver, 175; Samuel, 525; Thomas, 577

EVERHART: E.L., 379; John, 175

EVERITT: Isaac, JP, 151

EVERSON: George R., Capt., 175; Nathaniel, 164; Richard, 164; Thomas M., 175

EVERTS: Garnet, 344

EWALD: Charles J., 137

EWART: Robert K., JP, 340

EWEN: James Jr., JP, 407; Jesse, 552

EWING: Alexander, 175; J.A., 103; J.M., 64, 191; James, 176; Jane [HARBISON], 239; Jesse, 176; John, 208, 299; Jonathan H., 617; Jonathan K., 240, 557, 615; W., 93; W.D., 216; William, JP, 103, 167

EXEL: Jane [CAMPBELL], 85

EYERLY: Jacob, 380

EYLER: Jacob, 176; Peter, 176

EYSTER: George, 176

FACKENTHALL: Michael, 176; Michael Jr., 176

FADDAS: Catherine [STEWART], 541

FAGAN: Enoch, 176

FAGUNDAS: Catharine, 176; George F., 176; Mary, 176; Susan, 176

FAHNESTOCK: B.A., 350; B.L., 309; H.C., 60, 208, 214, 320, 414; Harris, 418; Harris C., 216, 329, 440, 621; Samuel, 254, 361

FAIR: Mathias, 587

FAIRCHILD: Elizabeth, 177; Stephen, 177; Stephen Jr., 177

FAIRMAN: Robert, 16

FAITH: Abraham, 176, 319

FALCON: Abram, 357

FALKER: George, 214

FALKNER: Ann, 177; Daniel, 177; Elizabeth, 177; Jane, 177; John, 177; Margaret, 177; Nancy, 177; Sarah, 177; Thomas, 177

FALLON: Christopher, 63

FALZINGER: Henry, 177

FANNING: Capt., 157, 463

FANSCHOVER: Col., 418

FANVER: Betsey, 177; Elizabeth, 177; George, 177; Samuel, 177; William, 177

FARAND: Lester T., JP, 459

FAREIRA: Joseph Jr., 341

FARMER: Lewis, Capt., 548

FARNELL: John, 201

FARNHAM: A.N., JP, 42

FARNSLER: Joseph, 39

FARNSWORTH: Moses, 177

FARQUHAR: A.M., 240

FARRAND: Jarad, 178

FARRAR: L.T., JP, 471; Mary L., 471

FARRELL: Alexander, 178; David, 178; George, 181; James, 416; John C., 178; Margaret [NAGLE], 416; Maria, 11; Mary, 178; Susannah Caire, 178; Thomas, 124

FARRON: John, 178

FARWELL: Isaac, Capt., 177

FASSETT: John S., JP, 480

FASSITT: Alfred, 423, 443, 601

FASY: John, 179

FAULK: John, 452

FAULKNER: Capt., 199; H.L., 131

FAUNCE: Capt., 495

FAUST: John, 178; Philip, 178

FAUSY: John, 179

FAUZEY: Mary, 313

FAWCETT: Robert B., JP, 104

FAWCY: John, 179

FAWROT: David, 179; James, 179; Mary, 179; Phebe, 179; Timothy, 179

FEATHER: Charles I., 332; Elizabeth, 179; Isaac, 179; John, 179

FEATHERLEY: Henry, 179

FEDDER: Henry, 75

FEE: Michael, 179; Rebecca, 179

FEGAN: Enoch, 176

FEGELY: John, 179

FEGLY: Phil, 390

FEISTER: John M., 173

FELIX: Peter, 180

FELKER: Elizabeth, 42; George, 214

FELL: Catharine, 180; Hannah C., 180; Jesse, 83; Jesse, JP, 28, 113, 209

FELLERS: Col., 496

FELLOWS: Abiel, JP, 476; Erastus, 105

FELTY: George, 180; George F., 180; Henry, 180; Magdalina [SAILOR], 489–90; Samuel, 469

FENN: Cynthia E. [BEACH], 34; Henry, 34

FENNER: John, 180

FENNIKLE: Peter, 515

FENNIMORE: Benjamin, 180

FENSTERMAKER: John, JP, 305

FENTON: Daniel G., 40; John, 381; Margaret [McKEE], 381

FERER: Henry, 657

FERGUS: Hugh, 619; Thomas, 52
FERGUSON: Alexander, 546; Dan, 339; David, JP, 546; Ebenezer, 181; Elizabeth, 181; J.B., 546; Jane, 277; John, 74, 181, 235; W., Capt., 237; William, 181
FERING: Elizabeth, 181; George, 181
FERRA: William, 227
FERRAND: Lester T., JP, 314
FERREE: Henry H., 389
FERRELL: George, 181; Mary, 181; William, 181
FERRIS: Augustus F., 297; John, 181
FERRY: Loman, JP, 286; Luman, JP, 30
FERTENBAUGH: Jane, 181, 638
FERTIG: Abraham, JP, 13
FESIG: Adam, 54
FESMIRE: Catharine, 182; John, 182
FESMORE: Catharine, 182; John, 182; Mary, 182
FETTER: George, 410; John C., 144
FETZER: Jacob, 182
FEVIER: John, 182; Mary Ann, 182
FIELD: William, JP, 614
FIELDS: William, JP, 62
FIERNAN: W., 112
FIFE: Andrew, 182; John, 182; Margaret, 182; Mary P., 182; Nathaniel, 182; William, 182
FIFFE: James, 182
FIGART: Benjamin, 564; John, 564
FIGGINS: James, 182
FIGHT: John, 181
FILER: Orris, 182
FILSON: Jeremiah, 254; John, 546
FINAFROCK: Daniel, 409
FINCH: Darius, 42; H., 576; Samuel, 182; William, 183
FINCHER: John, 193

FINDLAY: Daniel, 183; James, 369; John K., JP, 274
FINDLEY: D.W., JP, 313
FINE: Henry M., 230
FINFRICK: Andrew, 183
FINK: J.H., 332; Michael, 183
FINLAY: J.B., 254
FINLEY: Capt., 451; Daniel, 183; John, 183; Joseph, JP, 224; Nehemiah, 543; Polley [STOKELEY], 543
FINNEY: Capt., 236; James C., 321, 571; John F., JP, 63; John L., 183; Josiah, 183; Josiah Jr., 183; Lazarus, 184; Mary, 321; Sylvester, 184; Walter, JP, 71
FINNI: Mary, 321
FINSTEAD: Samuel, JP, 289
FISCUS: Abraham, 184
FISEMIRE: John, 184
FISH: B.F., 418; Ephraim, 184; John, 184; Michael, 184; Pardon, 184
FISHBURN: Capt., 335
FISHBURNE: Ann Mary, 185; Philip, 185
FISHER: Abel Jr., 185; Barbara [SUTTON], 550; Caleb, JP, 621; Capt., 101, 393; Charles F., JP, 275, 459; *Cisor*, 614, 663; Col., 101, 529; Emma [PATTERSON], 435; George, 185, 320; Henry, 185; Jacob, 108; James, Capt., 353; John, 45, 185–86, 511; L.G., 29; Linoley, 57; Margaret, 185; Martha, 185; Mary, 185; Mathias, 185; Michael, 186; Patrick, 195; Rachel, 185; Samuel, 550; Sarah, 404; T., 621; Thomas, 185
FISK: Lucia [DOUD], 152; Thomas, 152
FISS: Catharine, 186; Henry, 186
FISTER: Jacob, 75

FITCH: Andrew, Capt., 617; Gurdon, JP, 492; L.F., 131, 179; Talmon, 357, 428; Zalmon, 116, 418
FITTING: Catharine, 396
FITZGERALD: David, 359
FITZSIMM: David, 300
FITZSIMMONS: David, 12, 29, 74, 160, 193, 218, 325–26, 384, 407, 421, 432–33, 458, 538, 554, 583, 600; William, 186
FITZWATER: Jacob, 319, 387
FIX: Daniel, 392; Margaret [MILLER], 392
FLACK: James, 186; John, 260; Margaret, 186; Samuel, 178
FLANAGEN: James, 93
FLATHERS: Thomas S., JP, 211–12
FLATT: Andrew, 186
FLAUGH: Barbara, 186; Betty, 186; Catharine, 186; George, 186; Jacob, 186; John, 186; Mary, 186; Matthias, 186; Samuel, 186, 219
FLECK: Conrad, 187; Peter, 187
FLECKINGER: Joseph, 508
FLECKINGER: John, JP, 7, 197; Peter Jr., JP, 63
FLEESON: Matilda [CRAIG], 118
FLEET: David, Capt., 25
FLEISHER: Jacob, 186; Peter, 186
FLEMING: George, 181; Henry, JP, 166, 269, 378, 485–86; John, 362, 602; John E., JP, 253; Joseph, JP, 593; Oliver G., 146; Robert, 385
FLENNEKEN: R.P., 344
FLENNIKEN: R.P., 71
FLETCHER: Col., 39; Jacob, JP, 124; John, 53, 483; Robert, JP, 208; Simon, 187; Thomas, 640
FLICK: John, 510; Paul, 289, 359; Peter, 187

FLICKINGER: Catharine [FLAUGH], 186; Jacob, 186

FLIEGER: Theodore, 295

FLING: Elizabeth, 187; William, 187

FLINN: Catharine [WILT], 592

FLINT: Edward, JP, 253, 358, 432; Luke, 187

FLOOD: Jane, 187; John, 187

FLORY: Peter, 187

FLOWER: Col., 412, 485; Zephon, 187

FLOWERS: Benjamin, 103; Emeline, 188; Hannah, 188, 653; Jacob, 653; Julia, 653; Robert, 188; Sarah, 188; Thomas Jr., 188; Thomas Sr., 188

FLOYD: John, 539; John M., JP, 459; Thomas, JP, 450

FLUGER: John, JP, 133

FLYNN: Simon, 188

FOBES: Aaron, 188; Anderson, 188; Chloe, 188; Elias, 188; Henry C., 188; Joshua, 188; Levi, 188; Simon, 188

FOGEL: John, 145, 239, 407, 471, 613; Solomon, 407; Willoughby, JP, 149

FOGG: Joseph, 175

FOGHT: George, 188

FOGLE: Willoughby, JP, 486

FOLK: *Simeon,* 188

FOLMER: William, 64

FOLSZ: Joseph, 459

FOLTZ: Benjamin M., 72; George, 188; John, 188; Joseph, 459

FOLWELL: Charles S., 292, 513; John, 661

FONT: Catharine, 110

FOOR: David, 439; Leonard, 439; Margaret [PECK], 439

FOOS: Matthias, 189

FOOSE: Isaiah, 176

FOOT: Lucy, 189; Nathan B., 189; Simeon, 189; Timothy, 189

FORBERT: William, JP, 380

FORBES: Alfred, JP, 363; Arthur, 189; Charles, JP, 168; Hugh, 189; James, 189; Margaret, 189; Nathan, 189; Preceptor, JP, 76, 228, 574, 576; Robert, 177; William, 189

FORD: A.H.L., 453; Bela, 614; Betsy [KING], 313; C.H.L., 182; Christopher, 190; David, 190; Eleanor, 190; George W., 191, 613; Hopeful, 190; Jacob, 34; James, 182, 190, 453; John, 94, 421; Margaret, 190; Nathan, 190; P., JP, 127; Peter, Capt., 123; Richard, 614; Sarah A. [RODGERS], 478; Thomas, 190

FORDHAM: Francis, 614

FORE: John, 419

FOREBAUGH: Solomon, 358

FOREMAN: David, JP, 159; James, JP, 278; Peter, 159, 190

FORGERSON: Henry, 181; *Miriam,* 181

FORGISON: G.L., 190; John, 190

FORKER: Israel, JP, 2, 143, 161, 174, 324, 400, 414, 438, 561, 615

FORMAN: David, JP, 561; Martha B., 191; Nowell, 191; Thomas M., 191

FORMON: Col., 443

FORNEY: Catharine, 444; George, 444, 537; Jacob Jr., 221; Jonathan W., 508; Joseph, 444; Margaret, 444; Margaret [PHILLIPS], 444; Mary Elizabeth, 444; Peter P., 444; Samuel, 444

FORREST: Abigail, 191; David, 191; Elisha, 454

FORSTER: Amelia, 192; John, 191; Jonathan, JP, 54; Robert, 192; Thomas Jr., 352, 477

FORSYTH: Andrew, 60; John A. Jr., JP, 606; Joseph, 191; O., 260

FORT: Ann, 191; *Besphatin,* 191; Bisphaln, 191

FORTE: John, JP, 438

FORTENBEH: Jane, 638

FORTINBACH: Jane, 639; Philip, 638–39

FORTNER: Benjamin, 191

FORTNEY: George, 472; Jacob, 145

FOSTER: A.M., 119; Benjamin, 658; Catharine, 191; Charles B., 224; E., Capt., 591; E.B., 417; G.W., 172; H.D., 458, 565; Henry D., 185; Hiram W., 507; Hugh, 102; James, 129, 346, 383, 497; James W., 587; John, 191; Joseph H., 207; Robert, 192; Robert, JP, 123; Thomas, 192, 249, 617; William, 78, 129, 313, 316, 346, 497

FOULK: Capt., 480; Simon, 188

FOULKE: Caleb, JP, 264; Joseph, JP, 229, 556

FOULKROD: Isaac, 192; Jacob, 192; Jacob B., 192; John, 192; Mary, 192; Sarah, 192

FOUNTAIN: James, 312

FOUTS: Jacob, 532; William, 487

FOWLER: Augusta L., 192; Austin, 192; Caleb, 453; Edwin, JP, 470; Electa, 192; G.H., 358; George S., 192; Ira C., 192; Isaac, 215; Jonathan, 192; M.P., 358; Nancy, 192; Olive [PRATT?], 453; Sarah "Sally," 192

FOX: Aaron, 192; Abraham, 192; Andrew, 193; Catherine, 193; Chloe, 193; David, 193; Elisha, 193; G.R., 243; Jacob, 193; John, 368; Lydia, 192; Mary, 375; Nancy [FOWLER], 192; Reuben, JP, 202;

(FOX, continued)

Samuel, 330; *Sinkler*, 193; Thomas, 193; *Tinkeler*, 193
FOY: George, JP, 152
FRAILEY: John, 193
FRAKE: Aaron, 76
FRALEY: John N., 182
FRANCE: Peter, 194
FRANCIS: Charles, 194; Hannah, 194; James, 96, 194, 463; Samuel, 194
FRANCISCO: Elias, 428; Mary, 428
FRANCISS: James, JP, 78, 602
FRANK: Joseph S., 405
FRANKENFIELD: Henry, JP, 420
FRANKFORT: Henry, 194
FRANKINBURGER: John, 63
FRANKLIN: Addison, 194; Arnold, 194; John, Capt., 217; Joseph, 195; Louisa, 194; Lucinda, 194; Mary, 195; Rhoda [COLVIN], 108; Thomas E., 455; Walter, 534
FRANKS: Isaac, 195
FRATT: Henry, 195
FRAVEL: Abm., 105
FRAZER: Catharine, 195; Elizabeth, 195; John, 195; Lenah [MIDDAUGH?], 195; Louisa, 195; Margaret Cecelia, 195; Mary Ann, 195; Permelia [SEELY], 500; Peter, 195; Rosanna, 195; Thomas Patrick, 195
FRAZIER: Alexander, JP, 349, 372; David, JP, 411; John A., 117
FREAME: William, 195
FREAR: Nathaniel, 388
FREASE: Solomon, 123
FREAT: Jonas, 393
FREAZE: Amanda, 195; Catharine, 195; Elizabeth, 195–96; John, 195; Lorenzo, 195; Margaret, 195; Martin, 195–96; Mary, 195; Susanna, 195
FRECH: Joseph, 384

FRECKELTON: Martha, 278
FREDERICK: Elizabeth [LYNCH], 351; John, 17, 351; Joseph, 196, 330; Louisa, 195; Michael, 196; Peter, 485
FREEBORN: Cyntha Lorinda [THOMSON], 560
FREEDLEY: Ludwig, 196
FREELAND: Daniel S., 394; Garrett, 196; Robert, 196
FREELANHISEN: Col., 34
FREEMAN: Benjamin, 196; Charles D., JP, 43, 285; Ebenezer, 434; James B., 43; John, 202; Mary, 197; Matthew, Capt., 152; Philip, 197; Samuel, 219, 240, 309, 365; Sidney, JP, 220
FREEMAND: Smith, 247
FREESE: Elbridge G., 277
FREESTONE: Ann, 195; William B., 195
FREEZE: Elizabeth, 195; Martin, 195
FRENCH: Capt., 620; Daniel, 197; Francis, 521; James, 521; John, 355; Lucy, 521; Mary, 197; Nathan, 197; Sophia, 521; William, 197, 521; William B., 521
FRETHY: Charles, JP, 554
FRETZ: Clinton, 195; Jacob, 195–96; Reuben, 562
FREY: Capt., 339
FRICK: Charles, 229; George, 623; George A., 363; Jacob, 187, 225, 623; William, 229, 344
FRICKER: Capt., 325; Peter, 197
FRIDERICI: Henry, 151; Joseph, 195
FRIED: Abraham, 330; Catharine [LEE], 330
FRIEND: A., 316; K.T., 146, 347, 470; Kennedy T., 120, 297, 339, 415; Porter R., 32, 37, 74, 407;

William C., 246, 523, 568; William Charles, 67, 289, 315
FRIES: Henry, 553; Peter, 197
FRIETTCHEY: Peter, JP, 306
FRILL: John W., 25–26
FRINK: Francis, JP, 9, 34, 120; Tracy, 42
FRISBEE: Samuel J., 153
FRISBIE: Ann, 197; Charlotte, 404; Levi, 197; Luman, 197; *Lurman*, 197; Luther, 198; Mahitable, 198; Peter, 197; Sally, 198; Samuel J., 153; Theodore, 197; Zebulon, JP, 18
FRISHMUTH: E.H., 56, 281; Jacob, 276, 290, 588
FRITZ: Balzer, 198; Jacob, JP, 382; Philip, 342
FRIZZELL: Jason Jr., 177
FROST: Anna B. [KNEELAND], 317; Martha [BREWER], 64; Stuart, 472
FROTH: Henry, 125
FROW: James, JP, 132, 466
FRY: Benjamin, 503; Conrad, 198; Elizabeth, 198–99; George W., 198; Henry, 198–99; Jacob, 198; Joseph, 156; Lawrence, 198; Mary, 198; Mary [COX], 117; Mary [DOCK], 156; Nancy [COX], 117; Nathan, 199; Peggy [STENGEL], 63; Peter, 199; Ph. F., 287; Sally [SHAFFER], 503; Sarah, 199; Sarah [DAVIS?], 198; Thomas C., 376
FRYER: Eleanor, 199; Frances [RODES], 478; Jacob, 452; Leonard, 199; William, 10
FRYHOFFER: William, 547
FRYSINGER: George, 440, 477; Jesse, JP, 125
FUHR: Catherine, 199; George, 366; Joseph, 366; William, 199

FULKERSON: John, 199
FULKINSON: John, 199
FULLER: A.S., 153, 556;
Alfred, 93; Amizi S., 355;
Amzi, 604; Benajah, 200;
Catharine, 200; Consider,
200; Hannah [BIERCE],
46; Ichabod, 200; Isaiah,
200; James, JP, 71, 341,
401; John, 166; Joseph,
200; Lucinda, 71, 200;
Martha, 200; Ruth, 200;
Sarah, 200; William, 200
FULLERTON: Alexander
Jr., 612; Hannah,
200–201; Humphrey,
273; Thomas, 200–201
FULLWOOD: C., 181;
Charles, JP, 253; David,
181
FULMER: Casper, 201;
Elizabeth, 201; Mary, 201
FULTON: Alexander, 119,
239, 623; Ann, 201;
Elizabeth, 201; James,
201; James Jefferson,
201; Jesse, 201, 579, 662;
John, 201, 579, 662; John
B., 201; Joseph, 201;
Miller, 201; Rachel, 201;
Robert, 530; William,
637; William A., 623
FULWILER: John, 9
FUNK: George, 201; Henry,
590
FUNSTON: Henry, JP, 157,
256, 273, 556; Lavina,
157; Nicholas, 412;
Sarah, 273
FURMAN: Allen F., 12
FURNELL: John, 201
FURNISS: William, 202

GABLE: John S., 446
GADD: Joseph, 476
GADDES: Henry, 202
GADDIS: Henry, 202
GAGE: Col., 262
GAHAN: James, 462
GAILY: Robert, JP, 167
GAIWICKS: Daniel, 202
GALAWAY: Elizabeth
[CHAPMAN], 95
GALBRAITH: Alexander,
202; Ephraim, 83, 266,

401, 544; James, 544;
John, 442, 533, 599;
William B., 366
GALE: Charles, JP, 430;
Mahitable [FRISBIE],
198
GALI: R., 74
GALLAGHER: Ebenezer,
202; Mary, 202; William,
254
GALLAHER: Hugh, 413;
Robert C., 466
GALLAWAY: William, JP,
54
GALLENTINE: Abraham,
202, 215; Jacob, 202;
Susannah, 215
GALLOWAY: Adam, JP,
455; Jane, 482
GALLUP: Col., 68; James
D., 609; Josiah, JP, 232;
Vilaty, 232
GALT: John, 236
GALWICKS: Daniel, 202
GAMAGE: Elizabeth
[BALLARD], 23;
Horatio, 23; Julia A.
[DEWITT], 140
GAMBLE: Eunice
[WESTFALL], 594; J.C.,
292; James, 117; Samuel,
594; Sarah, 408
GANDER: Jacob, 202
GANDINER: Jacob, 203;
Sarah, 203
GANDY: Enoch, 203;
Martha, 203; Rachel, 203
GANGEVOIR: George,
230
GANGWER: Andrew, 203;
Anthony, 203; Catharine,
203; George, 203; George
A., 203; Jacob, 203;
Mary, 203; Solomon,
203; Susan, 203
GANS: Lebbeus B., 16
GANSALES: Richard, 203
GANSEVORT: Peter, Col.,
17
GANSON: Nathan, 203
GARARD: C., JP, 410
GARDEN: Andrew, 204;
Priscilla, 204
GARDINER: Daniel, 204;
Hannah, 204; Vincent,
Capt., 364

GARDLEY: Samuel, 265
GARDNER: Capt., 328;
F.J., 117, 192, 379; Isaac,
26, 376; James, 204, 640;
Jean, 204, 640; John, 71,
204; John Jr., 204;
Jonathan V., JP, 191, 207,
479; Martin, 440;
Nathaniel B., 204; Phebe,
204; Thomas, 204
GAREE: A., 64; Isaac, 64
GARESCHÉ: Anne, 161;
Gabriel, 161
GARLAND: George, 409
GARNETT: Obadiah, JP,
107
GARRARD: Corbly, JP,
254, 406
GARRETSON: Joseph, JP,
228; William, JP, 207
GARRETT: Andrew, 125;
David, 30, 538; John,
109, 568; Samuel, 351,
354; William E., 390
GARRISON: Benjamin,
204–5; Ephraim, 204;
James, JP, 526; John,
205; Leonard, 205;
Rebecca, 205; Sarah, 204;
William, 205; Zibbiah,
205
GARTNER: Edwin, JP, 388
GARVEY: John, 205
GARY: Catharine, 205;
Peter, 205
GASKILL: David, 504
GASKIN: Capt., 173
GAST: Henry, 293, 337;
Margaret, 205; *Matthias*,
205
GASTEN: Joseph S., JP,
245
GASTIN: Capt., 391
GASTON: Alexander, JP,
74; Daniel, 206; Nancy,
206
GATES: Albert, 162; Capt.,
422, 460; Erastus, 190;
Freeman, 206; Nathaniel,
206; Oliver, 206;
William, Capt., 195
GAUF: John, 206
GAUGH: Esther, 603; John,
JP, 603
GAUL: Christian, 206; John
F., 206

GAULLAGHER: Thomas, 515
GAY: Col., 26, 594; Easty, 203; Peter, JP, 53–54, 504
GAYLARD: Abigail, 206; Darius C., 206; David L., 206; Elihu S., 206; Harvey R., 206; Levi, 206; Margaret, 206; Polly P., 206
GAYLORD: Ambrose, 206; Benjamin B., 39, 126, 232, 588; Eleanor, 206; *Electa* [COOK], 112; Henderson, 47, 361, 582; Jennett, 207; John, 207; Levi, 206
GEARHART: Harman, JP, 612; Jacob, 84, 394, 402
GEARY: Julia [CARNER], 116
GEBHART: Herman, JP, 241
GEDDES: Jonathan, 74; Joseph, 207; Sarah, 207
GEE: David, 207; James, 295; Mary [REEVES], 465; Polly, 207; Zophar, JP, 465
GEEHR: Balzer, Col., 448
GEER: Asa, 207; Benajah A., 210, 642; Erastus, 207; George, 210, 642; Gurdon, 210, 642; James, 207; Lucy, 210, 642; Mary, 207; Roger, 207; Ruth, 210, 642; Samuel, 210, 642; Washington, 380
GEERY: John, 208; John Jr., 208
GEHO: Zibbiah [GARRISON], 205
GEHR: Baltzer, Col., 32–33, 625; Jacob, Col., 155
GEIB: Henry, 208; Peter, 208
GEIDNER: Timothy, 308
GEIER: Col., 1
GEIGER: Albertus, 166; Col., 80; Henry, Col., 224; Jacob, 227, 641; John L., 225; Mary, 227, 641; S., Capt., 212; Samuel, JP, 166

GEIP: Henry, 208
GEIR: John, 209
GEISE: Henry, 208; Jeremiah, 208
GEIST: Conrad, 443
GEITNER: Elisabeth [KEMMERER], 649; Timothy, 649
GELAT: George, 208; Jonathan, 208; Robert, 208
GELLER: George, 208
GELWICKS: Ann M., 208; Anna Maria, 208; Daniel, 202; Mary, 208; Nicholas, Capt., 208
GEMMILL: William D., 409
GENTZERMAN: Elizabeth, 208; Eve Ann, 208; George, 208; John, 208; Mary, 208; Susan, 208
GEOFF: Capt., 483
GEORGE: Catharine [ROTH], 482; John, 227; Matthew, 209; Robert, JP, 213, 474; Thomas, 489; William, 209, 578
GERE: Henry, 621; Simeon A., 602
GERHART: Marelious, 209; Peter, 209
GERHARZ: Capt., 130
GERHEART: Isaac, Rev., 589
GERMON: Francis S., 250, 347
GERODELLE: John, 216
GEROULD: Ephraim B., 99, 456; James, JP, 194, 491, 497
GERRARD: *Linten*, 344
GEST: John, 219, 338, 537
GETTER: John, JP, 535
GETTY: Thomas R., 92, 328
GETTYS: Thomas R., JP, 461
GETZ: -----, Mrs. [KEIFFER], 304; George, 269; John Sr., 212
GETZER: Samuel, 351
GEYER: Andrew, 304; Andrew, JP, 34; Col., 19, 506; David, 209;

George, 338; George C., 58; Isaac, 209; John, 209; Peter, 209
GIBBINS: Thomas, 260
GIBBNEY: George, 209
GIBBONS: Francis A., 603; Joseph, 304; Philip, 209
GIBBS: Hannah [VANARSDALEN], 571; J.W., 83, 89, 120, 308, 336, 515, 553; Joseph, 209; William, 209–10
GIBLEY: Amarillis [PARKS], 433
GIBONS: Catharine, 209
GIBSON: Col., 431; George A., 562; J.W., 120; James, 114, 125, 226, 240, 248, 253, 446; John, 152, 154, 210, 289–90, 322, 369, 566; O.L., 129; R.M., 447; Rachel, 147; Thomas, 298, 497; William, 82, 189, 289, 498
GIDDINGS: J.R., JP, 69; Joshua R., 215, 261
GIDEON: Ann, 210; George, 210
GIER: Gurdon, 210, 642
GIFFORD: William, 210
GILBERT: B., 336; Elizabeth, 210; Frederick, 28, 38, 220, 293, 394, 483; Heber, 210; Henry, 419; Johannes, 283; John, 155, 276, 291; Lucina, 210; Mahitable [SEELY], 500; Stephen, 210
GILCRIST: Joseph, JP, 453
GILDER: Capt., 109, 249
GILDERSLEEVE: William Camp, 49
GILES: Olive [BENNETT], 42; Thomas, 567
GILFILLAN: Margaret [FIFE], 182
GILKERSON: James, JP, 322
GILKISON: James M., JP, 294; James, JP, 83; Nancy, 83
GILKYSON: Elias, 42; James, JP, 436

GILL: Capt., 341; Erasmus, Capt., 351; Thomas, 355; William, 211
GILLAM: James, 97
GILLASPY: Mary, 211; William, 211
GILLELAND: James, 221
GILLEN: John, 216
GILLESPIE: John, 211; Samuel, 140, 195, 207, 262, 395, 544
GILLET: Abigail, 211; Asa, 211; Betsy, 211; Grove, 211; Henry, 211–12; Henry A., 211–12; John, 211–12; Mamre, 211; Olive [MASON], 364; Samuel B., 211–12; William, 211; Ziba [ROWLEY], 484
GILLETT: F.H., 601
GILLETTE: Caroline M., 18
GILLIAM: James, 97
GILLIES: John, JP, 546, 580
GILLSON: Daniel, 212; Eleazer, 212
GILMAN: A., 460; Edward, 193, 433; Hiram, JP, 94; S.M., JP, 583
GILMER: Albert, 387; James, 238; William, 185
GILMORE: A., 87, 239, 539; Alfred, 70, 73, 223, 281; Jonathan, 81; Samuel A., 281; Stephen M., JP, 164; Thomas, 212; William, 185
GILSON: Daniel, 212; Joseph A., 212; Rachel, 212
GINGERICK: Sarah [SAILOR], 489–90
GINGINER: David, 256
GITTING: David, 151; Lewis, 33
GITZ: John Sr., 212
GIVEN: Samuel, 517
GLADDEN: Solomon, 212, 621
GLANTZ: John, 214
GLASGOW: J.C., 555; James C., 158; James C., JP, 99

GLASS: Elizabeth [MYERS], 415; George, 212; Jonathan Sr., 481; Josiah Jr., 538; Robert, 372
GLASSMEYER: Jacob, 213
GLEASON: Edah, 574; Milo, JP, 268
GLEIM: H.A., 240; Joseph, JP, 400
GLENCER: Ann Margaretta, 213; John, 213
GLENDY: Thomas, 213; William, 213
GLENN: Benjamin F., 427; David, JP, 10; James, 213, 408
GLENTWORTH: George P., 92; James, 213; Mary, 213; Rachel, 213
GLESSNER: Jacob, JP, 122, 287, 546, 582, 584
GLEZEN: Augustus, JP, 311
GLIDDEN: B., JP, 568; Benjamin, JP, 22
GLIDDINGS: Aranda P., 213; Clark, 213; Elisha, 213; Joseph W., 213; Joshua, 213; Joshua R., 213
GLIME: John, 121
GLINES: William, JP, 126, 137, 273, 386
GLIZEN: Augustus, JP, 601, 617
GLONINGER: Jonathan, 227, 641; Jonathan W. Jr., 58
GLONTZ: John, 214
GLOVER: A., JP, 608; James, 214; Mary, 214
GLUNT: Jacob, 98
GLYMER: Jacob, JP, 274
GODARD: Betsey [DEWITT], 139
GODDARD: W.C., 18, 200, 301, 314, 505, 599; William C., 31, 554
GODEN: George, 13; Hannah [ANTRUM], 13
GODFREY: George, 214; W.B., JP, 48

GODMAN: Abigail [LONGSTRETH], 345; James H., 466
GOFF: Delia, 23; Huldah, 214; Lucy [FRENCH], 521; Oren, JP, 534; Samuel D., 214; Solomon, 214
GOHE: Adam, JP, 482
GOHN: Jacob, 214; Mary, 214; Philip, 214
GOLDER: Robert, 75
GOLDY: Aches, 215; Harriet, 215; John, 214; John B., 215; Joseph, 215; Mary, 214, 643; Samuel, 215; Sarah, 215; William, 215
GOLLENTINE: Abraham, 215
GONDER: Joseph, 452
GONE: James, 109
GONSANLUS: James, 215
GONTER: Elizabeth, 215; John, 215; William D., 208
GOOD: Jacob, JP, 381; John, JP, 255; Mary [McKINNEY], 382; Nathan, 382; Tilghman, 203
GOODALL: Ebenezer, 215; Jerusha, 215
GOODELL: Joel, 215; Jonathan Weeks, 215; Mary, 215; Micah Newton, 215; Nathan, 215; Phebe G., 215; William, 215
GOODELLE: John, 216
GOODENOUGH: J.D., JP, 146, 528; James D., JP, 144; Jared D., 46, 304
GOODHART: J.C., JP, 402, 516; Jacob, JP, 141, 269, 274, 587; Joel, 274, 402, 587
GOODING: James, 216; Jane, 216
GOODMAN: Jacob, 27, 197; Joanna [BOWMAN], 59; Rachel [JENKINS], 290
GOODRICH: Achsah [PARSONS], 434; Charles, JP, 258, 560;

(GOODRICH, continued)

Dwight, 428; E.S., JP, 485, 557; Elisha S., 434; Evelina, 560; George, JP, 12; William, 65, 165
GOODSELL: Isaac, 167
GOODSPEED: Charles, 249; John, JP, 330, 445, 467
GOODWIN: Abraham, 64; Emery, JP, 3, 212; Harriet [PRIOR], 455; Martha, 415; Myron, 272; Philip M., 192; William B., 509
GOODYEAR: George, 216
GORDEN: Mary, 216; Thomas, 216
GORDON: Alexander, 416, 623; Catharine, 217; David, 148, 461, 658; Harriet, 217; John, 216–17, 493; John 2nd, 216; Mahala, 217; Mary, 217; Samuel L., 217; Sarah, 216–17; Thomas, 217
GORE: Alfred, 217, 528; John, 217; Obadiah, 18; Samuel, 18, 217, 272, 527; Sarah "Sally," 217
GOREN: Daniel D., JP, 45
GORMAN: Charles R., 618
GORMLEY: Joseph, 215
GORMLY: Adam, JP, 597
GORSUCH: Robert, 331
GORTNER: John, 75
GOSE: Thomas G., 248
GOSHEN: Capt., 488
GOSNER: Capt., 412
GOSS: Abraham, 217; Beder, 218; David, JP, 217; Ebenezer, 217; Elizabeth, 217
GOSSLER: George, 394
GOSURTEN: John, 59
GOTTIER: John, 169
GOTWALT: Jacob, 618
GOUDY: Capt., 102
GOULD: Daniel, 218; John, JP, 168; Sarah, 218; William 1st, 218
GOURLEY: David, 218; Mary, 218
GOWAN: Capt., 624; George, 218; Hugh, 218

GOWER: John, 218
GOWESE: Robert M., 24
GRAAF: John, 206
GRACE: Jacob, 218
GRAEFF: Jacob, JP, 32, 363
GRAFF: Samuel, 219; Susanna, 219
GRAFIUS: Daniel, 64, 229, 556; I., JP, 429; Israel, 137, 409, 429, 536, 564; J.S., 577; Jacob, 245, 437, 533, 549, 577; Jonathan, 386, 549; Jonathan S., 533
GRAFT: John, 219; Mary, 219; Philip, 219
GRAHAM: Andrew, JP, 120; Daniel, 219; Elizabeth, 532; Frances, 219; Francis, 219; George, 219; Hannah, 220; Henry, 219; Hugh, 220; J.H., 251; James B., JP, 40; James H., JP, 243; John, 220, 318, 384; *M.,* 25; Mary, 219–20; Thomas, 74, 162, 276; William, 1, 219, 622
GRAM: Kezia [MYERS], 415
GRAMLIN: Adam, 220; Isaac, 220; Peter, 220
GRANFORD: Abraham, Capt., 182
GRANGER: Abner, Capt., 193; Capt., 265
GRANNIS: John, JP, 184
GRANNISS: Enos, 220
GRANT: Benjamin, 426; Deborah, 220; E.P., 416; George, 220; J.P., 346; Jonathan, 221; Parkinson, 221; Robert, 220, 291; Sarah, 221; Thomas, 220
GRATT: Nicholas, 221
GRAVATT: John, 221
GRAVES: Amos, 221; John, JP, 244, 497
GRAY: A., 424; Alexander, 221; Capt., 173, 250, 340; Catharine [CORN], 115; Charles, Capt., 56; Daniel, 608; David, JP, 202, 222, 276, 491; Elizabeth, 413;

Esther, 221; Ezra, 190; Fanny, 614, 663; Francis W., 276; Gibbons, 244, 497; Isaac, 225; Isabella [MURRY], 413; James, 83, 148, 159, 221–22, 233, 266, 341, 468, 513, 593; Joel, 222; John, 115, 222, 413; Joseph, 222; Margaret, 413; Mary, 222–23; Millison, 222; Nathaniel, 222; Peter N., 321; Peter W., 222; Phebe, 222; Polly, 221; Robert, 223, 394; Samuel P., 222; William, 222, 381, 413; William Jr., 183; William M., 222
GRAYDON: Andrew, 544; William, JP, 201, 233, 544
GRAYHAM: Col., 77
GRAYSON: John, 340
GRAZIER: Isaac, 619; John B., 619
GREATHEAD: Thomas, 144, 518
GREEN: Anson B., 444; Anthony, 72, 363, 437, 574; Asahel, 175; Benjamin, Capt., 607; Caleb, 223; Capt., 232; Elizabeth [LOWE], 555; H., 622; Henry, 223; James, 101, 561; James 1st, 223; Jehiel, 223; John, 223, 555; Joseph, 260; Letty, 223; Levina [COLVIN], 108; Mary [KELLY], 307; Matthew, 553; N.M., 99; Noah M., 74; Prudence, 223; Samuel, 307; Samuel J., 32, 383; Sarah, 191; Timothy, 223; *Tomothy,* 223; Willard, 224
GREENAMOYER: Capt., 551
GREENAWALT: Col., 251, 325
GREENE: Abigail, 223, 644; Alanson, 223, 644; Christopher, 223, 644; James, 223, 644; Nancy, 223, 644; Polly, 223, 644

GREENLAND: Abner, 335; James, 224
GREENLEAF: Israel, 224; Mary, 224
GREENSLIGHT: Sarah, 504
GREENWALD: Jacob, 224
GREENWALT: Abraham, 224; Nicholas, 224; Philip, Col., 329
GREENWOOD: Aaron, 503; Capt., 90, 456; Eliza, 503; Thomas, 352
GREER: Capt., 519; George F., JP, 107; John, JP, 262
GREFFEY: Col., 416
GREGG: Andrew, 341; Capt., 272, 419; James, Capt., 573; Thomas, JP, 16, 108
GREGORY: Alexander, 225; Ann [ROBERTS], 476; Asahel, 224; E., 476; Elizabeth, 225; Hubbell, 224; John, 225; Lorana, 224; Milly, 545; Ralph, 225; Samuel, 224–25; Stephen, 225
GREIGER: John L., 225
GRENDER: Nicholas, 570
GRESHAM: Elizabeth, 225; George, 225; John, 562
GRETH: John, 250
GRETT: John, 221
GREY: Isaac, 225
GRIBBON: John, 225; William D., 225
GRIDLEY: Capt., 416
GRIER: David A., 507; John C., 150; John G., 433; Michael C., 85
GRIFFETH: William, JP, 274
GRIFFIN: Clara, 226; Col., 35; Ezra, 226; Francis, 81; G.W., JP, 466; George, 81, 226; Joshua, 226; Lydia [BUTLER], 81; Margaret, 226; Reuben, 423; Robert, JP, 468; Samuel, 196
GRIFFIS: K/Haren, 226; Lydia, 226; Stephen, 226

GRIFFITH: Elisha, 226; Henry H., 226; John, 96, 227; Levi, 227; Nicholas, 473; Samuel P. Jr., Dr., 205, 359, 454; Thomas, 395; William, 227
GRIFFITHS: A.W., 322; E., 222; John, 234; Samuel P., 116, 525
GRIGNER: Jacob, 227
GRIMES: Elijah, 23
GRIMM: Elizabeth [COLLINS], 107
GRIMSOM: Samuel, 227; Sarah, 227
GRING: David, 227
GRISWOLD: Amanda, 228; Capt., 447; David, JP, 434; Diana [HUTCHINS], 281; Fanny, 228; Francis, JP, 227; Harriet A., 228; Hiram, 416; John, 227; Laura, 228; Solomon, 228; Ursula, 228
GROSCOTT: Daniel, 228; Jacob, 228
GROSCUS: Paul, Capt., 32
GROSS: Adam V. Jr., 227; Jeremiah R., 393; John, 228, 533–34; Joseph, JP, 284; Philip, JP, 393; Polly, 228; William, 459; William M., JP, 41
GROSSMAN: Samuel, 341
GROSVENOR: Col., 23
GROTEVANT: Emily, 490
GROUT: Capt., 334
GROVE: Alise N., 65; Philip, 228
GROVER: Davis, 255, 595; Edmund, 228; Elizabeth, 228; Isaiah, 228; Joseph, 229; Salinda, 228; Simon, 228
GROVIER: Isaiah, 229
GROVIN: Isaiah, 229
GRUBB: Capt., 343; Charles H., 84; Col., 4; Curtis, Col., 347; Edward B., 455; Jacob, 229; John, 47; Peter, 84; Polly, 229; Sarah, 229; Thomas, 284, 433, 618; Tobias, JP, 139, 167, 219, 409

GRUBER: Henry, 229; Valentine, 229
GRUFFY: Andrew, JP, 490
GRUMPH: Christopher, 229
GRUNENDIKE: Samuel, Capt., 25
GRYDER: M., 87
GUERNSEY: Joseph W., 131
GUEST: Alban, 229; James, 229; Margaret, 229; Richard, 229
GUFFY: Andrew, JP, 219
GUIRE: Polly [PLANK], 447
GULDY: Col., 588
GUMP: Benoni, 230; Elias, JP, 405; George, 245; John, JP, 245, 312, 517; William, 230
GUNDAKER: H.W., 336, 473; Henry W., 153, 510, 540; Samuel, 511
GUNGIVOIR: George, 230
GUNN: Lucy, 230; Noble, 230; Westrull W., 230; William O., 230
GUNNELL: Beverly, 230, 645; Catherine, 230; Corben, 230, 645; Jonathan, 230, 645; Kitty, 645; Pamelia, 230, 645
GUNNISON: E.D., JP, 481; Ebenezer D., 192, 534, 599
GUNSALUS: Manuel, 36
GUNSWOORT: Col., 2
GURNEY: Francis, 230; Mary, 230
GUSEMAN: Joseph, 36
GUSHERT: Detrick, 231
GUTHERIE: William, 231
GUTHRIE: Capt., 340, 462; Elizabeth, 231; James, 11, 231; Joanna, 231; John, 231; Joseph B., 231; Mary A., 490; Robert, 231; William, 231, 297
GUTHRY: John, 231
GUY: Barbara, 231; Jonathan, 231
GUYNN: William, 231
GWIN: John, 232
GYLVIS: Hiram, 42

HAAS: D.B., 497; Mary [LUDWICK], 349; Peter, JP, 239
HABERACKER: G., 203
HACHENBURG: Peter, JP, 232
HACKENBERG: J.P., 490
HACKER: William, 41
HACKETHORN: John, 585
HACKETT: Allen, 232; William, 300, 510
HADDEN: Thomas, JP, 279, 371, 593
HADLEY: Moses, 232
HADLOCK: Asa, 232; James, 232
HAFFERMAN: Catharine, 232; Hugh, 232
HAGANS: J.S., 98
HAGARTY: Patrick, JP, 592
HAGEMAN: John, 232
HAGER: C., 476; Christopher, 408; Jacob, 232; John, 232
HAGERMAN: James, 233
HAGERMEYER: Henry, 233
HAGERTY: Elizabeth, 379; James, 379; Jarret, 571; John, 379; Letitia [McGILL?], 379
HAGGINS: Henry, 233
HAGUE: Reuben, 125
HAHN: Abraham D., 317; Capt., 452; Catharine, 233; Daniel, 233; David, 233; Isaac, 233; Jacob, 233; John, 233; Joseph, 233; Mary, 233; Michael, 233, 509.; Samuel, 233; Sarah, 233
HAIGHT: Henry R., JP, 587
HAILING: Abram, JP, 230
HAILMAN: J.M., 25, 343; J.W., 312, 351, 486
HAIN: Philip, 233
HAINES: Benjamin, 233; Christiana [BIRCH], 47; Elizabeth, 234; Jacob, 234; John, 234; John Jr., 234; Roger, 233; Samuel, 234

HAIR: James, 234; John, 234
HALBACH: Augustus F., 61
HALBACK: John F., 308, 649
HALDEMAN: C., JP, 247; Christian, 450, 612; Peter, 394
HALE: Benjamin, 98; J.M., 28; R.C., 233; Samuel, 55
HALEY: John, 234
HALL: David, JP, 559; Ebenezer R., JP, 105; Edward, 559; Edward A., 498; Edward H., 491; Elias, 229; *Evenliner*, 234; Hezekiah, 234; Hiland, 331; J.C., 423; James, JP, 46, 350; Jane, 491; Jesse, 457; John, 155, 233–34, 491; Jonathan Jr., 457; Joseph, 445; Levi, 234; Lucy [WOOD], 614; Mahlon, 491; Margaret, 234; Moses, 234; Reuben, 234; Sally [JONES], 297; Salmon Jr., 212; Sarah, 234; Thomas W., 491; Timothy, 235; William, 235, 446, 491; William H., 614
HALLECK: Calvin, JP, 226; J., 236
HALLER: Col., 43, 264, 276, 334, 395, 458; George, JP, 494
HALLET: Ann, 235; Eliza, 235; Jonathan, 235; Martha, 235
HALLETT: Ephraim, 235; Isabella, 235, 305; Jonah, 235
HALLMAN: George, 235
HALLOWAY: Seth P., 114, 241
HALSTEAD: Edward, 235; Jacob, 235
HAMAKER: Jacob, JP, 580
HAMBLETON: Joseph, 123
HAMBLY: Thomas, 77; Thomas C., 36
HAMBRIGH: Henry, Capt., 236

HAMBRIGHT: Henry, Capt., 183, 236; Mary Ann, 236
HAMEND: Frederick, 62
HAMERSLY: William W., JP, 91
HAMES: H., 457
HAMILL: Hugh, JP, 327
HAMILTON: Aaron, 412; Abram, JP, 15; Capt., 377; Daniel, Capt., 236; David, 237; F.R., 4; Feny, 236; George, 236; George P., JP, 70; James, JP, 201; Jean, 237; John 2nd, 236; Jonathan, 289; Justus, JP, 76, 531; Martha, 236; Philip, 236; Rebecca Jane, 354, 652; Robert, 255, 382, 608; Robert A., 7; Silas, 236, 369, 652; Thomas, 236; William, 105, 237; William S., JP, 50
HAMLIN: E.W., 55; John, JP, 407
HAMMAN: John, 276, 509
HAMME: Christian, 278; Jonas, 278; Mary, 278
HAMMEL: Frederick, 237; Samuel, Capt., 465
HAMMELS: John George, 237
HAMMER: Jacob, 478; John, 390; Joseph, 390
HAMMON: Rebecca [MORGAN], 405
HAMMOND: Amariah, JP, 207; Charity H., 237; David, 237; John, 383; Loisa, 237; Martha W. [HOOD], 268; Phebe, 237; Polly [TUBBS], 566; R.H., 206; Robert H., 381, 448; William, 158
HAMPHILL: Joseph, 131
HAMPTON: Col., 328
HAMRICH: C.P., 194
HAMRICK: Adam, 237; Henry, 237
HAMSON: William, 237
HANCHET: Jonah, 238
HANCHETT: Eunice [SPENCER], 529
HANCOCK: Benjamin F., JP, 379; C.H., 297;

(HANCOCK, continued)

Cutlope, 238; J.H., 297;
Magdalena, 238; William,
297
HAND: Abraham, 238;
Alvah, 642; Col., 151,
565; Edward, Col., 247,
589; Samuel H., 30;
Seneca L., 642; Thomas
C., 49, 328, 345, 358,
360, 403, 427, 546, 563,
582, 596
HANDELL: John, 238
HANDRAKE: William G.,
254
HANDY: Capt., 106;
George, 100; William, 9
HANEY: Nancy, 616;
Samuel, 616
HANFIELD: William, 590
HANFORD: John, JP, 241
HANGBELL: Elizabeth,
569
HANKE: John, JP, 254
HANKERSON: Col., 91
HANKS: Clorinda, 238;
Elijah, 238; Esther, 238;
John, Capt., 560; Mary,
238; Patty, 238
HANLY: C., 464
HANNA: A., JP, 34, 291;
Benjamin, 505; James,
180; John, 289; Joshua,
413, 442, 590; Polly
[COVERT], 180;
Thomas, 7, 30, 33, 123,
159, 163, 205, 365, 389,
409, 432, 487, 517, 531,
563, 601
HANNAH: John, 238;
Robert, 238–39
HANON: Thomas, 259
HANSBURY: James, 382
HANSE: Leonard, 239;
Leonrad, 239
HANSELL: B., 499
HANSON: Ariel, JP, 102
HAOLIN: Thomas, JP, 346
HAPGOOD: George, JP,
392
HAPPALL: Adam, 239;
Alice, 239
HARBERT: William, 285

HARBESON: John, 239;
Massey, 239; Mathew,
239; William, 239
HARBISON: Catherine,
239; Francis, 239–40;
Jane, 239; John, 239;
Joseph, 239, 383; Mary,
239; Matthew, 239;
Robert, 239; William, 239
HARBOLT: Adam, 240
HARBOUGH: Elizabeth,
240; Henry, 240; Jacob,
240; Samuel, 620
HARDEN: Cato, 240; John,
240; N. Bonaparte, 240
HARDER: William, 240
HARDIN: John, 240, 275;
William, 241
HARDING: Charles, 434;
Curtis, 434; Dewitt, 434;
E., 241, 248; Isaac, 241;
Israel, 241; Jesse, JP, 241,
248; Lester, 147; Lydia,
241; Martha [PARRISH],
434; S.G., 241, 248;
Samuel, 241; Stephen,
241
HARDISTY: Francis, 241
HARDY: Elias, 241; James
F., 241; John C., 596;
Joseph, 570; Pary, 241;
William, 220
HARE: James, 242; John,
242; Margaret
[KRIDER], 320; Mary
Ann, 242; Michael, 242;
Robert, JP, 168; Samuel,
359
HARFORD: *James,* 191;
Jonathan, 191
HARGAN: Alexander B.,
179
HARGER: John M., 90
HARKER: Joshua G., 537
HARKIN: Jeremiah, 254;
Joseph, Capt., 326
HARKNESS: John, 242
HARLEY: Col., 515; Jacob,
237
HARMAN: Daniel, 552;
Jonas, 71; Lucretia, 242;
Martin, 242; Samuel, 75,
283, 324, 392, 530
HARMON: John, 254, 259;
Oliver, 242
HARN: Samuel D., 376

HARNED: Nathan, 223
HARNERI: Nancy
[SCOTT], 479
HARNIT: Nathaniel, JP,
114
HARP: Frederick, 242
HARPER: Adam, 242;
Alexander, 103; Daniel,
242, 565; Eliza Jane, 243;
Elizabeth, 242; James,
242, 365; John, 243;
Thomas, 188; William,
243; William S., 566
HARPLE: Catharine, 243;
Jacob, 243; John, 243;
Mary, 243; Nancy, 243;
Sarah, 243
HARPOUGH: Cornelius,
Capt., 84
HARRAR: Benjamin, 243;
Daniel, 243; Isaac, 243;
Jesse, 243; Joseph, 243;
Nathan, 243; William,
243
HARRINGTON: Mabel
[THOMPSON], 560;
Nancy [BREWER], 64
HARRIS: Abraham, JP,
171; David, JP, 198;
Eleanor, 243; Isaac, 46,
155, 400, 412; John, 194,
243; John 2nd, 243–44;
John H., 397, 614; Mary,
243–44; Matilda
[PATTERSON], 436;
Nicholas, 244; Priscilla
[COLE], 105; Sarah, 111;
Sidney W., 206; W.S.,
171; William, 244;
William C., 139, 422;
Winfield S., JP, 171
HARRISON: Alexander,
175; Catharine, 244;
George, 244, 544;
Harmaus, 244; Joseph,
244; Magdalena, 244;
Martha, 244; Peggy, 244;
Philip, 244; Stephen, 244;
Thomas, 244, 457;
William, 244, 398, 597
HARROFF: Jacob, 244
HARROLD: John, 416
HARRON: Thomas, 245
HARSHA: John, JP, 340
HARSHE: John, JP, 109

HARSON: Sarah
[HIGBEE?], 245;
Thomas, 245
HART: A., 190; Alva, 34;
Ambrose, JP, 40, 78, 275,
603; Christopher, 245;
Col., 176; George, 245;
James H., 24, 33, 132,
332, 478, 551, 624; James
M., 387; Jane [BAIRD],
20; Jesse, 427; John, 29;
John F., 245; Jonathan V.,
304, 361; Joseph, 297;
Joshua, 121; Josiah,
Capt., 373; Magdalen,
245; Martin, 245; Mary
[DEYO], 34; Michael, JP,
25; Nicholas, 245;
Rachel, 245; Seely, Capt.,
26; Susanna [BARR], 29;
Thomas, 56, 119, 152,
263, 465; William, 174,
400, 605; William K., 95
HARTCHY: Catharine,
245; Elizabeth, 245; John,
245
HARTLEY: Col., 516, 519,
541
HARTLINE: Jacob, 246
HARTMAN: Adam, 246;
Capt., 115; Catharine,
246; Conrad, 246, 270;
Daniel, 246; David, 51;
Elizabeth, 246–47;
Frederick, 246, 425;
George, 246; Hannah
[MORRIS], 406; Henry,
246; Jacob, 246; John,
246–47; Magdalina, 246;
Michael, 246–47; Nancy,
246; Peggy, 246; Philip,
246; Polly, 246; William,
246, 612
HARTON: G.M., 414, 561;
G.N., 259
HARTSHORNE: Capt.,
415
HARTUNG: Christopher,
247
HARTZEL: Col., 357;
Peter, JP, 603
HARTZELL: Isaac, 49,
633, 654; J.F., 243; Mary,
110; Peter, JP, 210; Sarah
[LEAS], 329

HARVEY: Elias, 165;
George N., 607; Joseph,
323; Mary [BROWN],
71; Mary Ann
[ROBERTS], 475; Ruth
[EDWARDS], 165;
Samuel, 323; William,
247, 646
HARWOOD: Thomas, 247
HASELTINE: Robert, JP,
169
HASKELL: Harriet, 247;
Prince, 247
HASKETT: Capt., 1
HASSINGER: Jacob, 229,
556
HASTINGS: Capt., 522;
David, 196; James, 247;
John, 247; O., 187, 495;
Thomas, 457
HATCH: Don, Capt., 422;
Sabin, JP, 86
HATCHER: Joshua, 563
HATCHY: Catharine, 245;
Elizabeth, 245; John, 245
HATESS: Lester C., 261
HATFIELD: Ann, 248;
Catharine [WEIGELL],
589; Elias, 248; William,
JP, 581
HATH: Sabin, JP, 523
HATHAWAY: James, 130,
168, 175, 259, 355, 498;
John C., 170
HATHEWAY: Joseph, JP,
361
HATRUNFT: John, 13;
Sarah [ANTRUM], 13
HATZ: Johannes, 248;
John, 248
HAUCK: Samuel, 47
HAUGHAWOUT: Sarah
[CAMPBELL], 85
HAUGHEY: Daniel, 95;
Francis, JP, 232
HAUGHT: Jacob, 215;
William, 230
HAUSE: Leonard, 248
HAVELAND: Grace, 375
HAVEN: Samuel, 12
HAWK: James, 248;
William, JP, 32, 348
HAWKENBERRY: John,
248
HAWKIN: H., 127

HAWKINS: Abigail, 248;
Benjamin, 220; James,
369; Joseph, 248; Nancy,
248; Thomas, 248;
William D., JP, 121
HAWLEY: Almon, 215;
Benjamin, JP, 519; Elijah,
507; Ozias, 249; Sarah,
249, 519
HAY: George, Capt., 466;
Henry, 100; John, 249;
Peter, 27; Peter, JP, 176;
Samuel, 332; William J.,
74, 193, 197, 263, 275,
537
HAYDON: Cornelia
[LUKER], 349; Zerah,
349
HAYES: Barney, 249;
David, Capt., 11; Manliff,
JP, 246; R., 337; Richard,
34; Robert, 84; Robert
G.H., JP, 25, 293; Sarah,
249
HAYLER: John, 249
HAYMAN: Isaac Wayne,
516
HAYMOND: Thomas S.,
JP, 31
HAYNES: C.Y., 426;
Catherine, 473; Selden,
JP, 473, 539, 548
HAYS: Adam, Dr., 249;
Charlotte, 249; Col., 235;
David, 249; Elias, 142;
George, 249; James, 250;
John, 101, 249; John L.,
8, 623; Pliny, 250;
Robert, 457; Sarah, 249;
Thomas, 367, 413;
William, 249; William P.,
303
HAYSLIP: Caroline, 277;
S.J., JP, 140, 273, 536;
Samuel J., JP, 277
HAZEN: Col., 159, 416; J.
Andy, JP, 526
HAZLET: Robert, 250;
William A., 41
HAZLETT: Capt., 425;
Robert, 250, 334
HAZZARD: T.R., JP, 107
HEACOX: William, JP, 431
HEAD: Benjamin, 438;
Gamaliel, JP, 143; John,
250

HEADLEE: Lewis, JP, 403, 448

HEADLER: Lewis, JP, 393

HEADLEY: Hannah, 250; J.B., 170; Jacob, 250; James, 250

HEALP: Catharine, 252; John, 252; Ludwick, 252; Mary Ann, 252; Susannah, 252

HEARING: Christiana [SHIVELEY], 509; John, 509

HEATH: Capt., 455; Charles E., 186; H., 399

HEATON: Elizabeth, 250; James, 250

HEAVENER: Col., 180

HEBARD: Adriel, 484; Lois [ROWLEY], 484

HEBBERLY: Frederick, 251

HEBERLING: D., JP, 590

HECH: O., JP, 299

HECK: Christian, JP, 387; Jacob, 254

HECKERT: Daniel, JP, 417

HECKMAN: George, 251; H.G., 166; H.S., 413; Jefferson K., JP, 110

HEDGES: Ellzey, 131, 287, 294; William B., JP, 291

HEEL: James, 119

HEFFELFINGER: Philip, 251

HEFFLEBOWER: Jacob, 251

HEFFLER: Barbara, 251; John, 251

HEFFLISH: Melchior, 251

HEFFNER: Benjamin, 237

HEGELE: Gottlieb, 233

HEGIN: Edward, 251

HEGLE: George, JP, 588

HEHN: John, 233; Philip, 233

HEIBER: George, 252

HEICKHOLD: John, 274

HEIDENREICH: William, 224, 234, 256, 482; William S., 322

HEILLENREICH: William, 588

HEINBACK: Philip, 324

HEINTZELMAN: H., 446; Henrietta [PINKERTON], 446

HEISAM: John, 252

HEISE: Conrad, 29

HEIST: Daniel S., 475; John, JP, 475

HEISTER: Col., 511; Gabriel, JP, 38; Joseph M., Dr., 416; *Wm.* Jr., 38

HEITLER: Richard P., JP, 530; Richard R., Col., 534

HEITRICK: Jacob, 252

HELFENSTEIN: E., 411; John P., 382, 399; S., Rev., 257

HELFENTEIN: John P., 216

HELFFENSTEIN: Albert, 471

HELFINGER: David, 235

HELLER: Ephraim, JP, 23; Frederick, JP, 347; George, 277; John, 252, 288; John M., JP, 293; Polly [JAMES], 288; Tobias, 252

HELLES: William, 230

HELM: Hiram, 252; Samuel, 252

HELMAN: Charles F., 182; J.H., 182

HELMICK: Nathan, 481

HELP: Ludwick, 252

HELPH: Ludwick, 252; Mary Ann, 252

HELVESTON: Thomas, 269

HELWIG: Joseph, 578

HEMET: John Jr., 268

HEMINGER: Anne Catharina, 253; John, 253; Mary, 253

HEMINGWAY: Samuel, 253

HEMMENS: J.B., 215

HEMPHILL: James W., 428; Joseph, 174, 370, 388, 403, 562

HENDEL: Capt., 444; Jacob, 176; William, 58

HENDERSON: A., 430; Ann, 253; B.H., 198; Capt., 451; Elizabeth [STEWART], 540; Harry Ellsworth, 254;

Hubbard, JP, 481; J.J., 513; James, 253; James S., 107; John, 253; John J., 296; Jonathan G., 518; Jonathan I., 54; Joseph, 253, 276, 296; Joseph W., 513, 659; Maria S., 254; Mary, 253; Sarah, 253; Wallace, 411; William, 253; William A., 254

HENDON: Samuel, 226

HENDRICK: Andrew, 254

HENDRICKS: George D., 600; Harriet [LUKER], 349; John, 349; John F., 615

HENDRICKSON: Cornelius, 254; Daniel, Col., 561; John, JP, 174; William, 254

HENDRIX: Adam, 459

HENDRY: Samuel, 16

HENDRYX: O.D., 97

HENEBERGER: John, 254

HENING: Abigail W. [PRIOR], 455; Barbara, 255; Esther, 255; James G., 455; John, 255; Robert M., 455; Susannah, 255

HENITZELMAN: *J.*, JP, 37

HENMAN: Emmanuel, 584

HENNEN: Matthew, 254; Thomas, 31

HENNER: Joseph, 254; Thomas, 254

HENNING: George, 255; John, 255

HENNON: Abel, 255; Joseph, 255

HENRICH: Adam, 618; Thomas, 624

HENRY: A.B., 554; B., 286; Capt., 197, 327, 493; Eliza, 255; Francis, 255, 388; Isaac, 558; Joseph R., JP, 621; Levi, 282; Lewis, 255; Mary M. [JACKSON], 286; Norton P., 286; Rebecca [LITTLE], 340; Samuel, 50, 55, 134, 176, 208, 288, 296, 347, 404, 468, 482, 488, 528, 544–45, 566, 607; *Sauttle* F., JP, 338; Sawtel F., JP, 106;

(HENRY, continued)

Thomas, 24, 88, 255, 264, 333, 356, 401, 463; William, 255, 340; William Jr., 134
HENSEL: William, 255
HENSEY: John, 255
HENTZ: Susan [RODES], 478
HENTZE: Frederick, 256
HEPBURN: J.F., 334; James, 214, 502; Morris, JP, 307
HEPP: Philip, 256
HERBERT: Ann [JACKSON], 285; Jonathan, 256; Samuel, 256; Stewart, 104, 256; Susan, 256; Thomas, 256; William, 256
HERCHELRODE: John, 21
HERIGERE: John B., 172
HERIN: Samuel, JP, 134
HERING: George, JP, 395
HERLESS: George, 188
HERMAN: Col., 34; Samuel, 209; Samuel, JP, 191
HERMANY: Christina, 256; Jacob, 256
HERNER: James, JP, 368
HERR: Daniel, 393
HERRICK: C.H., JP, 423
HERRIMAN: Jacob, 256; Sarah, 256
HERRING: Christian, 256; Elizabeth, 256
HERRION: Hannah [DAVIS], 133
HERRON: William A., 442
HERRSMITH: A., 488
HERSH: John Jr., JP, 163
HERSHBERGER: Jonathan, 159, 349, 412, 426
HERSHMAN: Elizabeth [CAMPBELL], 86; John, 86
HERSON: Moses, Col., 417
HERTZ: Charles, JP, 26; Conrod, 257
HERTZHOCK: Valentine, 270
HERTZLER: Christian, 33

HERTZOG: Capt., 124; Catharine, 355; Emily, 355; Frederick, 355; Hannah, 355; Lavina, 355
HERTZOGG: Valentine, 270
HESON: Moses, Col., 260
HESS: Barbara, 257; Daniel, 614; E.C., 221; George, 257; George Jr., 424; Jacob, JP, 27, 36; Mary, 257; Peter M. Sr., 257
HESSER: Frederick, 257; Henry, JP, 359
HESSOM: David, 252; Ellen, 252; John, 252; Mary, 252
HESTON: Bathsheba T., 257; Edward. Lt. Col., 257; Hannah, 257; Harriet C., 257; Isaac, 257; Jane, 257; Louisa, 257; Mary, 257; Matilda, 257; Rachel C., 257; Sarah, 257; Thomas, 257; Thomas J., 257; William P., 257
HETICK: P.I., 37; Paul, 409
HETRICK: Jacob, 252; John W., JP, 287, 328, 331; Philip, 252
HETSILGESER: John, 329
HEVINS: Henry, 364
HEWES: Elijah C., JP, 186; William, JP, 577
HEWETT: Abel, JP, 167, 226, 621; Israel, 258
HEWIT: Andrew, 254; Israel, 257; Nicholas, 401; Peter, 593; Polly, 257; Rebecca [KING], 313; Sally, 257; Samuel, 593; Thomas I., JP, 163, 189
HEWITT: Abigail, 258; Charles, 46; George W., 258; Israel, 258; Robert, 258; Sarah, 258; Thomas I., JP, 36
HEY: J. George, 156
HEYES: Robert G.H., JP, 326
HEYL: Conrad, 260
HEYSER: William, Capt., 516

HEYSHAM: Edwin, 3
HEZLEP: George, 19
HEZLESS: James, 520
HIBBERD: George, 265
HIBBIN: Chambers W., 74
HICE: George, 258; Henry, 258; Margaret, 258; Mary, 258; Robert, 258; Samuel, 258
HICHNEY: Joseph, JP, 39, 43
HICKERNELL: Sarah [MYERS], 415
HICKMAN: Elizabeth [MILLER], 395; George H., 276; Jonathan, 485
HICKOCK: Asa, 258; Betsey, 258; Clarinda, 258; Durlin, 258; Durlin W., 258; Eben F., 258; Esther, 258; Ezra, 258; Mariah, 258; Olive, 258
HICKOK: Betsey, 258; Durbin, 258; E.W., JP, 39, 126, 584; Esther, 259; Nathaniel, 259
HICKOX: Ebenezer, 259; Giles, 259; Larmon, 259; Ralph, 197; Wait, 259
HICKS: Daniel, 12; Joseph, 259; Julia, 259
HIDE: *Eliphelit*, 152; Marcia [DOUD], 152
HIERTER: Gabriel, JP, 213
HIESTER: Col., 179, 523, 551, 569, 624; Gabriel Jr., JP, 210, 252, 265, 347, 593; Gabriel, JP, 175, 181, 454, 623; Joseph, Col., 237, 482, 588; Mary [OTTO], 429; Sarah [OTTO], 429
HIGBE: Joseph, 245
HIGBEE: Sarah, 245, 259
HIGBIE: Mary Ann [STURGES], 548; Peter, 548; Rebecca [IRVIN], 283
HIGBY: Henry, 14, 140, 163, 222–23, 273, 277, 370, 444, 536, 570, 595; R.M., JP, 390
HIGGINS: Andrew, 259; Maria [SIDMAN], 512; Patrick, 647; Samuel P., 512, 527

HIGH: Frances, 249; George, 259; William, JP, 54
HIGINBOTHAM: James C., JP, 376
HIGLEY: Sabina [BROWN], 70
HILANDS: Alexander, 497; R., 663
HILDEBRAND: E.P., 374
HILES: Conrad, 260
HILGAR: Henry, 260
HILL: Betsey, 128; Capt., 414; Catharine, 260; Charles, 260; Charles H., 196; Elihu, 400; Elizabeth, 260; Emmy [DEYO], 143; Frederick, 260; Henry, 260; Isaac, 128, 258; Jacob, 483; James, 119; John, 260, 374; John G., JP, 377; Joseph, 261; Martha [CRAIG], 119; Phebe [COLE], 105; Rees, Col., 335; Rhoda, 260; Samuel, 213; Sanford C., 104, 352, 602; Simeon, 340; Thomas, 308
HILLARY: Ashburn, 261; Eleanor, 261
HILLEGOSS: Adam, 464
HILLER: George, 277
HILLIARD: Mary [LINE], 338; Samuel R., 148
HILLIS: W.D., 22
HILLMAN: James W., 205
HILLPOT: Frederick G., JP, 405; Jonas T., 543
HILLS: Joseph, 261; L.B., 139; Obed, 261
HILLYARD: Peter, 261
HILLYER: Clara, 261; Laura, 261; Nathaniel H., 261; Seth, 261; Sibel, 261; Tacy, 261
HILTON: Morris, JP, 366
HILZ: Richard, 487
HIMES: Edward, 307
HIMMELL: Joseph, 260
HINCKEL: Joseph, 456
HINCKLY: A.H., JP, 423
HIND: John, 261
HINDS: Bartlett, Capt., 262; Charlotte [SEELY], 499

HINE: Charry [BEACH], 34; Daniel, 34; George, JP, 269, 435; Jared, JP, 76, 571; Warren, 554
HINING: James G., JP, 295
HINKLE: Casper Jr., 550; Catharine [PUDDING], 456
HINOR: William E., 358
HINSDALE: Albert, 262; Elisha, 262; Elizabeth, 262; Jacob, 262
HIPPLE: Conrad, 262; Frederick, 262; George, JP, 6; John, 262; John Jr., 262
HIRSH: James M., 390
HIRST: James M., 177, 524–25; William, JP, 225, 578
HISTED: Benjamin, 262; Thaddeus, 262
HITCHCOCK: Israel, 158; J.K., 577
HITE: Conrad, 262; David, JP, 262
HIXSON: James, 263
HOADLY: George, 2, 37, 126, 203, 234, 277, 294, 380, 433, 451, 569; Samuel, Capt., 263; Silas, 263
HOAGLIN: William, Capt., 93
HOAN: Christopher, 57; Jonathan, 56
HOARD: Simeon, 263
HOBBEY: Capt., 408
HOBBS: Athen W., 495; Dorcas A. [EDWARDS], 165
HOBORN: Elizabeth [McELROY], 377
HOCKER: Martin Jr., 185
HOCKEY: George, 471
HOCKINGBURY: Hurman, 263
HOCKLEY: J., 155, 563
HOCKLY: Thomas, Col., 580
HODGDON: Samuel, 167, 262
HODGE: Andrew, 254; Capt., 167, 268; J., 296; Moses, 46; *Velons*, 215
HODGENS: Isaac, JP, 381

HODGES: C., 21; John A., 92
HODGKISS: William D., 356
HOEMS: E., Capt., 565
HOFF: Abraham, Capt., 415; Capt., 339; Henry, 263; John, JP, 85
HOFFEDITZ: Juliana [ROTH], 482
HOFFER: Andrew, 54; Jacob, 54
HOFFMAN: B.F., 392; Barbara, 263; Christian, 263; Cornelius, 263; Elizabeth, 264; George, 91, 282, 537; Henry, 264; Isaac, 264; Johannes, 536; John, 264, 321, 392; John C., 237; John H., 16; Joseph, 264; Lewis, 264; Ludwick, 264; Maria, 264; Mary [WOLF], 613; Philip, 542; Philip H., 150; S., 100
HOFFMANN: Frederick, 523
HOFFORD: James C., 591
HOFFSTOT: John W., 485
HOFIUS: John H., Dr., 113
HOGAN: Jacob, 598
HOGE: A.H., 467; Benjamin, 360; Frances [MERSHIMER], 360; Jacob, 598; James, 264; Jonathan, 264; Mary, 264; William, 264
HOGELAND: Joseph, 265; Nancy, 265
HOGG: James, 265
HOGGE: James, 265; Rachel, 265
HOGUE: Mary [SMITH], 520; William, 520
HOIT: Mary, 273; Nicholas S., 273
HOKE: Elias, 518; Henry, JP, 518
HOLBAN: Lorentz, 265
HOLBEN: Lorentz, 265
HOLBEND: Lorentz, 265
HOLBROOK: W., JP, 5; Warum, JP, 589
HOLCOMB: Alexander T., 475; Joel, 265; Levi, 265;

(HOLCOMB, continued)

M., JP, 84, 249; Marcus, 265; Sarah, 265
HOLDEN: Jacob, 265; *Octavius* A, 266; Sartile, 266; Sartin, 266; Thomas, 427
HOLDER: Jacob, 265
HOLDERBAUM: Michael, Col., 480
HOLDICK: Lydia [KOLLOCK], 319
HOLDSHIP: Charles A., 430
HOLEMER: Col., 414
HOLENSHEAD: James, 266
HOLFORD: Isaac, 419
HOLGATE: John, 548; M., Capt., 266; Rebecca, 266; Reuben, JP, 72, 217; William, Lt., 266
HOLIDAY: Capt., 29
HOLLAND: Ann, 266; Capt., 479; John, 262, 266; Joseph, 266; Phebe, 266; Thomas, 266
HOLLENBACK: Jacob, 301; Rebecca [KAMP], 301
HOLLENBECK: Chastine, 206; Sarah, 206
HOLLENSHEAD: Ann, 266; James, 266; Nancy, 266; Psyche, 266; Sarah, 266
HOLLER: Mathias, 260
HOLLIDAY: Adam, 560; Daniel, 207; John, 266
HOLLINGSWORTH: Henry, 224; Levi, JP, 147
HOLLINSHEAD: James, 266; Peter, JP, 404
HOLLISTER: Elijah, 267; Elisha, 267; Erastus B., JP, 428; Jeremiah, 16
HOLMAN: Mary, 267; Samuel, 73; Thomas, 267
HOLMES: A.G., 49; Capt., 361, 457; James, 267; Jane, 267; John, 336; John K., 453; John M., 361; Matthew, 267; Robert, 267; Seth, 267; Susan [BRICKELL], 65;

Thomas R., 230, 403, 434, 443, 481; William, 93, 216, 267, 315, 410
HOLROYD: Robert, 273
HOLSON: Nancy, 267; William, 267
HOLSTEAD: Timothy, 268
HOLSTEIN: M., 123, 388; Samuel, 375, 388
HOLT: Thomas, 268
HOLTONS: James, 19
HOLTZINGER: Barbara, 268; Jacob, 268; Mary [WAMBACK], 582
HOMAN: John, 268; M., JP, 435
HOMER: John, 36, 90
HOMMEL: Frederick, 470
HOMMER: Jacob, 268
HONAKER: Catherine [JACOBY], 288
HONEY: Samuel, 314
HOOBAUGH: John, 176
HOOD: A.W., 553; Catherine, 268; George, 268; John, 100; John M., 255; Martha W., 268; Samuel, 163, 305, 479; Samuel B., 280, 479; Thomas, 565
HOOK: Daniel, 49, 308–9, 362, 443, 485; James, 268; James Jr., 268; John, JP, 343; Samuel, JP, 232; Stephen, 325; Thomas, 308
HOOPER: John, 124; Nancy [CUMMING], 126; Polly [REAGAN], 465; Simeon, 126
HOOPS: Adam, 269
HOOTEN: A., JP, 375
HOOTON: Andrew, 592
HOOVER: Ann, 269; Armand, 531; Christian, JP, 233; George, 185; Henry, 269, 616; Isaac, 419; Jacob, 269; Philip, 269
HOPKINS: A., 178; Charles L., 128, 370, 396, 405; Daniel, 294; Ebenezer, 269; Esther [JOHNSON], 294; Lucinda [BIERCE], 46; Martha [GANDY], 203;

Rachel, 269; Stephen, 128, 370, 405, 461, 527; T.R., 95, 345; Thomas, 436
HOPKINSON: John, JP, 460
HOPPER: Joshua M., 363; Paul, 402
HOPSON: Samuel, 470
HORDER: William, 269
HORFNOGGLE: George, 269
HORN: Abraham, 269; Charles, 270; Eliza Ann, 270; Franklin Pierce, 270; Hannah Alice, 270; Henry, 152, 507–8, 602; John Jr., 467; Jonathan, 63, 248, 269–70, 323, 467, 590; Maria, 269; Syman, 270
HORNBERGER: Jeremiah, 468
HORNER: Alfred, 17, 22, 173, 187, 267; J., JP, 210; James T., 209, 283, 324; John, 66, 250, 327, 362, 429, 490, 536, 576, 597; William, 98
HORNING: Samuel, 619
HORR: Adam V., 325
HORRELL: John, 307, 336
HORSE: Valentine, 270
HORSFIELD: Letitia, 589; Rebecca [WEISS], 590; William, 590
HORTMAN: *Conrad*, 270; Elizabeth, 270; George, 270
HORTON: Alonzo, 270; Chauncey B., 270; Henry, 270; J.C., 353; L.L., 465; Lois, 270; Louisa, 270; Mary Ann, 270; Samuel, 270
HORTUMAN: Peter, Col., 576
HORTZHOY: Valentine, 270
HOSKIN: Noah, 258; Olive [HICKOCK], 258
HOSKINS: John, 270
HOSKINSON: Basil, 270; Thomas, 216
HOSTEN: Henry, 270

HOTCHKISS: Betsy [GILLET], 211; Cornelius B., 348; Harris, 271

HOTTENSTEIN: David H., JP, 448; Henry, 175

HOUCK: Polly [ERB], 172

HOUGH: Benjamin, 604; Enoch, JP, 572; George S., 204, 249, 300, 365, 437, 446, 479, 555, 565; John, 67, 271

HOUGHTON: Alonzo, 270; Chauncey B., 270; Henry, 270; Lois, 270; Louisa, 270; Mary Ann, 270; Rowland, 103; Samuel, 270

HOUSE: George, 271; Matthew, 129; Nathan, Capt., 575

HOUSEGGER: Col., 120

HOUSEKEEPER: John, 603

HOUSEL: Julia [JOHNSON], 293; Philip, 103; William L., 293

HOUSEMAN: Amah, 271; Bela S., 271; E. Finley, 271; Jacob, 271; John G., 271; Sarah [NORRIS], 422

HOUSER: Jonathan, JP, 188

HOUSTON: Samuel, 246–47, 427; W.C., 47; William, 7, 280

HOUTS: Adam, 271; Barbara, 271; Catharine, 271; Jacob, 271; Margaret, 271

HOUTZ: Beltzer, 272

HOW: H.L., 108; Hannah [BISBEE], 47

HOWARD: John, 272; John Jr., 272; N.G., 350, 465; Peter C., 143; Samuel, 272

HOWD: Asahel, 259

HOWDEN: Alexander, 272

HOWE: Asa, 272; Curtis, 548; Daniel, 272; Freelove [METCALF], 399; Horace, 221; Priscilla, 272;

Thomas M., 106, 218, 548; William, 272

HOWELL: Hannah, 273; J.D., JP, 425; John D., JP, 391; Jonathan, 272; Nathaniel, 273; Reuben, 273; Timothy, 23; William, 273; William Sr., 273

HOWENSTEIN: J., 382

HOWMAN: Ira, Col., 92; William, 103

HOWSER: Benjamin, Col., 606

HOXIE: Capt., 234

HOXWORTH: Edward, 273; Peter, JP, 542; William J., JP, 542

HOYT: Elias, 45; Mary, 273; Nicholas S., 273

HUBBARD: Asa, 273; Axy [STONE], 543; Col., 615; David, 606; Ebenezer W., JP, 193; F.B., JP, 87, 594; Franklin D., JP, 375; H., 210; Israel, 273; John, JP, 64

HUBBELL: Jesse, JP, 538; John Jr., 274

HUBBER: Jonas, Capt., 188

HUBBERT: Anthony, 274; Benjamin, 274; Christian, 274; Elizabeth, 274; John, 274; Juliann, 274; Mary, 274; Rebecca, 274; Samuel, 274; William, 274

HUBER: Andrew, 274; Christian, 274; Col., 551; David, 274; George, 274; Jonathan, 81; Peter, 394

HUBERT: Casper, 274, 306; Elizabeth Jane [RODGERS], 478; Mary Ann, 274

HUBLEY: Bernard, Capt., 441; Capt., 201; Col., 101; Elizabeth [PERKINPINE?], 441; Elizabeth R., 441; Eve Mary, 441; Frederick, 275; John A., 441; Sarah Ann, 441; Tamor, 441

HUBNER: Catharine, 275; Frederick, 275

HUDSON: Charolett [BOWMAN], 59; Joshua, 275

HUEY: George, 275; Margaret, 275; Robert, 367

HUFF: Andrew, 174; Benjamin, 275; George, 225; Jesse, 473; Peter, 275

HUFFMAN: Christian, 275

HUFFNAGLE: Catharine, 275; Jonathan, 552; Michael, 275

HUFNAGLE: Christian, 276

HUGGINS: Patrick, 276, 647

HUGH: Joseph, 131

HUGHES: Abner, 48; Capt., 109; Daniel, 276; Ellis, 636; Ellwood, 583; Emily [EARLE], 162; James, 204, 276, 406; John, 276; Parley, 276; Polly, 276; Remembrance, 222; Robert, 612; Susan B., 276

HUGHEY: John, 277; Mary W. [EARLE], 162

HUGHS: William, 297

HUGO: Mary Ann [SPANGLER], 527; Samuel B., 527

HUHLER: George, 60

HULBARD: Asa, 273

HULBERT: Fanny C., 564; Richard O., JP, 103, 427, 602

HULDEMAN: C., JP, 29

HULER: George, 277; Maria, 277

HULET: Hannah, 277; John, 277

HULINGS: David W., 495; Doroll, 495; Ellen, 495

HULL: Abner, 277; Capt., 543; John, 492; P.P., 289; W., Col., 339; Wakeman, 277; William, 87

HULME: Isaac, 53; Richard, 544

HUM: Catharine, 277; Henry, 277; John, 252, 277; Susannah, 277

HUME: John, 278
HUMEL: Henry, 367
HUMES: James, 37, 201,
559; John, 24; Samuel,
385, 423; Thomas, 201
HUMME: Christian, 278
HUMMEL: Daniel, 237;
Henry, 278, 500; Jacob,
161; John George, 237;
Sarah [SCHATZ], 500
HUMMER: Rachel
[CAMPBELL], 85
HUMMESON: Roxeina
[WILLIAMS], 603;
Samuel, 603
HUMNICH: Christian, 121
HUMPHREVILLE:
Samuel, JP, 444
HUMPHREY: Elijah,
Capt., 16; Elizabeth, 278;
Ellehu, Capt., 324;
George, 278; Harvey H.,
17; Hiram, 278; Horace
J., 278; Jacob, Capt., 278;
James O., 278; Jane, 278;
Roswell, 278; William N.,
278
HUMPHREYS: D., 230;
Jonathan, 198
HUNCKHOUSE: Thomas
J., 185
HUNGER: Alexander, JP,
625; Joseph, 625
HUNGERFORD: L.P., 112
HUNSINGER: Solomon,
586
HUNSUKER: Abraham,
354
HUNT: Absalom, 14, 628;
Ann, 320; Byrum, JP,
578; Charity, 13; Daniel,
278; David, 278–79;
Ebenezer, 279; Elijah, 14,
628; Elizabeth
[HAGERTY], 379;
Hannah, 13; Henry V.,
279; Horace, 279, 615;
Isaac, 279; J.S., JP, 413;
Jacob, 279; James, 315;
Josiah, 14, 628; Lois,
279; Lydia, 279; Nancy
M., 279; Samuel, 5;
Sarah, 14, 278–79; Seth,
JP, 604; Thomas, 197,
274; William, 14, 279,
628

HUNTE: William, JP, 268
HUNTER: Alexander, 157;
Ann, 279; Capt., 397;
Col., 87, 242, 443; David,
540; Jacob, 65; James,
150, 255; John, 279;
Joseph, JP, 552; Robert,
Capt., 279; S., Col., 465;
William, JP, 204, 362
HUNTINGTON: Asher,
280, 648; Charles O., 280,
648; Christopher, 280;
Col., 2, 88, 595; Eunice,
280; Julian C., 102;
Lydia, 648
HUNTLEY: Rufus, 174
HUNTRINGER: Jacob,
257, 318, 323, 625; Jacob,
Jr., 19, 264, 302
HUNTZINGER: Charles,
523; George W., 466;
Jacob, 524
HURD: Daniel, 583; Hiram,
JP, 585, 619; Robert, JP,
100
HURST: Edward, 314
HUSTER: Joseph, Col., 259
HUSTIN: William, Capt.,
433
HUSTON: Anne, 280;
Charles, JP, 240; Daniel,
280; James, 280; John,
405; John Jr., 280; Mary,
280; Mary Ann
[PHILLIPS], 444;
Nathan, 547; Philip, 280;
Sarah [LARNED], 326;
Thomas, 128, 405, 461;
William, 280, 444
HUTCHESON: James, JP,
71
HUTCHINS: Caleb, 281;
Henry J., 559; Jacob,
280–81; Moses, 281;
Sally, 281; Samuel, 50,
76, 97, 143, 312, 330,
365, 380, 396, 403, 433,
552, 564, 579
HUTCHINSON: Benjamin,
JP, 304; E. Jr., 447;
Edward Jr., 447; John,
281; Mary, 281; Mary
[TILDEN], 562; Miron,
JP, 16, 129, 194, 242
HUTCHISON: A.J., 661;
E., 283; James, JP, 87,

201; John A., 580; John,
JP, 231, 549; Joseph, 313;
Thomas, 577
HUTTEN: Capt., 233
HUTTON: Frederick, 624;
T.H., 323
HUVLER: Sarah [NOLF],
422
HUY: Catherine, 281; John,
249, 281; Margaret, 249,
281
HUYCK: William, 281
HUYLER: Capt., 249; John,
249
HUZZARD: Rudolph, JP,
170
HYDE: Seril P., JP, 423
HYLE: Conrad, 260

IBACH: Gustavus W., 151
ICKES: Jonas, 71
IDDINGS: William, 281
IDEL: Conrad, 282;
William, 282
IDLE: Barney, 281;
Catharine, 282;
Christiana, 281; Conrad,
282; Ellenor, 281;
George, 282; Jonathan,
282; Susanna, 281;
William, 282
IGO: Daniel, 557; Mary
[TEVIS], 557
IHRIE: George, Capt., 465
IKELER: Johnson H., JP,
476
ILGENFRITZ: Elizabeth
[BURK], 77; John, 77;
W., 528
IMHOFF: Henry, 167
IMMAN: A., 282; Henry,
282
IMMEL: Alexander, 584;
John, JP, 58; Leonard,
251, 282
IMMON: Henry, 282
INGALLS: J., 215; Smith,
JP, 415
INGALS: Amos, 93
INGERSOLL:
Artemadores, 282; Capt.,
606
INGHRAM: Alexander Jr.,
622; B.F., 292, 401; B.T.,
205; John, 443; P.T., 116

INGLES: Andrew, JP, 602
INGMAN: Lanslot, 465
INGRAHAM: Esther
[HICKOK], 259; Jane
[CARNES], 87; John,
362; Lydia, 259; P.T.,
116; Samuel, 87
INNERS: Daniel, 282
INNES: Edward, 553
INNOIS: Jacob, 282
INSKEEP: Abraham H.,
283; Ann, 283; Eliza,
283; John, Lt., 282–83;
Sarah, 282–83
INSWORTH: Catharine,
283; Edward, 283
INVILLIERS: C.D., 308
IREDELL: Seth, 210
IRELAN: William L., JP,
158
IRELAND: A.C., 391, 478;
Deborah, 201; Elizabeth,
283; Hetty, 283; John,
283; Molly, 283; Rufus,
283; Velle, 283; William,
283; William W., 344
IRISH: Timothy, JP, 164
IRONS: John, 240
IRVIN: Andrew, 283, 587;
Henry, 173; James, Capt.,
283; Margaret, 283;
Mary, 173; Rebecca, 283
IRVINE: Capt., 47; Hood,
193, 469; John 1st, 283;
John 2nd, 283; John G.,
JP, 582; Thomas, JP, 495;
William, JP, 143, 166,
333, 411
IRWIN: Col., 97; Connor,
173; Elizabeth, 173;
George, 173; Henry, 172;
Isaac, 173; James, 63,
156, 273, 284, 331, 468,
540; John, 61; John C.,
JP, 35; John G., JP, 470;
Margaret, 284; Margaret
2nd, 284; Maria, 172;
Mary, 173; Matthew, 284;
Nathaniel, 284; Sarah,
173; Thomas H., 635;
Thomas, JP, 282, 529;
William, 355, 549
ISAMAN: Michael, 284
ISARD: Charles, JP, 199
ISBELL: Garner, 284;
Mary, 284

ISEMAN: Christian, 284;
Michael, 284
ISENHOUR: Philip, 284
ISRAEL: Joseph, 213;
Mary [GLENTWORTH],
213
IVERSON: P.P., JP, 42
IVES: Levi, 400
IVESTER: Elizabeth, 285;
George, 285; Jane, 285;
John B., 285; William,
285

JACK: James, 285; James
Jr., 285; Matthew, 231,
429; Wilson, 224
JACKMAN: James, 66, 443
JACKSON: Abigail, 285;
Abraham, 71; Ann, 285;
Ann Willing, 285; B., JP,
426; Benjamin B., 286;
Betsey, 285; Caleb, 285;
Capt., 49, 122, 522;
Caroline, 285; Catharine
[DENIKE], 140; Col.,
122, 522; Daniel, JP, 39,
275, 378; David, 286;
Ebenezer, 285; Eleanor,
285; Elizabeth Willing,
285; Ellenor, 285;
George, 188; George B.,
71; Hannah [FLOWERS],
188; Henry, 408, 481;
Jacob, 140, 377; James,
94; John, 285; John W.,
425; Joseph, 29, 285–86;
Joshua, 285; L.H., JP,
289; Lyman, 286; M.E.,
164, 583; Margaret, 178;
Margaret [SOLLIDAY],
525; Mary M., 286;
Michael, 46, 105, 274,
415; Peggy, 286; Polly,
286; Richard, 286; S.S.,
JP, 602; Samuel, 286,
341, 387; Sarah
[BROWN], 71; Seviah,
286; Sophia, 286; Susan,
286; Thomas, 7, 15, 41,
48, 62, 64, 76, 80, 88–89,
95, 111–12, 128, 132,
143, 147, 154, 166, 182,
184, 189–90, 213, 219,
223, 228, 238, 244, 247,
250, 269, 272–73, 286,

314, 317, 319, 336, 345,
385, 388, 398, 415, 418,
428, 430, 433, 435, 444,
446, 449, 455, 459–60,
463, 466, 468, 473, 493,
496, 514, 543, 550–51,
571, 585, 591, 611, 619,
622; William, 285–86
JACOBS: Adam, 287;
Daniel, 287; Dorothea,
287; Dorothy, 287;
Elizabeth, 287; George,
287; George L., 399;
Henry, 287; Jacob, 287;
James, 287; Jonathan,
287; Nicholas, 287; Peter,
287; R., 65; Samuel, JP,
601; Sarah, 287; Sarah
[MILLER], 395; Thomas,
144; William, 287
JACOBY: Andrew, 288;
Barbara, 288; Catherine,
288; Elizabeth, 288;
George S., 422; Henry,
288; Jacob, 288;
Jonathan, Capt., 80;
Louisiana, 439; Margaret,
288; Marietta, 439;
Nicholas, 288; Philip,
288; Robert N., 439
JAEGER: Dan, 43; Daniel,
JP, 83; Jonathan, 83
JAMES: Abraham H., 334;
Capt., 40, 482; Catharine,
288; George, 517; Isaac
T., 288; J.D., 288; John
D., 169; John O., 185;
Jonathan, 288; Julia, 288;
Nathan, 288; Polly, 288;
Sarah, 288; Thomas, 288;
William, 288
JAMESON: Samuel, 15,
52, 633; Thomas, 124
JAMIESON: Rachel
[NOLF], 422
JAMISON: Capt., 355;
Elizabeth, 289; Hugh, JP,
26; Jane, 289; John, 289;
Joseph C., 289; Margaret,
289; Mary Catharine,
289; Samuel, 289
JANNEY: Benjamin S., 150
JANVIER: Isaac, 289;
Matilda, 289; William
W., 289

JAQUET: Elizabeth, 289; John Daniel, 289; Margaret, 289

JARVIS: Dwight, 364

JAY: Catharine, 207; Charlotte, 207; Jesse R., 207; John, 253; Mary [HENDERSON], 253; Sally, 207

JAYNE: Sophie, 619; Timothy, Capt., 322–23

JEFFERIES: William W., 408

JEFFERIS: Isaac, 244

JEFFERS: John, 33; John, JP, 71; Robert, 137; Sarah E. [BAYLIE], 33

JEFFERSON: Tiberius, JP, 66

JEFFREY: Demarius, 289; John, 289

JEFFRIES: John A., 134; John P., 116

JENKINS: Algernon S., JP, 418; Bethiah, 290; Cynthia [TUBBS], 566; Eve, 290; Falla, 290; J.G., 37; James, 290; John, 290; Rachel, 290; Samuel T., 566; William, 290

JENKINSON: Henry, 239

JENKS: Abraham S., 249; Adam, 290; John, 290; *L.N.*, 290; R.J., JP, 126

JENNINGS: Alpheus, 133; Ann, 291; Benjamin, 116, 160, 180, 290–92, 326, 345, 358, 360, 391, 443, 522, 596, 598, 600, 611; David, 34, 291; Henry, 290; Isabel J., 291; Israel, 291; James, 291; Jesse, 291; Jonathan, 133, 290; Margaret, 291; Mary, 291; Mary [DAVIS], 132–33; Nathan B., 291; Olie, 291; Rhoda, 291; Rhoda Ann, 291; Sybil [COREY], 114; Thomas, 290–91

JERAULD: Eleanor, 291; James, 291; Ray G., 291

JETT: Capt., 20

JEWEL: Levi, 291; Seth, 291; William, 291

JEWELL: Jane, 291; Seth, 291; William, 291

JEWETT: Francis F., JP, 161; Holland, 292; Jonathan, 292; Joseph M., 292; Sarah, 292

JOB: Alice, 292; Amy, 292; Dennis, 292; Elizabeth, 292; Jacob, JP, 470; James, 292; Lydia, 292; Peter, 292; Robert, 292

JOBES: Ruth, 292; Samuel, 292

JOBS: Richard, 292

JOHN: August, 166; Lemuel, 545; Robert, JP, 169; William, 545

JOHNS: August, 166; Elizabeth, 292; Jacob, 292; John, 145; Leonard S., JP, 312; Mary "Polly" [DIFFENDERFER], 145

JOHNSON: Abel, 293; Ann, 293; Baker, Col., 415; Barney, 292; Benjamin, 28, 206, 293–94; Bernard, 292; Capt., 2, 190, 461; Christopher, Capt., 293; David, 88, 264, 293–94, 356, 382; Esther, 294; George, 293; J.B., 210; Jacob, 293; James, 87, 161, 293–94; James H., 293; James J., 365; John, 293–94; John Jacob, 294; Jonah, 203; Jonas, 77; Jonathan C., 293; Julia, 293; Lydia, 294; Margaret [GAYLARD], 206; Mary, 293; Mary "Polly" [SHAFFER], 503; Mary Ann, 293; Moses, 227, 294, 579; Robert, 139, 294, 618; S.H., 616; Samuel, 294; Sidney, 294; Simon, 389; Thomas, 294, 446; William, 293–94, 382; William K., 185

JOHNSTON: A., 125, 284, 419, 463; Abraham, 338; Alexander, 59, 96, 260, 283, 361, 481, 602; Baker, Col., 268; Benjamin, 294; Col., 463,

623; David, JP, 427; Eben, 473; George W., JP, 592; Gideon, 294; Henry, 1; Hugh, 295; James, 63, 220, 295, 344, 532; James P., 369; Jane, 295; John, 133, 290, 295, 297, 344, 441; John 2nd, 295; John L., 284, 338; Joseph, 21, 295, 463, 548, 568, 580; Margaret, 294–95; Mary, 294–95; Samuel, 295; Thomas, 156, 449, 467; Thomas P., 32; Walter, 295; William, 183, 237, 295, 308, 472; William B., 548, 574

JOHNSTONE: Christopher, Capt., 25

JOINER: Michael, 296

JOINERS: Michael, 296; Sarah, 296

JOLLY: James, 202

JONES: Abraham, JP, 96, 99, 191, 306; Absalom, 47; Amasa, JP, 427; Apphia, 297; Asa, 334; Asaph, 296; Benjamin, 186, 296; Betsey [PELTON], 441; Caleb, 545; Capt., 22, 130; Catharine [RODES], 478; Charles B., 58; Charles S., 105; Crocker, 296; David, 116, 297; Dennis, 296; Edward L., 418; Eleanor, 296, 342; Ethel, 296; Flavel, JP, 350; George W., 416; German, 541; Hannah, 296; Isaac, 228, 338, 401, 435, 464; Isaac T., 58; Isaiah, JP, 456; J. Richter, JP, 283; J.A., JP, 80; J.L., 246, 479; James, 296, 344; James H., 56; James M., 2, 13, 60, 213, 288, 547, 589; Joel, 297; John, 62, 410; John M., 303; Lemuel, JP, 140, 432, 560; Loisa, 297; Loyd, 358; Lucy, 297; Lucy [GUNN], 230; Lynds, 16; Mary, 298; Mary P., 58; Nelson, 607; Noah, 70; O.W., 423;

(JONES, continued)

Perregrine, 297; Philip, 297; Phineas, 297; Rebecca, 298; Reuben, 296–97; *Reubin*, 297; Rhoda, 297; Richter, 283; Sally, 297; Samuel, 190, 552; Sarah [HESTON], 257; Sarah [SUTTON], 550; Sarah [VanKLEEK], 498; Soma, 660; Tayler, JP, 529; Theophilus, 75; Thomas, 44, 140, 174; Thomas 2nd, 297; Thomas H., 249; Volney, 297; W.T., 12, 350; Walton, 230; Washington, 604; William, 278, 296, 298, 498, 550; William C., 298; William D., 358; William J., 47
JORDAN: A., 321; Alexander, 183; Catharine, 299; Edward, 42; Francis, 326, 444, 556; Frederick, 4, 288; Henry, 288; Hugh, 298; Jacob, JP, 287; James, 298; John, 90, 200, 322, 424, 439, 606; John Jr., 8, 468, 535, 573; Margaret, 298; Michael, 298; Robert, 299; Samuel, 299; Seaman, 165; Soloman, 299; Solomon, 299; Susan [EDWARDS], 165; William, 394; William C., 303; William H., 52, 144, 169, 189. 192, 215, 218, 415
JOSIAH: Elizabeth, 299; James, 299
JOSLIN: Darius Jr., 78
JOY: Ebenezer, 299; Girsham, 299; Horatio Arad, 23, 71, 96, 105, 228, 377, 476, 479–80; Hubbard, 555; Ruth, 299
JOYCE: John, 406
JUDD: Alfred B., 300; Arunah, 300; Freeman, 300; Reuben, 300; Sally, 300; William, Capt., 126
JUDSON: Amos, 50, 190, 314, 365, 396, 403, 433,

536, 579; J.S., JP, 447; John, 204; John P., 242; P.P., JP, 50
JUDY: John, JP, 90
JUSTICE: George W., 41, 63, 80, 110, 137, 155, 171, 216–17, 225, 248, 251, 261, 269, 306, 315, 327, 335, 359, 466–67, 480, 482, 491, 505, 508, 510, 513, 515, 524, 541–42, 556, 570; Jacob, 300; Jane, 300; John, 300; Joseph, 300; Margaret, 300; Peter, 300; William, 300

KACHLEIN: David, 300; Elizabeth, 300; John, 300; Margaret, 300; Michael, 300; Peter, Lt., 300
KACHLIN: Col., 513
KAEMMER: William B., 519
KAHAM: Michael, 301
KAHE: Frederick, 43
KAHL: Frederick, 1, 70, 212, 270, 355–56, 418, 435, 451, 504, 564
KAHM: Elizabeth, 301; Michael, 301
KAIN: William, 58
KALEHOFF: Frederick, 301
KALLAM: Amy, 301; Betsey, 301; Comfort, 301; Lucinda, 301; Lucretia [ELDRIDGE], 167; Luther, 301; Temperance, 301
KAMP: Andrew, 301; Daniel, 301; David, 301; John, 301; Rebecca, 301
KANE: Patrick, 301
KANNADY: John, Capt., 52
KAPPES: George, 301
KARBAUGH: Rachel [RIMMEY], 473
KARNEY: Thomas, 498
KARPER: Frederick, 463
KARR: James, 302
KARTMAN: Elizabeth [SKIMER], 515; Frederick, 515

KATZ: William, 229
KAUFFMAN: Abraham, 199
KAUFMAN: J.B., 77, 320, 395, 482
KAUP: Peter, 302
KAUTZ: Catharine, 302; Dorothy, 302; Elizabeth, 302; George, 302; Thomas, 302
KAUVANAGH: Catharine, 302; Jeremiah, 302
KAUVANAUGH: Catharine, 302; Jeremiah, 302
KAYLOR: John, JP, 138
KEAGY: A.L., 589
KEAN: Dennis, 302; James, 302; John, 302; Mary [ADAMS], 2
KEARNE: Mary, 303; Patrick, 303; Timothy, 303
KEARNEY: Capt., 164; John, 217
KEARSLEY: Samuel, Capt., 303
KEATING: Joseph, 457
KEATLEY: William, JP, 28
KEE: Porter, 311; Sarah, 303, 311; Stewart, 303, 311
KEEDER: *Valentine*, 303
KEEFER: Ann Maria, 303; Frederick, 303; William, 303
KEEHN: H.N., 2
KEELER: Chlora M., 304; Ebenezer, 303–4; John, 303; Lucy, 303–4; Nehemiah J., 303–4; William C., 304
KEELOR: William, 91
KEEMLE: Caroline, 304; Isaac A., 304; John, 304; Maria M., 304; Rebecca, 304; Samuel, 304
KEEN: Andrew, 304; Capt., 569; Charles, 362; George M., 15; Jacob, 304
KEENAN: Edward J., 465; James, JP, 379
KEENE: Henry E., 578
KEEP: Sarah [COLE], 105
KEGERRIER: John Jr., 508

KEHL: Catharine, 304; Jacob, 304
KEHLNER: Jacob C., 304–5; Maria, 304; Matthias, 304
KEIFFER: Angeline, 304; *Ann* M., 304; Anna, 304; Frederick, 304
KEIM: Daniel M., 25–26; Levi, 96; Peter, 212; William H., 13
KEISEL: Christopher, JP, 127
KEISTER: Jacob, 305, 458
KEIZER: Lewis, 311
KELCHNER: George, JP, 358; Jacob, 75
KELLAM: Lucretia [ELDRIDGE], 167; S.L., JP, 165, 402
KELLER: Amelia, 305; Catharine, 305–6; Catharine [SAILOR], 489–90; Conrad, 305; Daniel, 305; Elenor, 638; Eliza, 305; Elizabeth, 305–6; Frederick, 305; George, 305–6; Henry, 305–6, 319; Jacob, 305–6; John, 305–6; Margaretta, 306; Maria C., 306; Mary, 305; Peter, 275, 305–6; Philip, 310; Rebecca, 305; Samuel, 281; Simon, 306; William, 306
KELLEY: -----, Mr., 430; James, JP, 123; Julius, 137; Lucy T. [-----PACKER], 430; Matthew, 287; Peter, 275; William, JP, 270, 346, 396
KELLOG: Samuel, 306
KELLOGG: A.W., 529; Abner, JP, 326; Asenath, 307; Eldad, 306; Eliphalet, 306; George, 79, 210, 465, 534, 576, 579; Josiah, 307; Ledway, JP, 42; Lumen, JP, 443; Martin, 307; Nathan, 299; Philena, 307; Readway, JP, 42; Ruth, 307; Samuel, 306, 443;

T., JP, 18; Thomas, 307; Wells, JP, 144; Wills, 562
KELLUM: Isaac, 354, 598
KELLY: Abraham, 307; Ann Grizella, 307; Col., 173; Cornelius C., 307; David, JP, 399; Grizella, 307; Isabella, 307; Jane, 307; John, 50, 307, 448; Joseph, 660; Lewis, 91; Lucy Ann, 63; Margaret, 307; Mary, 307; P., Jr., JP, 5; Patrick Jr., JP, 87, 387; Patrick Sr., 307; Patrick, JP, 9; Robert, 49; Samuel, 307; William, 308
KELSEY: Jonas, 407
KELSY: Fanny C. [MERSEREAU], 390
KELVEY: James W., JP, 185
KEMMERER: Elizabeth, 649; Frederick, 308, 649
KENDALL: Capt., 21; Christopher, 313; John, 312; Rhoda [BALLARD], 23; Ursula, 23
KENEGY: John, JP, 202, 448
KENIG: G.F., 42
KENN: Charity [HUNT], 13, 628
KENNADY: Samuel, 74
KENNAN: James, JP, 365
KENNEDY: James, 253; James D., 379; James H., 433; James M., 132, 400; James S., 276; John, 125, 253, 280, 308; Leonard A., 529; Loren, 215; Margaret [ALLISON], 6; William, 89, 563; William C., JP, 587
KENNETT: Thomas, JP, 59–60
KENNEY: Amos, 308; David, 519; Jane [SMITH], 519; Jonathan B., JP, 3, 309; Rebecca, 308; William, JP, 121
KENSINGER: Isaac, JP, 345
KENT: Bela, 308; Lucretia, 308; Thomas, 308–9; William, 246

KENTFIELD: Ebenezer, 309
KEPHART: Margaret, 309; Martin, 309
KEPLAR: Jacob Jr., 550
KEPLER: William, JP, 36
KEPLINGEL: Christian, 309
KEPLINGER: Christian, 309; Elisabeth, 309
KEPNER: Bernard, JP, 264
KERBAUGH: David, 319; Mary, 319
KERBY: Isaac, 309; Phebe, 309
KERFOOT: George B., 327, 621
KERLIN: Abraham, JP, 344
KERN: Col., 197; Jonathan, 309; William, Lt., 309
KERNACHAN: William, 309
KERNER: George, 310; John, 310; Magdalena, 310
KERR: Alexander, 310; Andrew L., 63; Ann, 310; Betty, 310; Hannah, 310; Jane, 560; John, 118, 310; Margaret, 310; Martha, 310; Robert, 310; Robert H., 259, 363; S.A., 227; Samuel, 310; Sarah [ANDERSON], 9; Thomas, 310; William, 221, 310
KERSCHE: George, 310
KERSCHNER: Daniel, 43
KERSHAW: John G., 194
KERWOOD: Richard, JP, 344, 398
KESSINGER: Adam, 310
KESSLER: Catharine, 310; Charles, 528; Elizabeth, 310; George P., 310; Jacob, 310; Juliann, 310; Philip, 310; Susanna, 310; William, 310
KESTER: Mary, 310; Peter, 310
KETCHAM: John, 311
KETCHUM: Loisa [HAMMOND], 237
KETLER: Adam, 492; Hester [MURRY], 413; William, 492

KETT: Samuel, 183
KEY: Sarah, 303, 311; Stewart, 303, 311
KEYES: Daniel, 311
KEYS: Barbara, 311; Catharine, 311; Daniel, 311; David, 311; George, 311; Peter, 311; Philip, 311
KEYSER: Benjamin, JP, 267; Jacob, 58
KIBBER: George, 311
KIBLER: John, 372
KIDD: A., JP, 29
KIEZER: Ann Elizabeth [SMITH], 311; Lewis, 311
KILGORE: David, Capt., 176; Jesse, JP, 271
KILLAM: Ephraim, 311; Joseph, Capt., 70
KILLÉ: Samuel K., 124; William H., 521, 547
KILLIAM: Henry, 641
KILLMER: Isaac, 286
KILLUM: Isaac, 109
KILPATRICK: Thomas S., JP, 548, 568
KIMBALL: Abel, 311; James, 560; Jared, 312
KIMBER: Samuel, 535
KIMBLE: Jacob, 312; Mary, 312; Sarah, 222; Stephen, Col., 618
KIMMEL: Jacob, 122; Jacob, JP, 77
KINDALL: John, 312; Joseph, 312
KINDER: Philip, 312
KINESMAN: John Henry, 312; Margaret, 312
KING: -----, Mrs., 646; Abraham, JP, 39; Achsah, 314; Alexander, 312; Barbara, 313; Benjamin, 312; Betsy, 313; Capt., 57, 119; Charles, 532; David, 352, 601; Elias, 246; Eliza [DOUGLASS], 153; Elizabeth, 313–14; Francis, 313; George, 247, 313, 536, 646; H.C., 55; Henry, 332; Hiram, 601; James, JP, 4, 144; John G., 313; John M., 4;

John S., JP, 618; Jonathan, 313, 491; Joseph, 313; Leicester, 79, 132, 161, 339, 566; Lockwood, JP, 385; Lois, 313; Maria, 313; Mary, 313; Philip, 314; Rebecca, 313; Robert, 188, 284, 313–14, 540, 556; Sampson S., JP, 21, 49, 92, 176, 219, 288, 382, 487; Sampson W., JP, 379, 387; Samuel, 313; Sarah, 313; Simeon, 314; Stephen, 314; Thomas, 312; W.C., 451; William, 174
KINGLEY: John, 314; Lucinda, 314; Lucretia, 314; Rufus, 314
KINGSBERY: Joseph, 315
KINGSBURY: Burton, 250; Lemuel, 314; Louisa, 314; Payson, JP, 470, 561; William, 616
KINGSLEY: Joseph, 217; Martin, 314
KINKAID: Jane [McCULLOCH], 373
KINKEAD: David, 374
KINNEAR: Carter V., JP, 344, 588, 606
KINNEY: George, 217, 315; Jacob, 315; Joseph, 315; W.W., 598
KINSEY: David, 315; Simon, 614
KINSMAN: John, 556
KINTER: John, 315; Philip, 312
KINTS: Lewis, 315
KINTZ: Lewis, 315
KINTZING: Tench C., JP, 428
KIP: Peter, 315
KIPP: Jane, 315; John C., 315; William, 315; William B., JP, 85
KIRCHLIER: W.H., 580
KIRK: Alfred, 578; G.A., 597; Isaac Jr., 102; Isaac, JP, 102; James, 315; John, 316; John Jr., 289; Juliana, 315; Mary, 315; Timothy, 211, 378

KIRKENDALL: Capt., 215; Samuel, Capt., 263
KIRKES: John, 120
KIRKHAM: William, 368
KIRKLAND: William, JP, 102
KIRKMAN: Mary [McBRIDE], 367
KIRKPATRICK: George A., JP, 396; John, 164; William, 358
KIRKUM: George, 44, 437
KIRKWOOD: Robert, Capt., 323
KIRPER: Daniel, 275
KIRST: George, 310
KIRTLAND: Henry T., 539
KISENCEDERS: Martin, 316
KISINER: Jacob, 289
KISNER: Samuel, JP, 5, 96
KISSINGER: James M., 316; Reuben C., 316
KISTLER: Jonathan, JP, 19
KITCH: Catharine [KAUTZ], 302
KITCHEN: Col., 482; William, JP, 124, 150, 413
KITTS: Catharine, 316; John, 316; Maria, 316
KLETT: Frederick, 13, 36, 232
KLINE: A.P., 474; Elizabeth [SHINDEL], 508; Peter, 33, 301, 316; Peter A., 33, 301, 624; Peter Jr., 316; Samuel, 316
KLINESETTER: George, 33, 71, 131, 282, 308, 318, 336, 396, 418, 450, 456, 553, 613
KLINESMITH: Andrew, 316; Barbara, 316
KLOCK: David K., JP, 384
KLUGH: Frederick, 142
KLUNCH: Henry, 317
KLUNK: Elizabeth, 317; Henry, 317
KLYNE: Catharine, 317; Dorothy, 317; Gabriel, 317; Maria, 317
KNAPP: Abigail, 317; Avery, 474; Irene [DART], 131;

(KNAPP, continued)

John, 317; Joshua, 317; Justus, 184
KNAUSE: Hannah, 4
KNAUSS: David, JP, 171
KNEELAND: Anna B., 317; John, 317
KNEP: George, 317; Mary Ann, 317
KNIGHT: Catharine [SPANGENBURG], 527; Ezra C., 410; Jeremiah, 94; Samuel M., 568; Samuel Mason, 22
KNITTAL: Elizabeth, 318
KNITTLE: Adam, 318; Frederick, 318
KNOKLE: Lawrence, 319
KNORR: Jonathan, 52
KNOUSE: John, 318
KNOWLTON: Willard R., JP, 342
KNOWS: Jacob, 164
KNOX: A., 69, 207, 265; Archibald, 489, 499; George, 318; Jane, 318; John, 4, 112, 134, 136, 179, 211, 221, 353, 366, 421, 472, 519, 537, 609; Joseph, 249
KOCH: Adam, 318; John E., 232
KOCHENDERFFER: John, 319
KOCK: Adam, 630
KOEVLER: Adam, 319; Elizabeth, 319
KOHL: Frederick, 197
KOHLER: Edward, JP, 203; Elizabeth [MILLER], 394; F.W., JP, 295; Jacob, 395; Valentine, 318
KOKOGAI: Samuel, 318
KOLLOCK: Henrietta, 318; Jane, 319; Lydia, 319; Mary, 318; Shepard, 318; Shepherd, 319; Susan, 318–19
KONKLE: Lawrence, 319
KOOCKOGEY: Rebecca, 318
KOOKENDERFER: John, 319

KOOKER: Jacob, 137; Jane [DEAN], 137
KOONS: Barcroft, 123; Charles, 551; Daniel Jr., 540; Frederick E., 504; Isaac, 32, 173, 213, 224, 249, 253, 256, 290, 297, 301, 316, 320, 322, 350, 353, 394–95, 429, 443, 448, 482, 540, 553, 577, 581, 588; Michael, 45, 206, 434, 613; Richard, 350, 581
KOPP: George, 319; *Ludovic*, 319
KOPPS: *Ludwie*, 319
KORBAUGH: David, 319
KOUGH: Adam, 319
KOUGHER: Daniel, 319
KOVELER: Adam, 319
KRAM: Rebecca [ROTH], 482
KRAMER: Allen, 141; James W., 316; Thomas, JP, 325
KRANMER: Harriet [SPANGLER], 528; Philip, 528
KRAUSE: D.O., 166; David, Capt., 480; John, 269; John J., JP, 56, 119, 177
KRAUSS: Jacob, 407
KRAUT: Mathias, 124
KREAMER: Elizabeth, 320; Frederick, 320
KREBS: Catharine [BOWMAN], 59; George, 320
KREIDER: Catharine, 121; David, 121; Paul, 320; Tobias Jr., JP, 44; Tobias, JP, 257
KREMER: John, 320; Michael, 180
KREPPS: Solomon G., 647
KREPS: George, 320
KRESS: Benjamin, JP, 222; Catharine, 320; George, 320
KREWSEN: Simon, 320
KREWSON: Ann, 320; Lydia, 320; Margaret, 320; Mary, 320; Rebecca, 320; Simon, 320

KRIDER: Anna, 320; Elizabeth, 320; Harriet, 320; Jacob, 320; Margaret, 320; Sarah, 320; William, 547
KRIEBEL: Jacob, 13
KRISS: Conrad, 320; Mary, 320
KROAN: John, 321
KROESEN: Garrett, 321
KROESON: Garrett, 321
KROLL: Margaret, 199; Zebulon, 199
KRUG: Mary, 321; Philip, 321
KRUM: Capt., 19
KRUMBHAAR: L., 577
KRUMBINE: Peter, 125
KUDER: *Valentine*, 303
KUFOVER: Caroline, 355; Lavinia [HERTZOG], 355
KUHL: Henry, 73, 353
KUHN: Augustus, 482; Michael, 321
KUHNS: Jacob, JP, 369; Julian, 321; Michael, 321
KULP: Henry, 126, 495
KUMPS: George, 321
KUNCKEL: Christian, 94
KUNKEL: Capt., 198
KUNKLE: Jacob, 614
KUNTZ: John, 321
KUNTZE: Christian, 309
KURTZ: Capt., 180; Charlotte, 321; Elizabeth, 322; Henry H., JP, 321; Israel A., 274; John, 321; Josiah, JP, 532; Peter, 322; Sarah, 322
KUTER: Capt., 274, 394
KUTZ: Peter, JP, 478
KYCENCEDER: Margaret, 316
KYLE: James, 601; Matthew, 608

LABAR: Cornelia, 322; Daniel, 322; Samuel, 322
LABENGOOD: Christopher, 236
LACEY: Henry, 259; Isaac, JP, 150; John, Capt., 217
LACKEY: Henry, 322; Margaret, 322;

(LACKEY, continued)

Mary, 322; Robert, 322; Sarah Ann, 322; Thomas, 322
LACY: Col., 102; Elizabeth, 322; Ellen, 322; Isaac, 322; James, 322; Jesse, 322; John, 322; Mary [LESLIE], 334; Thomas S., 325
LADD: W.A., 239
LADIG: Peter, 323; Solomon, 323
LAFOURCADE: C., 251
LAHEY: John, 323
LAIRD: Harrison P., 596; J.M., JP, 596; Joseph, 115; William, 536
LAKE: Adam, 323; G.B., 435; Hannah [SONDAY], 525; James, 352, 585, 602; Joshua, JP, 60; Samuel, 237, 323; William, 323
LAMB: B.F., Dr., 150; C.B., 335; Clayton B., 167; Daniel, JP, 77; David, 323; Elizabeth, 323; Joel, JP, 208; Lemuel, 452; Reuben, 296; Silvanus, JP, 174; William, 479
LAMBERSON: Samuel, JP, 535
LAMBERT: Dorothy, 323; G.W., 22, 126, 588; Gersham W., 114; Jacob, 323
LAMBERTON: James, JP, 43; W., 89
LAMBERTSON: James G., 71; *W.J.*, 71
LAMBORN: Lawrence, JP, 124; Townsend, JP, 243
LAMPHAR: Samuel, 323
LAMPHIER: Benjamin, 323; Calista, 323; William D., 323
LAMSON: *E. Thomas*, 324; Ebenezer, 324
LANBUR: Johannes Georg, 469
LANCASTER: Richard, JP, 3
LANCER: Abraham, 324

LANDALE: James B., 324; Mary, 324
LANDER: Peter, 326; Samuel M., JP, 377
LANDES: Jacob, 367; John, 188; Samuel, JP, 208, 624
LANDIS: Benjamin, 458; Christian, 566; David, 324; Jonathan, 399
LANDON: Rebecca [BOWMAN], 59; S.B., 597
LANE: Ebenezer, JP, 19; Gustavus, 324; Henry, 324; Jesse, JP, 396; John, 324; John Jr., 324; Julia, 324; Mary, 290; Rachel [TYLER], 569; Susan [GANGWER], 203
LANENBERGER: Catharine, 324; George, 324
LANG: John D., 264; William, 35; William F., 505
LANGBERG: Joseph, 652
LANGDALE: James B., 324
LANGDON: Benjamin, 325
LANGHAM: Capt., 324
LANGLY: James, 29
LANGSHORNE: Ann F. [WILSON], 609
LANGSTON: James, 456
LANING: C.H., JP, 172; M.H., 154
LANIUS: Benjamin, JP, 208, 528
LANMAN: Philip, 325
LANS: Jacob, 325; John, 325
LANSERT: Abraham, 324
LANSLEY: John, JP, 20
LANTZER: Abraham, 324
LAPHAM: J., 190, 235; Jonathan, 1, 234, 278
LARCOM: Arvillus C., 325; Comfort, 325; Paul, 325
LARIMER: James, JP, 239; John, JP, 8, 156
LARKINS: James, 325; Seth, 325; Thomas C., 325
LARNED: Abijah, 326; Ann, 325; Anna, 326;

Asa, JP, 101; Sarah, 101, 326; Sylvanus, 326
LARRABEE: Capt., 236
LARWILL: John, JP, 397
LASHBAUGH: Susannah [SHAFFER], 503
LASHELLS: George, 326; Jonathan, 326
LATCH: Francis H., 326; Jacob, Capt., 326; Jane, 326; Tacy, 326
LATHISER: Hartman, 326
LATHROP: Charles J., JP, 257; James, JP, 52, 110; Lydia H., 257
LATHROPE: Dwight N., 165
LATIMER: Henry, 585
LATROSS: Dyer, 122
LATTA: Charlotte, 326; John, 326; William, 326
LATTIMORE: Elizabeth, 326; William, 326
LATTY: Mary [TUNISON], 567
LAUBACK: Christian, 515; Susanna [SKIMER], 515
LAUCKS: Israel R., JP, 625
LAUDER: John, 326; Peter, 326
LAUGHEAD: Robert L., 154; Robert L., JP, 90
LAUGHEY: William, JP, 327
LAUGHLIN: James, 313, 382; Joseph, 82; M.W., 47; T.J., 79, 99, 121, 432, 483, 557, 605; Thomas J., 39
LAUGHRY: William, JP, 400
LAUKS: Henry, 327
LAURENCE: Capt., 374; John J., 321
LAURENSON: John, 253; Sarah [HENDERSON], 253
LAUSCH: Henry, 327
LAVELY: William S., 335
LAVERY: John, 327
LAVICH: Gabriel, 330
LAW: Benjamin, 359, 619; D.L., 619; David L., 359; Sarah [DULIN], 158; William, 158

LAWDON: Lathrop, JP, 558

LAWER: Capt., 523

LAWLY: James M., JP, 59

LAWRENCE: Amos, 327; Benjamin, 59, 617; Capt., 600; Daniel, 327; I.J., 45; Julia, 429; Lyman, 145; Margaret, 327; William, 327, 429; William P., 242; Zachariah, Jr., 4

LAWS: Jonathan, JP, 33, 201

LAWSON: Hugh, 327; James, 153, 327; James, JP, 94

LAWYER: Peter, 328

LAYMAN: Henrich, 328; Henry, 328

LAZARUS: Frederick, JP, 536; Leonard, 245

LAZEAR: Jesse, 364, 618

LAZELL: Loly [WHEELER], 595

LAZIER: John, 328; William, 328

LEACH: Hezekiah Jr., 328; Hezekiah Sr., 328

LEADER: Frederick, 328

LEARD: John, Capt., 108; William, 328

LEARNING: Robert W., 180

LEARNS: Lewis, JP, 339

LEARRY: Daniel, 328

LEARY: William, 328

LEAS: Elizabeth, 329; George, 329; Jacob, 329; John, 329; Leonard, 329; Margaret, 329; Mary G., 329; Sarah, 329; Sophia, 329; William, 329

LEASURE: Abraham, 329; Henry, 328; John, 233, 329; William, 329

LEATHER: Sam, 630

LEATHERMAN: Francis, 333

LEAVITT: Hart A., 139, 145, 392, 571, 607; Humphrey H., 234

LEAVY: Michael, JP, 88

LEAZEAR: Henry, 328

LEBER: Jacob, 329; Nicholas, 329

LEBKECHER: Michael, 329

LEBKEEHER: Michael, 329

LEBO: Henry, 329

LECKEY: Daniel, JP, 609

LECONTE: Alphonse, JP, 109

LEDMAN: Daniel, 284

LEDYARD: Hiram, 330; Joseph Sr., 330; Robert, 330

LEE: Anna, 330; Capt., 419; Catharine, 330; Col., 106; Daniel, 330; Dolly, 330; Elizabeth, 330; George, 330; Hannah, 330; Hugh, 369; Hugh, JP, 73; Polly, 330; Rachel, 330; Stephen C., 330; Thomas, 438; William, 330

LEECH: Archibald, 330; Henry, JP, 491; Joseph S., 408; M., 49, 181, 375, 565; Malcolm, 436; Malcomb, 12

LEEDER: George, 331

LEEDOM: Charles, 572

LEEDS: D.W., JP, 142; Daniel W., JP, 141

LEESE: Daniel, JP, 263

LEET: Luther, 331; Sybil, 331

LEFEVER: John E., 391

LEFFAR: John, 331; R.L., 331

LEFFERD: Adam, 536

LEGGET: Thomas, 331

LEHEW: David, 331; Elizabeth, 331

LEHMAN: Abraham, 68; Anthony, 331; Capt., 547; Catherine, 331–32; Charles, 98; George, 331; George W., 127, 317; Henry, JP, 116, 134, 158, 469–70, 566; Jacob, 332; John, 331; Nancy, 331; Philip, 331; Polly, 331

LEHR: Philip, 332; Sarah, 332

LEIBENGOOTT: Jacob, 336

LEIBERT: John, JP, 102

LEIBINGOOD: Jacob, 336

LEIDEY: Samuel, 332

LEIGHTON: Andrew, 75; Mary [BUEL], 75

LEILIN: Jonathan K., 344

LEITHAUESER: Elizabeth, 332; Hartman, 332

LEITHEISER: Ann, 332; Elizabeth, 332; Hartman, 326, 332

LEITNER: Ignatius, JP, 100

LEITZ: Henry, 332; Jacob, 332

LELAND: Aaron, 222; Erastus, 617

LEMMON: James, 327; John, 332; William, 333

LEMON: John, 332

LENCE: Peter, 513

LENHART: H., JP, 412; Henry, 64, 150, 320; Philip, 333

LENHARTZ: H., 318

LENOS: David, Capt., 359

LENOX: Andrew, 221; Capt., 218, 517; George C., 333

LENT: John, 333

LENTHERMAN: Francis, 333

LENTZ: Capt., 538; Nancy [SILK], 513; Peter, 513

LEONARD: Alfred, 333; Alva, 333; Cynthia, 499; Esther, 333; Ezekiel, 333; Fanny [WILLIS], 606; George, 208, 333; Jonathan, 256, 274, 305; Lewis, 123; Marcus, JP, 424, 556; Milton A, JP, 218; Patrick, 562; Philip, 333; Rhoda, 333; Thomas, 333; William, 320, 333

LERAH: Jacob, 334

LERCH: A.W., JP, 80

LESHER: Jane, 156

LESLIE: Alexander, 334; James, 334; Jane, 334; Mary, 334; Thomas, 334; William, 334

LESLY: Catharine [DAVIS], 135

LESSIG: David, 334; Elizabeth [DEUTZLER], 142; John C., 142

LEVAN: Jacob, Col., 625; Samuel, 54, 197, 213, 220, 249–50, 304, 311, 318, 320, 347, 353, 357–58, 395, 416, 429, 443, 445

LEVANGOOD: Capt., 39

LEVENGOOD: Daniel, 410

LEVY: Joseph, 229

LEWIS: Abner, 48; Benjamin, 334; Betsey [MEEKER], 388; Catharine, 335; Charles, 351; Curtis, JP, 197; Elijah, 334; Ellis, JP, 56; Ezekiel, 337; George W., JP, 434; George, Capt., 53; H.J., 51, 63, 73, 532; Harry, 297; Henry, 174. 334; Henry M., JP, 194, 361; Henry W., JP, 365; Isaac, 334; Isaac, Capt., 5; Jacob, 334; Jehu, 334; John, 241, 335; John B., JP, 289; Lewis, 335; Mary, 335; Nathan, JP, 550; Oliver, 335; Phineas, 439; Richard, 335; Robert, 63; Samuel, 335; Samuel A., 142; Sarah, 335; Sharp Dalany, 296; Susannah [SYPE], 553; Thomas, 335; W.D., 55; William D., 350, 428

LEX: Charles F., 592; Jacob, 89, 143, 147, 187, 194, 203, 260, 330, 341, 353–54, 359, 364, 368, 383, 437, 480, 506, 516, 533, 549, 577

LIAS: John, JP, 254

LIBENGOOD: Jacob, 336

LIBINGOOD: Jacob, 336

LIDDY: Matthew, 336

LIGGET: Joseph, 385

LIGGETT: James, 336; John, 336; Samuel, 336; Thomas, 336; William, 336

LIGGIT: James, 331; John, 331; Mary, 331; Samuel, 331; Thomas, 331; William, 331

LIGHT: Catharine, 336–37; John, 336–37; John Sr., 238; Sarah, 336

LIGHTCAP: Mary, 337; Samuel, 337

LIGHTNER: Jonathan, JP, 436; Nathaniel, 394

LIKENS: George, 337; Hannah, 337; Israel, 337

LIKES: Jacob, 337; Rebecca, 337

LILLEY: John, 337

LILLIE: Abraham, 137

LILLY: John, 337; Samuel, 412

LINCOLN: John, 337; Michael, 337

LIND: John, 351; Matthew, JP, 313, 382

LINDEMUTH: Col., 538

LINDENSMITH: George Jr., 337; George Sr., 337

LINDERMAN: Capt., 155; Isaac, JP, 28, 206, 243; John J., 335

LINDLEDAKER: Martin, 344

LINDLEY: Joseph, JP, 289; William, 14; William, JP, 133, 136

LINDLY: Caleb, 337; Elizabeth, 337; William, 441, 471, 486, 488, 578, 607, 628; William Sr., JP, 337

LINDSAY: James, JP, 47, 56, 114, 121, 176, 196, 226–27, 248, 337–38, 376, 381, 425, 475, 549, 557, 611, 616; John, 7, 338; Judith B., 616; Mary [ALSWORTH], 8

LINDSEY: David, 338; James, 90; Mungo, 338

LINDSLEY: Caleb, 337

LINDY: Eliza, 338; Jacob, 338; Susannah, 338

LINE: Anna, 338; Elizabeth, 338; Joseph *Serring*, 338; Mariba, 338; Mary, 338; Rachel, 338; Samuel, 338; *Sernin*, 338; William, 338

LINEBOCK: Joseph, 338

LINELLY: William D., 102

LINES: Ebenezer, 338; Frederick, 2, 74, 339; Mercy, 338; Rufus, 339; Tamer, 339

LINK: Solomon, 129

LINN: A.P., 386; Andrew P., Dr., 388; Dewalt, 339; Esther [McGEE], 378; James F., JP, 44, 84, 317; James Sr., 339; James, JP, 372; John E., 30, 298, 389, 409, 432, 531; Samuel, JP, 328, 552

LINSCUTT: Samuel, 339

LINSLEY: Stephen, 339

LINT: Eliza, 339; Gillian, JP, 350; Isaac A., 339; John, 339; Joseph E., 339; Margaret Jane, 339; Sarah Elasan, 339

LINTON: J., 212, 225; Robert P., 612

LINVILLE: Sarah [SWAZE], 552

LIPKEY: Elizabeth, 339; Henry, 339

LIPPINCOTT: Aaron S., 459; Benjamin, 28, 83, 209; George, 176; Henry, 253

LISH: Philip, 340

LISKE: John, 340; Nicholas P., 340

LIST: Lewis, 188; Sarah [FLOWERS], 188; William, 467

LISTON: Thomas, 430

LITCHEN: Cornelius, 62

LITCHFIELD: E.B., 595

LITEHARD: Joseph, 340

LITTELL: Leech, 597; Thomas, 340; William, 340

LITTLE: Alexander, Lt., 340; Capt., 600; David, 368; Jane, 340; John, 38, 311, 340; Major, 612; Margaret [JACOBY], 288; Martha, 340; Mary, 340; Matthias, 341; Nancy, 340; Rebecca, 340; Samuel, JP, 38; Sarah, 341; Susan, 157; Thomas, 340–41; William, 296, 340

LITZINGER: Barnabas, 416; Honor [NAGLE], 416
LIVELY: Andrew, 650; Elizabeth, 650
LIVENBURG: Frederick, 341
LIVERMORE: Daniel, 301
LIVINGOOD: Peter, 341
LIVINGSTON: Daniel, 341; J.B., 581; Joseph, 93; William, 28, 31, 341
LIVINGWOOD: Mary, 341; Peter, 341
LIVLEY: Andrew, 342; Elizabeth, 342
LLEWELYN: John J., 542
LLOYD: Col., 344; David, JP, 186; Elizabeth, 342; George, JP, 135; Hannah R., 342; Jane A., 342; John, 342; Lecester, 1; Mary, 342; Thomas, 342, 569, 643
LOAD: Andrew, JP, 354
LOCHMAN: Ann [LEITHEISER], 332; Christian, 326; William J., 332
LOCK: Ayres, 342; James, 342; William, 342
LOCKARD: John, 342
LOCKART: Robert, Capt., 131
LOCKE: Charles H., 342; Ebenezer, 342; Francis, Capt., 25; Molly, 342
LOCKERMAN: John, 343
LOCKERT: John, 342
LOCKMAN: George, Dr., 275; Henry, 343
LOCKWOOD: Lucy [THOMPSON], 560
LODER: Levi L., JP, 204
LOFT: Elizabeth [ANTRUM], 13; George, 13
LOGAN: Alexander, 343; David, 343; James, 88, 167, 255, 264, 343, 382, 608; John, 258, 302, 457, 619; Samuel, 343; Samuel Jr., 343; William, JP, 149
LOGNE: Hugh, 226

LOMISON: Abigail [BARNES], 27; Jacob, 186
LONG: Alexander, 343; Benjamin, 117, 343–44; Capt., 210, 260, 563; Col., 241; Cooksey, Capt., 365; Cookson, Col., 377; Daniel, 608; David, 343; Elial, 343; George, 186, 344; Gideon, 344; Hannah, 344; Henry G., JP, 302; Jacob, 304; Jacob M., 344; Jacob Sr., 344; James, 36; James, JP, 182; John, 344, 418; Joseph, 344; Mary, 343; Mary P. [FIFE], 182; Matthew, 344; Samuel S., JP, 137; William, 49, 183, 344
LONGAKER: Peter, 622
LONGENECKER: David, 212, 269, 306, 511; Jacob, 531; John, 24
LONGSTREET: Capt., 179
LONGSTRETH: Abigail, 345; Joel, 345; John, 344; Martin, 345; Morris, 370, 470; Nancy, 345; Philip, 345; Salome, 345; Thomas, 345
LONGWELL: Hamilton, 117, 228; Jane, 345; Stephen, 345
LOOFBOURROW: David, 345; David Jr., 345
LOOMIS: Andrew, 282; Asa, 345; Betsey [HICKOCK], 258; Elizabeth, 346; George, 346; James, 258, 584; John, 346; Martha, 345
LOPER: Abraham, 346
LORAH: Jacob, 334
LORAIN: John, 346; Robert, 346
LORD: Daniel, 17, 196; Isaac, JP, 141; Samuel, 112, 232
LORENTZ: Joseph, 346; Mary, 346
LORENZ: Frederick, 396
LORRANCE: Elizabeth [KAUTZ], 302

LORRES: Franklin L., 457
LOSE: George, 346
LOSEY: Jesse, 346
LOT: Capt., 573; Nicholas, 347
LOTT: George W., 81; Jacob, 347; Maria, 347; Martha A. [BUTLER], 81; Nicholas, 347; Philip Jacob, 347
LOTZ: Christiana, 347; Conrad, 347; Elizabeth, 347; Emma, 347; Henry, 347; Jacob, 347
LOUCKS: G.W., 624; George W., 21
LOUDON: Matthew, 264
LOUGHBOROUGH: David, 345
LOUGHHEAD: James, 251, 423
LOUGHIN: Jeremiah, 184
LOUIS: Jane, 623
LOURY: Michael, 347
LOUTZENHISER: J., 475
LOVE: Henry, JP, 8, 206, 223, 348, 477; James, 225; John, 119
LOVEARE: John, 148
LOVELAND: Abner, 193, 347; Frederick, 348; L.H., 347
LOVELESS: David, 348; Polly, 348
LOVELL: Frederic S., JP, 106
LOVETT: Erastus, 193; Rhoda, 348; Samuel, 348
LOW: Andrew, JP, 53; Christian, 98; Eliza [BARNES], 78; Elizabeth [BARNHART], 28; Hugh, 54; John, 78; Nicholas, 78; Polly [BARNES], 78
LOWDEN: James, JP, 117; Mary [HOGE], 264
LOWE: Elizabeth, 555; Gilbert D., 348; Isaac, 212; Samuel, 555; William, JP, 17
LOWELL: Capt., 171
LOWER: Capt., 452; Peter, Capt., 24; Susannah [WILT], 592

LOWERY: Josiah, 640; Josias, 204; William, 640
LOWMAN: Philip, 325
LOWMASTER: Jacob, 417
LOWN: M.B., 374
LOWNES: Thomas C., 496
LOWNSBERRY: Samuel, 348
LOWREE: M.B., 327
LOWREY: Alexander, Col., 24; John G., 457; William, 348
LOWRIE: John, 10; M.B., 21, 221, 346; Matthew B., 56, 183, 312, 376; W.B., JP, 157, 607; Walter, 187; Walter H., 160, 614
LOWRY: F.M., 499; Jacob, 348; James, Capt., 82; John F., 83, 266; William, 348
LOWSON: Capt., 407
LUBOLD: Jacob, 319
LUCAS: Berridge, 349; Elijah, 583; Isaac, 349; John, 349; Margaret, 349; Martha, 349; Thomas, 349; William, JP, 418
LUCE: Artemas, JP, 583
LUCUS: Isaac, 349
LUDINGTON: Ruth, 349; William, 349
LUDLOW: Stephen, 136
LUDWICK: Catharine [MUSE], 413; Elizabeth, 349; John Martin, 349; Mary, 349; Susan, 349
LUDWIG: Capt., 334, 624; George, 632; Henry, 175; John, Capt., 246; Michael, 410; William C., 566
LUKENS: Abraham J., 387; Charles, Dr., 460; Edward, 217
LUKER: Benjamin, 349; Catharine, 349; Cornelia, 349; David, 349; Elizabeth, 349; Harriet, 349; Mary, 349; Sarah Ann, 349; William Craig, 349
LUKRE: David, 349
LUMEREAUX: Joseph, 349

LUMM: Hampton, 350; Jesse, 350
LUND: Oliver W., 68
LUNDER: John, 337
LUNKLE: Michael, 116
LUPER: Catharine, 464; Philip, JP, 464
LURE: Shubach C., 17
LUSHBAUGH: Henry, 350
LUSK: Hugh, 350; John, 350; R., 74, 251; Robert, JP, 24; Thomas, 350; William, 74
LUTTMAN: Jacob, 546
LUTZ: Jacob, 293; Joseph, 350; Margaret [RUSK], 487
LYBERGER: Nicholas, 350
LYBRAND: Joseph, Rev., 462
LYE: Henry, 284
LYMAN: Burrel, 350; Francis, 351; Harry, 350; Isaac, 350; Laura, 350; Laura D., 350; Otis, 350
LYN: Anna Maria, 351; Catharine, 351; Elizabeth, 351; John, 351; Peter, 351; Susanna, 351
LYNAM: William R., 494
LYNCH: Elizabeth, 351; Michael, 351; Rees, 351; Robert W., 351; Samuel, 351
LYND: James, 451, 612
LYNN: John, 351
LYON: Benjamin, 351; Elizabeth, 351, 651; Franklin, 352; Gartsey, 351; H.D., 18; James, 351; Jaspar, 352; Jediah, 351; Jonathan, 609; Joseph E., 224; Mary, 351; Robert, 351, 651; Thomas, Lt., 352; Walter, JP, 146; William, 352
LYONS: Capt., 55; James, 352; John, 352; Nicholas, 260; Samuel, 352; William, 47; William S. JP, 263
LYTLE: Andrew, 352; Cyrus, 352; John, 352; Margaret, 352
LYTTLE: Capt., 529

MABLEY: John, JP, 192
MacBRIDE: Robert D., 623
MACK: Capt., 15; Horace, 303; Lois [ROBINSON], 477; Nicholas, 492
MACKALL: Benjamin, 352; James, 352; Rebecca, 352
MacKAY: Daniel, 373
MACKENEY: William, 343
MACKET: Charles, 352
MACKEY: Jeremy, JP, 520; R.W., 406
MACLAIN: John, 353
MACLEAN: David, 197
MacPHERSON: John, 387
MADARA: William C., 41
MADDEN: James, JP, 36, 259
MADDOCK: William A., 20, 39, 55, 72, 117, 293, 369, 393, 447, 490, 587, 616
MADDON: Joseph, 353
MADEIRA: Elizabeth, 353; Michael, 353
MADER: George, 25
MADERA: Caspar, 353; Margareth, 353
MADISON: Anna [SUMMERS], 549
MADON: Joseph, 353
MAFFET: David, 353; Sarah, 353
MAFFETT: David, 353
MAGAHY: Mary, 238
MAGARVEY: Francis, 353; Olin, 353
MAGAW: Col., 620; William, 353
MAGINLEY: Amos W., 369
MAGLAUCHLIN: John, 310
MAGLAUGHLIN: Andrew, 353
MAGOFFIN: William M., 53
MAGUIRE: John, 101
MAGUNNIGAL: Samuel, JP, 97, 190, 263, 560
MAHAFFEY: Samuel, 354
MAHAN: Robert, 224
MAHEU: Richard, 354
MAHEW: Richard, 354

MAHOLM: John, 375
MAHONEY: Daniel, 354;
James, 354
MAHUS: Richard, 354
MAIN: Ezekiel, 354; Isaiah,
258
MAINS: William, 355
MAIRY: Lewis, 204
MAKEPEACE: Elijah,
355; *Keathy*, 355; Lydia,
355; Nelson, 375;
Roxana, 355; Seth, 355
MAKINS: Samuel, 355;
Sarah, 355
MALABY: Amy, 355;
Elizabeth, 355; Frederick
L., 355; George W., 355;
Harriet, 355
MALABZ: Amy, 355
MALCOLM: Angelica,
355; Ann P., 355; Donald,
355; Henry, 355–56;
Henry Jr., 355; Joseph G.,
JP, 355; Rebecca, 355;
Robert M., 355; William,
355
MALEBY: Henry B., 355
MALIX: Gideon, 406
MALLBIE: Benjamin, 356
MALLERY: G.N., 444;
Garrick, 81, 429; Rachel
[WILLIAMS], 604
MALLORY: Gideon, 356;
Harvey, JP, 388;
Nathaniel, 356; Sarah,
356
MALONE: John, 356
MALTZBERGER: John,
163
MANAHAN: William, 236
MANAN: John, 356
MANEBECK: Catharine,
356–57; Elizabeth, 356;
Henrietta, 356; Levan,
356; William, 356–57
MANKINS: William, 357
MANN: Andrew, Capt.,
121; Job, 260; John, JP,
247, 350; Susan
[BORROW], 56
MANNAN: John, 356–57
MANNER: Seth, Col., 371
MANNIN: Allissannae,
357; William, 357
MANNING: George, 328;
James, 15, 561; John,

356–57; Nancy, 357;
William, 357
MANSFIELD: Capt., 411;
Jonathan, 357
MANSPEKER: Daniel, 124
MANVILLE: Almira
[WOODRUFF], 616
MAPES: Elsworth, JP, 529;
William, 358
MAPLE: William, 358
MARBOURG: Alexander,
332
MARCH: Charles, 358;
John M., 358
MARCHAND: D., 220;
Daniel, 131
MARCY: Howland, 89;
John, 202
MARKEL: George, 358
MARKELL: Elizabeth,
358; Peter, 358
MARKER: Andrew, 358
MARKLAND: John, 358;
John Henry, 358; Sophia,
358
MARKLE: Christian, 358;
Gasper, 117
MARKLEY: Capt., 245;
John, 418
MARKS: Jacob, 359;
Johannes, 359; John, 359;
Samuel, Rev., 461;
William, 107
MARONY: L., Capt, 35
MARPLE: M.M., 152
MARQUIS: Andrew, 134;
David, 401; Mary
[MOORE], 401; Samuel
Jr., 118
MARRELL: Harriet, 359;
Hugh, 359
MARSDEN: John, 359
MARSDON: John, 359
MARSH: Boswell, 455;
Casper, 359; David, 359;
George, 359; J.H., 496;
James, 403; John, 180,
359, 551; Joseph, JP, 443
MARSHALL: Abigail, 360;
Andrew E., 359; Ann
[WESTFALL], 594;
Athe, 360; Capt., 535;
Christopher, Capt., 68;
Col., 57, 599; David, 360;
Hezekiah, 360; Isaac,
360; Jacob, 594; James

C., 299; Jane [LESLIE],
334; Jesse, 360; John, 40,
236, 239, 360, 400;
Joseph, 360; Joseph W.,
349; L.H., 227; Margaret,
360; Mary, 227, 360;
Mary [BELL], 40;
Rogers, JP, 195; Samuel,
101, 349, 389; Sarah,
360; Sarah E., 359;
William, 362
MARSHAMMER:
Sebastian, 360
MARSHEL: Justin, JP, 618
MARTIAL: Thomas, Capt.,
262
MARTIN: A., 527;
Abraham, 113;
Alexander, 231, 360, 362,
385; Anna, 361, 383;
Balsar, 360; Bernhart, JP,
367; Capt., 357, 596;
Catharine, 362; Claudius,
361; Col., 78; David W.,
361; Elizabeth, 362;
Ephraim, Col., 5; George
W., JP, 136; Henry, 361;
Hezekiah, 383; Isaac,
361; Isaac M., 361; J.M.,
333; Jacob, 361; James,
179, 361, 363, 402; Jehiel
P., 361; Jeremiah, 554;
John, 319, 361–62, 396;
Joseph, 426; Joseph R.,
JP, 102; Julia Ann, 362;
Lewis, 362; Magdalen,
362; Mary, 361–62;
Patrick, 362; Peter, 362,
533; Philo, 361; Richard,
362; Robert, 363; Robert
H., 136; Robert M., 363;
Roger, 363; Sophia, 362;
Thomas, 362–63; Thomas
J., 354; W.T., JP, 418;
William, 363, 426
MARTZ: Charles, JP, 237;
George, 363
MARVIN: Barzilla, JP, 555;
E.C., 226; Hosiah, Capt.,
445; John, JP, 484; Mabel
[ROBERTS], 476; P.F.,
30; R.E., 1; Roswell E.,
42, 128; William, 476
MARX: William, 363
MASON: Aaron, 363;
Calvin, 363, 395; E., 241;

(MASON, continued)

Elihu, 273; Elijah, JP, 70, 101, 146, 157, 417, 594; Henry, JP, 119; Isaac, 363; James, JP, 186; Nathan, 363; Olive, 364; William, 364
MASSER: Barbara [WAMBACK], 582; Henry, JP, 620
MASSEY: Caleb, 364; Elizabeth, 364; Leah, 364; Sarah, 364
MASTEN: C., JP, 378; Cornelius Jr., JP, 223
MASTERS: Capt., 425; Clement, 364; Daniel M., 362; George, 476; Judith, 364; Mary, 364; Stephen, 364; William, 364
MASTICK: Benjamin, 364; Cynthia, 364; Edwin B., 472
MATCHETT: John, 111
MATEN: F.A., JP, 531
MATHAW: John, 151
MATHENY: Joseph, JP, 427
MATHER: Abner, 364; Eleazer, 365; Samuel, Capt., 365
MATHERS: James, 421; Jonathan A., 421
MATHEWS: Anson, 413; James M., JP, 175; John, 538, 612; Levi, 365; Sally [MUSE], 413; William, 365
MATHIAS: James, 365
MATHIOT: G.F., 365; George, 365; John, 153, 236, 372; Samuel, 612
MATLACK: Timother, Col., 48
MATSINGER: Adam, 366
MATTER: George, JP, 552
MATTESON: David, 365
MATTHEW: J., 142
MATTHEWS: Ann Emily [BAKER], 21; Garret, 365; S., 228; Samuel, 59, 108, 516; Theodoshea, 87; Thomas B., 58; William, 365

MATTISON: Mary [McKINLEY], 382; Nathan, 382
MATTLEY: Joseph, 14
MATTOCK: Mary C. [RUGAN], 485
MATTOCKS: Abigail, 308; Jacob, 366; Jacob C., 366; James, JP, 229, 308, 433, 608; Richard, 365; S.P., JP, 242; Samuel P., JP, 367
MATTSON: Mary [BAUGH], 32
MATZINGER: Adam, 366
MAUCK: John, 66, 142, 170, 272, 310, 329, 581
MAULSBY: Samuel, 135
MAURER: Jacob, 320; John, 326; Peter, 366; Peter C., 366
MAUREZ: Solomon, 109
MAUSER: Jacob, Capt., 25
MAXFIELD: William R., 60
MAXON: Elsey, 366; Nathan, 366
MAXWELL: Ann, 366; Capt., 101; David, 353; Gen., 586; James, 366, 375; James 3rd, 366; John, 74, 159, 366; Michael, 59; Rebecca [DUNCAN], 159; S.A., 127; Thomas, JP, 127, 573; V.L., 180; Volney L., 97, 189; W., 594; William, 107, 112, 159, 244, 395
MAY: David, JP, 255; George, Capt., 458; John, 534; Thomas, 410
MAYBERRY: Col., 504; Maria [HOFFMAN], 264
MAYBERY: Elizabeth, 614, 663
MAYBURY: Isaac, Capt., 618
MAYER: John R., 425
MAYERS: Margaret [WILT], 592
MAYES: Isaac, JP, 3; Joseph F., 3; Susanna [KESSLER], 310; Thomas, 186

MAYHEW: Ann, 367; Azeuba, 367; David, 367; Enoch, 367; Hazel, 367; Holmes, JP, 312
MAYLAND: Jacob, 85
MAYNARD: A.J., 228; Almira C., 291; Thomas J., JP, 291
MAZE: Mary, 367; Thomas, 367
McAFEE: Benjamin, 367; Joel P., 367; Rachel, 367
McAFFEE: Hetty [IRELAND], 283
McALEER: Thomas, 450, 522
McCALISTER: Col., 108; H.F., JP, 40; Hugh T., JP, 47; Hugh, JP, 163; John Jr., 274; N.W., 163
McALLISTER: Charles, 554; Col., 180; John Jr., 70; W.Y., 606
McAULEY: James, 94, 238
McBRIDE: Alexander, 367; Ann, 367; George, 495; Hugh, 367; James, 367; Mary, 367; Neel, JP, 381; Peter, 368; William, 31, 117, 235
McCABE: R.B., 237
McCAFFERTY: Matthew, 91
McCAFFERY: Bernard, 372
McCAIN: Daniel, JP, 42
McCALISTER: Col., 272
McCALL: John, 11; Peter, 448
McCALLA: Alexander, 93, 435
McCALLISTER: James, JP, 247
McCALLMONT: George, 9
McCALMONT: J.B., JP, 591; S.E., 591
McCAMANT: Isaac, 368
McCAMENT: Isaac, 368
McCAMMON: Thomas, 459
McCANDLESS: James, 214
McCANE: R.J., 168
McCANN: Daniel, 368; George, 287, 350

McCAR: John, 368
McCARMICK: James, JP, 156
McCARNAHER: Alexander, 579
McCARRELL: Lemon, 381
McCARTER: Charles, 368; Rachel, 368
McCARTHUR: George, Capt., 208
McCARTNEY: Andrew, 607; Eleanor [WILSON], 607; Samuel, 371
McCARTY: Amanda, 368; Daniel, 368; Dennis, 368; Laura [LYMAN], 350; Sarah, 368; Thomas, 369
McCASLIN: John, 406
McCAULY: Mary [SYPE], 553
McCAW: Charles, 608; William, 609
McCAWLEY: G.G., 497
McCAY: Mathew, 570; Robert, 43, 53
McCELLAN: James, 369
McCHESNY: William H., 268
McCLAIN: Alexander, 369; Capt., 392, 422; Esther, 369; Margaret, 369; Mary, 383; Mathew, 369; Robert, 369
McCLAN: Robert, 162
McCLANE: James, 60, 199, 343, 357; John, 353; William, 609
McCLAREN: Thomas, 369
McCLASKEY: James, 597; John, 78
McCLAUGHAN: James, 369, 652; Samuel, 369, 652
McCLAY: Samuel, 83
McCLEAKEN: Samuel, 20
McCLEAN: Capt., 549; Jacob, 369
McCLEAR: Martha, 471, 657
McCLEARY: Ewing, 121; William, 454
McCLEAVE: Catherine, 369; James, 369
McCLEERY: Jonathan, 324
McCLEES: A.E., JP, 373

McCLELLAN: John H., 607; Joseph, Capt., 370; Robert, 342; Thomas, 370; William, JP, 196, 463
McCLELLAND: Ebenezer, 597; Elizabeth [LINE], 338; Fergus, 338; George, 255, 384; George W., 98. 559; James, JP, 343, 597; John, 370; John, JP, 205, 249; Joseph, Capt., 475
McCLENAHAN: Andrew Jr., JP, 184
McCLENIGHEN: John, 370
McCLINTICK: John, JP, 320; William, 320
McCLINTOCK: A., 544; Francis, 378; Huldah, 532; James O., 322; Otis, 532; William, 532
McCLLELAN: Joseph, 370
McCLOUD: Esther, 370; George, 370; John, 370; Lucy, 370; Phebe, 370; Sally, 370; Samuel, 355
McCLUGAN: Samuel, 369
McCLUNEY: W., 348
McCLUNG: Alexander, 371
McCLURE: Andrew, 384; James, 131, 368; John Jr., 384; Mary, 653; R.P., 307, 444; Robert, 255; Tabitha, 370, 653; Timothy R., 440; William, 370, 374, 384, 653; William M., 49
McCLYMONDS: James, 238
McCOFFEY: Susan, 148
McCOLLOCK: Joseph, 373
McCOLLOUGH: Benjamin, Capt., 458
McCOLLUM: Thomas, 227
McCOLLY: Baler, JP, 279
McCOMB: Malcom, JP, 368; Robert, 294; William, 589
McCOMBER: Zenos, 370
McCOMBS: Samuel, 235
McCONAGHY: John, 371
McCONAHEY: Samuel, 399

McCONAUGHY: D., 376; Hugh, 366
McCONLEY: John, 371; Mary, 371
McCONNAUGHEY: Robert, 185
McCONNEL: James, 36
McCONNELL: Alexander, 66, 82, 130, 262, 418, 429, 604; David, 102; Francis, 371; George, Capt., 410; James, 158; John, 334, 371, 400; Levi, 102; Mary [DULIN], 158; Mary [PELLING], 440; Nancy, 371; William, 371
McCOOK: Daniel, 602
McCOOL: William, 327
McCORD: Andrew, 16; Archibald S., JP, 101; Charles O., 589; James S., 262; Margaret [CARNES], 87; Robert, 87; Sarah, 371; William, 371
McCORKLE: Edward, 40; Thomas, 414; William, 110, 343
McCORMIC: James, 371
McCORMICK: Elizabeth M., 372; Grissel, 372; Hannah, 39; Hugh, 39, 51; James, 181; John, 372, 578; N.C., 108, 422; Noble C., JP, 260, 422, 553; Robert, 372; Sarah, 372; William, 372; William T., 553
McCOY: Angus, 372; B., 542; Capt., 34; Catharine, 372; Charles, 372; Charles Jr., 372; Christiana, 373; Daniel, 372–73; Elizabeth, 373; Ephraim, 372; George, JP, 397; Isabella, 413; James, 280, 373; John, 373; John C., 476; Joseph, 372; Kenneth, 373; Margaret [KELLY], 307; Margaret [MURRY], 413; N.A., 550; Nancy, 373; Patrick G., 307; Robert, 25, 413; Ruth Elizabeth, 372; Sarah, 372; Thomas, 484

McCRACKEN: Alexander, 503; John, 373; Lavinia [SHAFFER], 503; Rachel [STRAW], 546; Robert, 546

McCRADY: Robert, 373

McCRARY: William, JP, 463

McCREADY: Daniel, 373; David, 373; Jeremiah, Dr., 229

McCREARY: R., 293; R.G., 447; Robert G., 53; Thomas, JP, 92, 428

McCREERY: Thomas, 316

McCREIGHT: Alexander, 194

McCRERY: John, JP, 113; Joseph, JP, 60

McCRUM: William, 373

McCULLOCH: Abraham, 374; Elizabeth, 373; George, 126; James, 10, 360; Jane M., 373; Joseph, 373; Mathew, 187

McCULLOUGH: Elizabeth, 373; Henry, 211, 588; James, JP, 602; John, JP, 455; Joseph, 27, 373; Thomas, 160; William Jr., 176, 211

McCULLY: Ephraim, Capt., 609; John, JP, 141

McCUNE: Ann Grizella [KELLY], 307; Archibald S., JP, 610; Archibald, JP, 368; J.A.C., 9; James, 497; John, 307

McCURDY: Alexander H., 151; Daniel, JP, 54, 133, 612; Hugh, 239; James, 371, 374; Jane, 374; Joseph, 117; Robert K., 4, 134; Samuel, 540; Samuel R., 374

McCUTCHEN: William, 354

McDADE: James, 374; Mary, 374

McDANIEL: Archibald, 189; John, 184, 366

McDANNELL: John, Capt., 120

McDARMOTT: Daniel, 374

McDERMIT: James, JP, 447

McDERMOT: Daniel, 374; Jane, 659

McDERMOTT: Daniel, 374; Joseph, 374

McDERMUT: James, 374

McDEVITT: Daniel, 375; Margaret, 375

McDIVETT: James, 375

McDONALD: A., JP, 611; A.O., 611; Capt., 450; Catharine, 375; Edward, 375; Francis, 375; Hugh, 276; J.K., JP, 340; James, 375; Joseph, 375; Mary, 375; Oliver, 72; Rebecca [McGEE], 378; Robert, 375; Samuel, 215; Theophilus, 375; William, 378

McDONNALD: Hugh, 647

McDONOUGH: Anthony A., JP, 327; Henry, JP, 262; Hugh, 375

McDOUGALL: A.L., 560; Samuel, JP, 182, 453

McDOUGLE: Alexander, 376; J.B., 608; Samuel, 376

McDOWELL: Catharine, 376; Henrietta [KOLLOCK], 318; James, 11, 67; James Jr., 171; Jane [KOLLOCK], 319; Jane V., 376; John, 106, 319, 376; John 2nd, 376; John P., 67; Margarett, 376; Mary, 376; Nancy [COLEMAN], 106; Robert, 376; Robert S., 505; Samuel, Capt., 233; Thomas, 376; William, 376; William S., 67

McELHANY: William G., 123; William, JP, 123

McELHATTEN: Capt., 29

McELHENEY: William, JP, 388

McELNAY: Agness, 376; Hannah, 376; James, 376; John, 376; Joseph, 376; Margaret, 376; Mary, 376; Rebecca, 376; Samuel, 376

McELREVEY: Hugh, 362

McELREVY: Hugh, 377

McELROY: Capt., 323; Catharine, 377; Elizabeth, 377; Elizabeth A., 377; Hannah, 377; James, 634; John, 377; Mary, 377; Sarah, 377; Thomas H., 377

McENTYRE: Henry, 110

McEWEN: Alexander, 366; F., 394; Henry, 377; John, 4; T.C., 252; Thomas, 217; William, 394

McFADDEN: Catharine [RAMBLE], 459; Henry, 459; John, 377; Thomas, 128

McFADDIN: Samuel, JP, 386

McFADDON: John, 377

McFALL: Thomas 2nd, 377

McFALLS: Henry, 406

McFANE: A.B., 102

McFARLAND: Capt., 393; James, 157; James B., 530; John, 540; William, 135

McFARREN: James, JP, 118

McFERRAN: Joseph, 373; Robert, 373, 617

McGALL: Col., 113

McGATHERY: Isaac, 378

McGAUGHY: Archibald, JP, 152

McGAW: Alexander, 378; Hannah, 378; James, 378; John, 378; Margaret, 378; Sarah, 378; William, 378

McGEE: Alexander, 378; Esther, 378; Henry, 378; James, 378; John, 159, 378; Margaret, 378; Rebecca, 378; Samuel, 378; Thomas, 378; William, 378

McGERRY: Mary, 378; Neal, 378

McGILL: James, 378; Lelitia, 379; Letitia, 379

McGINLY: Ann W., 53

McGINN: M., 449

McGINNESS: Charles, 227; John, 634; Margaret, 227

McGINNIS: William, 8, 379, 623
McGLANEN: Capt., 27
McGLATHERY: Eli P., 378; Isaac, 378–79; Rachel, 378–79
McGLAUGHLIN: Eliza, 331; Hannah, 331; John, 331; Mary, 331; Mary [LIGGIT], 331; Thomas, 331
McGLINN: Anthony, 525
McGONIGLE: Bernard, 308; John, 386
McGOUGH: Peter, JP, 150; Thomas, JP, 335
McGOWAN: Peter, 16; Robert, JP, 362
McGOWN: James, 333
McGRAIL: Sarah Ann [LUKER], 349; Thomas, 349
McGRATH: Laurence, 285
McGREGGOR: James, 379
McGREGOR: James, JP, 4
McGREW: James, 370, 653; Rebecca, 379; Samuel, JP, 477
McGRIGGER: James, 379
McGUIN: John G., JP, 352
McGUINNES: James, 379
McGUIRE: Barney, 379; John G., JP, 417; Mary, 380; Mary [LUKER], 349; Robert, 380; Samuel, 349
McHENRY: Edward, 380; Eli, 542; Mary, 380; *R.*, 117; Thomas, 380
McILHANEY: William, 184, 198
McILHENNEY: William, 198, 407
McILRATH: Alice, 380; Andrew, 380
McILVAIN: Greer, 85; Jane [CAMPBELL], 85
McILVAINE: E., 617
McINTIRE: Andrew, 380; Catharine, 197; Henry M., 380; Hugh, 380; Thomas, 59
McINTOSH: E.S., 137; Esell, 502; John, JP, 595
McINTYRE: Archibald, 180; David, 248

McKAIN: Sarah [SHAW], 504
McKANE: William, 292
McKAY: Neal, 380
McKEAN: Allen, 323; James, 90, 557; John, 126; William W., 518
McKEDNER: V., 561
McKEE: Abigail [GREENE], 223, 644; Andrew, 380; Francis, 381; George, 381; George C., 310; Henry, 381; Hugh, 381, 661; Isaac, 175; J.W., JP, 75, 411; James Gorton, 644; John, 223, 371, 381, 644; Margaret, 381; Mary, 381; Samuel, JP, 541; Sarah, 381; Susanna, 381; Thomas, 380; William, 381
McKEEN: Thomas, 381
McKEEVER: John, 381; Thomas, JP, 386
McKELVEY: James, 565; Thomas, JP, 385
McKELVY: Mary, 382; William, 382
McKENNAN: P., JP, 619; Patrick, 421; Thomas T., 340
McKEOWEN: John, 382
McKERN: Cornelius, 211
McKEWN: A.E., JP, 199
McKEY: John, 435; William, 435
McKIBBEN: Nancy, 148
McKIM: Alexander, 382; James, 382
McKINLEY: C.J., 46; Capt., 470, 474; David, 382; Elizabeth, 382; James, 382; John, 335; Martha, 382; Mary, 382; Rachel, 382; Sarah, 382; Stephen, 382
McKINNEY: Ann, 382; John, 382; M., JP, 181, 278; Mary, 382; Mordecai, JP, 181; Sylvanus, 382; William, JP, 148, 157, 474
McKINSTRY: Jesse, 495
McKINZEY: James, 382

McKINZIE: Helen, 383; John, 383; Margaret, 383
McKISSICK: James, 383
McKOWN: Capt., 108, 122, 495; D., Capt., 271; Daniel, JP, 63, 231; James, JP, 618
McLACHLAN: Colin, 383; Elizabeth, 383
McLAIN: Alexander, 383; Capt., 553; Charles Jr., 383
McLANAHAN: John, 104; Johnston, 43, 115, 517; Jonathan B., 115
McLANE: David, JP, 264; John, 353
McLAUGHLIN: Anthony, JP, 267; Capt., 180; Catharine [HARTCHY], 245; Catharine [KELLER], 305; Dunlop, 223; George, 363; James, 75; Nancy [DAVIS], 135; Randal, 53; W., 339; W.C., 146; William, JP, 407
McLEAN: Capt., 335; Catharine, 384; D.H.A., 214; H., JP, 475; John, 383; Jonathan D., 199; Mary, 383; Mary [GLOVER], 214; Samuel, 383; Sarah, 383; William, 75, 214, 384, 458
McLEES: Hannah, 252
McLELLAND: George, 384
McLEOD: John, 384
McLOUGHLIN: Capt., 31
McLOUTH: Cyrus, JP, 451
McLURE: Andrew, 384; Joseph, Capt., 417; Mary, 384; William, 384
McMACHAN: William, Capt., 65
McMAHAN: Capt., 173; John, 281
McMAHON: Abraham, 340; Thomas, 109
McMAKIN: Andrew, 196
McMANNERS: John, 384; Lucy, 384
McMANUS: Francis, 216
McMASTER: James, 385; Samuel, 385

McMASTERS: Edward, 384; John, 277; Rhoda, 384
McMATH: Daniel, 385
McMEANS: Joseph, JP, 303
McMICHAEL: Fanny [SANDERSON], 491
McMICKEN: Andrew, 373; James, JP, 420
McMILLAN: Ester, 385; John, 385; Nancy, 385; Samuel, 385; Washington, 603; William, 131, 134, 211, 233, 385
McMILLEN: Jonathan, 374, 385, 438; Thomas, 385
McMULLEN: John, 386; Michael, 386
McMULLIN: Michael, 386
McMURDY: John, 386
McMURRAY: Andrew, 214; Robert A., 215, 643; Sarah [GOLDY], 215, 643; William, 386
McNAIR: James, JP, 555; Samuel, JP, 87; Thomas S., 555
McNAMEE: Sarah, 386; William, 386
McNARY: Matthew, JP, 263
McNAY: Samuel, 362
McNEAL: Curtis, 278
McNEEL: Joseph, 374; William, 431
McNEELEY: William, 386
McNEELY: James, 386; Samuel, 386; William, 386
McNEIL: Andrew, JP, 199, 580; Capt., 84; Frank P., 140
McNICOLL: -----, Mrs., 580
McNINCH: Charity [CAMPBELL], 85
McNULTY: C.J., 423
McNUTT: Francis, 50
McPATRICK: Daniel, 386
McPHAIL: John A., 21, 48; Jonathan, 552
McPHERRAN: Andrew, 387; Susan, 387

McPHERRIN: Clark, 387; James, JP, 430
McPHERSON: Abigail E., 387; Archibald, 387; James, 409; John, 387; John B., 387; William, 387
McQUAID: Margaret [DAVIS], 135
McQUAIDE: Thomas, 133
McQUINN: John, 387
McQUISTOR: William, 291
McQUISTOW: Elizabeth [SINGLEY], 514; Samuel, 514
McREA: John, 588
McREVEY: Hugh, 377
McREVY: Hugh, 377
McREYNOLDS: Emily B. [WHEELER], 595; R., JP, 253
McSHARRY: Michael, 546, 599
McVAUGH: Jacob, 387; John, 387; Mabary W., 387; Mary, 387
McVAY: James F., 4; James T., 549
McWAUGH: Col., 179
McWHIRTER: John, 375; William, 411
McWILLIAMS: Jonathan, JP, 191
MEACHAM: Hosa M. [EDWARDS], 165
MEACHUM: Shelden, 598
MEAD: Col., 416; Israel, 388; John, Col., 607; Peter, 111
MEALMONT: A., 368
MEALS: Catherine [VARNUM], 575, 661
MEANS: Daniel, 388; Edward, 388; George, 388; Hannah, 388; Henry, 388; Hugh, 388; John R., JP, 125; Nancy, 388; Philip, 388; Robert, 388; Rosanna, 388; Thomas, 388; William, 368
MEARS: William, 480
MECK: Magdalina [HARTMAN], 246
MECKLING: George, 11, 645

MEDARY: David, 54, 59–60, 170, 356, 462
MEDBURY: Almira, 600; Asahel, JP, 600
MEDLAR: Morgan F., 24, 26
MEDLER: George, JP, 43, 103
MEED: Capt., 41
MEEDS: Cato, 388
MEEK: M.S., 363; Samuel, 254
MEEKER: Betsey, 388; Carey, 389; Catharine, 388; George, 388; J.D., JP, 308; Jonathan D., JP, 203; Lucy, 388; Robert, 388–89; Robert Sr., 389
MEESE: Baltzer, 509
MEGGS: Mary, 389; Richard, 389
MEGOGNEY: Catharine, 311
MEIGGS: Richard, 389
MEIGS: Col., 94; Return Jonathan, Col., 16, 94
MEIXSELL: C., JP, 541
MELICK: John, 177, 389; Mary, 389; Nancy [FALKNER], 177
MELLINGER: Capt., 274
MELLON: T.H., 141
MELLOTT: John, 266, 400; Obadiah, 266; Psyche [HOLLENSHEAD], 266
MELROY: Bartholomew, 389; Keziah, 389
MENDENHALL: James, 389; Joseph, Capt., 389
MENGEL: Matthias, 2, 163; Matthias, JP, 13, 213, 547
MENGLE: Matthias, JP, 393
MENING: Jacob, JP, 523
MENIUM: Barbara [FLAUGH], 186; Johannes, 186; John, 186
MENNIG: Jacob, JP, 523, 538, 624
MENOLD: Andrew, 338; Susannah [LINDY], 338
MENSCH: Adam, JP, 225
MERCER: Hall W., 367
MERCUR: H.S., 452

MEREDITH: Thomas, 70, 389

MEREUR: M.C., 346

MERGERGEE: Jonathan, 541

MERRIAM: Marshall, 389; Marshall L., 390; Sylvester, 390

MERRIAN: Marshall, 389

MERRIFIELD: Lemuel, 9

MERRILL: Almond, JP, 163; Jesse, 390; M.E., Capt., 99; Polly [ROOT], 481

MERRIT: Gilbert H., 598

MERRITT: Anna, 390; Thomas, 390

MERSCH: John, JP, 405

MERSEREAU: Fanny, 390; Henry D., 390; John L., 390; Joshua B., 390

MERSHEIMER: Henry, 34; Sebastian, 34

MERSHIMER: Adam, 360; Anna C., 360; Catharine, 360; Frances, 360; Henry, 360; Peter, 360; Peter Jr., 360; Sebastian, 360

MERSHON: D., 290

MERVIN: William N., JP, 86

MESSENGER: Bille, 390; Ebenezer, 208; Hiram, 390, 544

MESSENKOP: Charlotte [BAUSMAN], 33; George, 68; John A., 33

MESSER: James, Capt., 540

MESSERSMITH: Capt., 23; Henry, JP, 136

METCALF: Charles H., 399; Dan, 398–99; E., JP, 125; Freelove, 399; Ira, JP, 441; Isaac H., 399; Jonathan C., 399; Lucily, 398–99; Mehitable, 399; Orlando, 100, 107, 114, 167, 194, 256, 330, 357, 364, 482, 577, 597, 611

METTER: Elizabeth [CAMPBELL], 85

METZ: Jacob, 31; John, 379, 390

MEYER: H.M., 400; Jacob, 390

MEYERS: Henry, 589, 621

MICHAEL: William, JP, 149

MICHENER: James G., 322

MICK: Johannes, 391; Philip, 390–91

MICKLE: Elizabeth, 391; Reuben, 391

MIDDAUGH: Asher, 391; Hannah Ann [DECKER], 138; Henry C.T., 391; Isaac, 138; John, 391; Joseph, 391; Lenah, 195; Sarah, 391

MIDDOUGH: *Henry T.C.*, 391; John, 391

MIEKE: Lewis, JP, 488

MIFFLIN: Jonathan, 391; Samuel W., 391

MILBURN: Andrew, 391

MILEHAM: William, 392

MILEPAM: William, 392

MILES: A., 479; Caleb, 392; Col., 224, 343; Evan, 457; G.M., 392; James, 392; Joseph, JP, 442; William, 392

MILEY: Barbara, 392; Charles, 392; Jacob, 392; John, 392; Margaret, 392; Samuel, 392; Sarah, 392; William, 392

MILL: George, JP, 587

MILLER: A.J., 527; Aaron, 69; Abraham, 164, 208; Abraham, Capt., 56; Abram, 208; Adam, 360; Alexander, 351, 394; Alexander M., JP, 122; Ann, 585; Ann Elizabeth, 392; Arnold, 392; Barbara [SINGLEY], 514; Benjamin J., 457; Benjamin, JP, 372; Burton, 212; Capt., 76, 198, 247, 419; Catherine, 394–95, 654; Charles, 394; Charles P., 154; Christian, 392, 395; Christian 2nd, 392; Christian Jr., 396; Christiana, 654; Col., 556; Conrad, 393; Daniel, 248; David, 71, 331, 393, 532; David W., 385;

Desiree, 52; Effy, 654; Eliza, 394; Elizabeth, 395–96; Elizabeth [HARTMAN], 246; Elsey, 396; Eve, 395; F.B., 393; Frank B., 316, 483; Frederick, 393; George, 321, 393, 511; George H., 397; George P., 295; Godfried, 394–95; Henry, 394–95, 530; Hugh, 163; J.F., 484; J.W., 450; Jacob, 313, 394, 587; Jacob 2nd, 394; Jacob F., JP, 309; Jacob H., 584; James, 22, 171; James H., 395, 397; James L., JP, 279; James W., 135; Jane, 394; Jemima, 396; Jeremiah, 235, 394; Johannes, 395; John 2nd, 394; John 3rd, 394, 654; John F., 392; John H., JP, 155; John M., 209; Jonas, 392; Jonathan, 299, 353, 363, 392, 394, 396, 426, 431, 446, 469, 514, 616, 618, 654; Joseph, 395; Joseph P., 396; Joseph William, 534; Josiah T., JP, 126; Julia Ann, 393; Lewis, 392–93; Linus H., JP, 177; Ludwick, 395; Mahlon, 557; Margaret, 392, 395, 397; Margaret [MITCHELL], 398; Maria, 395, 397; Martin, 395; Mary, 392, 395; Mary [BURDUE], 76; Mary [MORRISON], 406; Mary Magdalen, 392; Matilda, 396; Matthew T., 606; Moses, JP, 41, 314; N., JP, 40; Nancy, 394–95, 397, 654; Nancy [ANDERSON], 9; Nicholas, 396; Peggy, 394, 654; Peter, 395–96; Philip, 273, 396; Rachel [LINE], 338; Reuben, 510; Reuben Jr., 258; Richard, 396; Richard Jr., 396; Ruby [ROGERS], 480; S.C., 237; Samuel, 149, 184, 255, 396, 429;

(MILLER, continued)

Samuel H., JP, 607; Samuel
W., JP, 160; Sarah,
394–95; Sarah
[COTSMOYER], 117;
Stephen, 396; Susan, 395;
T.C., 176, 395, 397; T.R.,
JP, 127, 145, 299;
Thomas C., 395, 397;
Thomas R., JP, 237;
Thomas, JP, 76; W.H.,
594; William, 177, 395,
397; William L., 194, 437
MILLIGAN: David, 397;
John, 455; Mary, 397; S.,
JP, 31
MILLIKAN: Samuel, 56
MILLIKEN: David, 10, 32;
James, 386
MILLIRON: Jacob, 258;
Margaret [HICE], 258;
Peter, 258
MILLS: B.H., 398; Capt.,
479; Constantine,
397–98; Daniel, Capt.,
181; E.A., 397; Eben A.,
398; Elias, 397;
Elizabeth, 398; James,
306, 311, 601; John,
Capt., 8; Josiah, 398;
N.S., 398; Philiota, 398;
William, 191, 398
MILLYARD: Benjamin,
174; Betsey
[EATINGER], 174;
Joseph, 174; Rachel
[EATINGER], 174
MILNE: Ann [BARNES],
27
MILNOR: Mahlon, 255
MILTON: James, 199;
Sarah [FRY], 199
MILWORTH: Samuel, 552
MINARD: Orlando, 67
MINER: Abye, 398;
Elnathan, 398; Jane, 398;
John, 275, 398; O.T., 9;
Rhoda, 398; William, 398
MINES: Joel, 78
MINGUS: Benjamin, 76;
Hieronimus, 398; Jacob,
76; Rebecca, 398;
Rebecca [BURDUE], 76
MINIER: Anne
[CAMPBELL], 85

MINNIGH: *Dani(el*, JP, 55;
Eveline L., 55; Henry T.,
447
MINNISS: James D., JP, 70
MINOR: Abia, JP, 571;
John, JP, 187
MINT: Col., 551
MINTER: Mary G.
[LEAS], 329
MIOCK: Asa D., 22
MIRICK: Ephraim Jr., 558
MISH: Charles C., 582;
John W., 269
MISK: Catherine
[BICKEL], 45; Jacob, 45
MISSEMER: Capt., 528
MISSIMER: John S., JP,
193
MITCALF: Dan, 398;
Jedidah, 398
MITCHELL: Adam, 414;
Ann, 586; Capt., 82;
Catharine, 399, 414; G.,
JP, 66; H.W., 289; Henry,
170; Horace B., 230;
Isabella, 398; J.B., 339,
396; James, 399; John,
399, 471; John A., 414;
Joseph B., 1, 22, 65, 144,
226, 398, 440, 497, 507,
526, 561, 564, 621;
Joshua, JP, 398; Margaret
[MITCHELL], 399;
Mary, 399; Nathaniel,
109, 290, 399; Polly
[WARNER], 583;
Randolph, JP, 434;
William, 639; William B.,
71
MITMAN: Barbara, 399;
Charles, 399; Daniel, 399;
Magdalena, 399; Samuel,
399; Susanna, 399
MITSCO: Conrad, 400
MITTMAN: Barbara, 399;
Charles, 399
MITZCO: Conrad, 400
MIX: Amos, 400; George
A., 82, 258, 317; Hiram,
160; Josiah, 400; Kezia,
400
MIXSELL: Philip, 436
MOAST: Elizabeth, 400;
John, 400
MOELLER: William F.,
JP, 403

MOFFAT: Alexander, 400;
John, 400
MOFFATT: John, 38
MOFFET: Robert, 350;
Thomas, 640
MOFFITT: Lemuel, 193,
300, 325–26, 384, 421,
433, 538, 554
MOHR: Daniel, 471
MOLOTT: John, 400
MONAGHAN: James, JP,
123, 368; W., 383
MONDAY: Thomas, 410
MONOGHAN: James, JP,
190
MONROE: *Loly,* 242
MONSON: Theophilus,
Capt., 428
MONTELIUS: Peter, JP,
321; William, 200, 380,
430, 463, 490, 496
MONTGOMERY:
Amanda, 236; Col., 417;
David, JP, 94; J., JP, 236;
James, 211, 392, 565;
John, 400; Robert, 90,
250, 271, 383; Samuel,
251; *Sarepta* [BROWN],
71; William, 11, 184, 245,
251, 423, 473, 530, 568
MONTIETH: James, Capt.,
421
MONTON: Leverett, JP, 18
MONTONYE: Nathan, 427
MOODY: Catharine, 400;
Joseph, JP, 493;
Nathaniel P., 400;
William, 376
MOOK: Orange, JP, 301
MOON: Col., 361, 425;
Elizabeth, 401; James,
401; John, JP, 309
MOONAN: Mary, 412
MOONEY: Artis, 401;
Cornelius, 301; Dennis,
401; Elizabeth [SCHIEB],
493; John, 535
MOOR: Chambers, 375
MOORE: A., Capt., 620;
Alexander, 401; Andrew
Y., 150, 616; Andrew,
Capt., 401; Anna, 226;
Capt., 224, 381, 477;
David H., JP, 125;
Deborah, 402; Eli, 403;
Elisha, JP, 579;

(MOORE, continued)

Elizabeth, 226, 402–3;
Ezekiel, 45; George, 445;
Hannah, 401; Hannah
[CUMMINGS], 127;
Hannah [SUTTON], 550;
Hannaniah, 550; Henry,
287; Isabella, 401; J.
Irwin, 619; James, 88,
401–2, 481; Jane, 402;
Jesse, 284, 401; John, 82,
257, 268, 402, 564; John
3rd, 402; John Jr., 550;
John R., 226; Johnston,
462, 501; Lewis, 404;
Mary, 401–2; Mary
[PATTERSON], 435–36;
Matthew, 249; Nancy,
401–2; Nathaniel, JP, 89;
P.A., 44; Patrick, 44, 338;
Phineas, 402; Polly, 402;
Robinson R., 39, 94, 129,
177, 207, 275, 378, 451;
Rosannah, 646; Samuel,
401–2; Seth B., 198;
T.A., 101; Thomas, 401,
403; William, 226, 312,
401–3, 646; William Jr.,
403
MOORHEAD: James, 150,
279, 556; Joseph, JP, 366;
Samuel Jr., 236; Samuel,
JP, 236
MOOSE: Capt., 89;
William E., Rev., 380
MORAN: Peter, 403; Susan,
403
MORDOCK: Capt., 32
MORE: P.A., 24, 146, 241,
417, 558; Peter A., 594
MORELAND: Moses, 403
MORELEDGE: Hannah
[WESTFALL], 594; John,
594
MORELY: Ezekiel, 403
MOREY: Charles, 403;
Elizabeth, 404; Lewis,
404
MORFORD: John, 404
MORGAN: Abel, 404;
Anna, 404; Asahel, 404;
Benjamin R., 567; Capt.,
68; Catharine, 405;
Chapman, 86; Col., 275;
Daniel, 404; David T., 10,

189, 302, 457, 602; E.W.,
535; Edwin W., 75, 224,
286, 423; Elizabeth,
404–5; Enoch, 404–5;
Harry, 46, 91, 106, 160,
224, 613; Isaac, JP, 330,
369; James, 86, 352, 405;
Jane, 330; Jesse, 404;
John, JP, 69, 90, 302,
619; Rebecca, 405;
Samuel, 405; Susannah,
405; Thomas B., 405;
William C., 225
MORGERT: Peter, 405
MORHARD: Capt., 358
MORISON: William T., JP,
35
MORLEY: Ezekiel, 403;
Isaac, 405; John, 405;
Thomas, 405
MORNINGSTAR: Mary
[GELWICKS], 208
MORRIS: Andrew, JP, 177;
Ann, 406; Anna, 512;
Anthony, 149; Anthony
H., 44–45, 188, 277, 319,
480, 499; Christiana
[IDLE], 281; David, 212;
Dennis, 247; George,
298; Hannah, 406;
Isabella, 406; James, 406;
Jonathan, 6, 128, 183,
272, 357, 406, 440, 465;
Joseph, JP, 36; Levi, 199;
R.W., 202; Samuel W.,
99, 512; Thomas, JP, 63;
Warder, 138, 149, 257,
510, 520; William, 406;
William Jr., 406
MORRISON: Alexander,
406; Andrew, 487; Capt.,
335, 337; Catharine A.,
406; Daniel, JP, 87, 113;
James, 406–7; James R.,
391; John, 168, 407, 580;
John R., 406; Joseph S.,
240; Julia Ann
[MARTIN], 362; Mary,
406; Noah, 611; Riley,
334; Robert E., 498;
Sarah, 407; Thomas, 407,
442; William, 85, 363
MORROW: J.H., 42;
James, 73–74, 152, 516;
John, 149; John, Col., 6;

R., 86, 153, 230; Richard,
231, 355
MORSE: Ansel, 407; Asa,
365; Elias, 407; Elijah,
407; Joel, 2; Joseph, JP,
223; Mary, 407; Olive,
569; Sarah, 407; Seth,
407; Solomon, 272;
Stephen, 407
MORT: William, 509
MORTON: A., 497; James,
477; Joseph, JP, 477;
William, JP, 412, 541
MOSELEY: Col., 569
MOSER: George, 407;
Henry, 408; John, 408;
Solomon, 408
MOSGROVE: Alexander,
377
MOSHER: Isabella, 408;
Jeremiah, 408; Joseph,
343, 408, 525; Susannah,
408
MOSHIER: Jeremiah, 407
MOSS: Sally [JAY], 207;
Solomon, 408, 655;
Solomon, Jr., 408, 655
MOSSER: George, 407;
Henry, JP, 616
MOSSES: Philip B., JP, 156
MOTT: Capt., 586; Edward
Jr., 598; H., 335; H.L.,
457; H.S., 358, 551;
Isaac, 408; Samuel 1st,
408; Samuel C., 539
MOULANZE: E.D., 23
MOURER: Nicholas, JP,
578
MOWER: Jonathan, 156
MOWLAN: Amos, 408;
Charles, 408; Mary, 408;
Rachel, 408; Rachel Ann,
408; Richard, 408; Sarah,
408; William, 408
MOYER: Catharine, 409;
David, 625; Elizabeth,
409; Frederick, 409;
George, 414; Henry
George, 409; Jacob, 409;
John, 409; Mary, 409;
Mathias, 409; Nancy,
409; Nicholas, 409; Peter,
409
MOYERS: Jonathan, 196,
409

MUCHMORE: Alexander, 532
MUCKEL: Ludwig, 536
MUEHLER: William, 476
MULETT: George, 355; Roxana [MAKEPEACE], 355
MULFORD: James M., 88; John, 127, 620; John Jr., 575; Julia Ann [WALTERS], 581
MULHOLLAND: George, 83
MULL: Aaron, 281
MULLEN: John P., 69; John, JP, 280; Michael, 410; William, 410
MULLER: Peter, 395
MULLIN: Robert G., 292; W.D., 292
MULLISAN: John, 30
MULLISON: Elizabeth [PARRISH], 434; William, 434
MULLONER: Margaret [BEECHER], 630
MUMFORD: J.L., 617; James, JP, 490, 529; William, 599
MUMMEY: Christopher, 410; John, 410
MUMMY: Christopher, 410
MUNDAY: Thomas, 410
MUNDELL: Abner, 410
MUNDLE: George, 410
MUNFORD: John, 169
MUNGER: Anna [WOODCOCK], 615
MUNN: Joseph P., 613; Samuel, 297
MUNROE: Newton E., 132
MUNSON: Almond, 410; Betsy A., 23; Calvin, 603; Isaac, 411, 463; Mary Ann [BALLARD], 23
MUNSS: A., 62, 67, 307
MUNTZ: Henry, 261
MURCK: Joseph, 2
MURDOCK: Capt., 529; Matthew, 377; Robert, 411
MURPHEY: Aaron, 399; Lindley, 69
MURPHY: Daniel, 464; Elizabeth, 411; James, 174; Jeremiah, 411;

John, 252, 411; Nancy, 411; Owen, 411; Ruth, 411; Samuel, 411; Sarah [EATINGER], 174; Sarah [REED], 463; William, 372, 411; Wright, JP, 215
MURRAY: James, 173, 412, 465, 498; James B., 3, 31, 106, 130, 202, 215, 247, 432, 498, 614; James F., JP, 608; Jeremiah, 412; John, 51, 412, 474; Mary, 412; Matthew, 412; Michael J., 412; Samuel, 13; Sarah [EATINGER], 173; Seth, Capt., 12; Thomas, 412; William, 412, 558
MURRELL: William, 412
MURREY: Anthony, 413; Elizabeth, 413; William A., 413
MURRY: Ann, 413; Elizabeth, 413; Hester, 413; Isabella, 413; Jacob, 413; James J., 413; James P., 413; James, Col., 260, 413; Jane, 413; John, 413; Margaret, 413; William, 413
MUSCH: Charles, 521; John, JP, 141, 521, 535, 547
MUSE: Catharine, 413; Fauntley, 413; John, 413; John J., 413; Joseph, 413; Margaret, 413; Sally, 413
MUSER: Paul, 413
MUSGRAVE: Isaac W., JP, 175; William, 43, 81, 113, 122, 130–31, 149, 232, 278, 377, 396, 429, 463, 533, 541, 545, 590
MUSHLER: Adam, 414; Catharine, 414; John A., 414
MUSKETMUSS: Adam, 414; Catharine, 414
MUSSELMAN: John, JP, 590; Samuel, 621
MUSSER: Capt., 380; George, 185; John, 68; Samuel, 417
MUZZEY: Robert, 414
MUZZY: Nathan, 414; Robert, 414

MYER: Alvin T., JP, 333; E.R., JP, 599; John P., 408
MYERS: Abraham, 533; Barbara, 415; Barbara [MILEY], 392; Catharine, 415; Catherine [SPONG], 531; Charles W., 414; Conrad, 414; Elizabeth, 415; Frederic, 392; Henry, 415; Jacob, 7; Jesper, 529; John, 144, 151, 218, 225, 415, 573, 605, 607, 609; John C., 415; John L., 415; Joseph, 529; Kezia, 415; Margaret, 415; Mary, 415; Peter, 415; Philip, 415; Philomena, 415; Sarah, 415; Susannah, 415; William, 58
MYRICK: Joseph, 415

NAGEL: Georg, 416; Philip, 415
NAGINEY: Sarah [HAHN], 233
NAGLE: George, 99, 210, 252, 265, 271, 347, 428, 454, 589, 593, 623; Honor, 416; Jacob, 416; John, 416, 566; Margaret, 416; Mary, 416; Mary [WILLIAMS], 604; Peter, 263, 304, 320, 416; Peter Jr., JP, 193; Philip, 416; Richard, 416; Rudolph C., 604; Sarah, 416
NAILER: William, JP, 589
NAILOR: Capt., 478; William, 141, 161
NASBY: Mary, 104
NASH: John, 312; Mary [KOLLOCK], 318
NATHANS: Judith [RUSSELL], 488; Rebecca [RUSSELL], 488
NAVE: Benjamin, 162; Henrietta, 162
NEAD: Matthias, JP, 343
NEAGY: John, 35
NEAL: Caldwell, 10; Maria [ANDERSON], 10; William, 416

NEALE: William, 416
NEAVEL: John, 17
NEEDHAM: Hannah G., 570
NEEL: Anne [WILLIS], 606; Henry, JP, 307, 366, 486, 606; Samuel, 349
NEELY: John, 16
NEFF: Isaac, 651; Margaret [RUGAN], 485; Robert K., 459
NEGGEL: Michael, 318
NEGUS: J. Engle, 536
NEICOMER: David, 159
NEIDER: Abraham, 417; Henry, 417
NEIL: Margaret [DEUTZLER], 142; William, 142
NEILL: James, 417
NEILSON: Capt., 542; Joseph, 417
NELL: Jacob, 417
NELLIS: William, 417
NELSON: Capt., 91; David, 470; Elizabeth [FALKNER], 177; James, 109; John, Capt., 163, 253; Josiah, 587; Major, 391; Robert J., 177; Samuel, Capt., 35; William, 417
NENDAY: Nicholas, 261
NEPHEW: Matthias, 417
NES: Henry, 611
NESBET: John, 167
NESBIT: John, JP, 54, 300
NESMITH: Thomas J., JP, 446; Thomas, JP, 335; W.D., 335
NESSLE: Conrad, 418; Laomi, 418
NETTERFIELD: Wiliam, 418
NEUSCHWENDER: Barbara [BEECHER], 630; Michael, 630
NEVEL: Henry, 418
NEVINS: James L., JP, 246
NEW: Adam, 418; Christopher, 418; Elizabeth, 418
NEWBURY: James, 418; Sarah, 418
NEWCOM: Samuel, 418; Samuel Jr., 418

NEWCOMB: Benjamin C., 354; Betsey [KALLAM], 301; Eliphal, 418; Simon, 418
NEWCOME: Samuel, 418
NEWCOMER: John, 310; Joseph, 532
NEWEL: Capt., 196; Samuel, 364
NEWELL: Agnes, 419; Alexander, 419; Barnard, 367; Elizabeth, 419; George, 419; James, 419; John, 419; Mary, 419; Nicholas, 419; Susannah, 419; Thomas, 88; William, 40, 419
NEWHALL: Joseph H., 42
NEWHARD: Edmund R., 308
NEWHAUS: Richard, JP, 157
NEWHOUSE: Anthony, 419; Anton, 419
NEWILL: William, 419
NEWINGHAM: David, JP, 430
NEWKIRK: Garret, 383; John J., 45; Matthew, 291, 321
NEWKOMER: David, 159
NEWLAND: Matthias, 419
NEWLEN: James W., 491
NEWLIN: James W., 272
NEWMAN: Capt., 53; Ezekiel, 466; Henry, 420; Jacob, 420; Jonathan, 419–20; Mich, 21; Philip, 420
NEWNAN: G., 14
NEWORK: Ezra, Capt., 451
NEWPORT: R.C., 497
NEWTON: Eben, 577; Hananiah, 420; John, JP, 311; Mary [BABCOCK], 18; N. Jr., 158
NEY: Adam, 147; Susanna [DETRICH], 147
NICE: William, Capt., 263
NICHERSON: Isacher, 420
NICHOL: Robert, 44
NICHOLAS: Capt., 541; George, 420; James, JP, 419; William, 586
NICHOLLS: James, 420

NICHOLS: Col., 130; Elibe, 420; Enos A., 129; James H., 420; Johanna, 421; Jonathan, 420; Robert, 421; Sarah [MORSE], 407; Susannah, 421; William, 323, 421; William C., 168
NICHOLSON: A.S., JP, 370; John, 421
NICKEL: M.R., 421; William, 421
NICKERSON: Hezekiah, 420; Isacher, 420
NICOLA: Margret [JENNINGS], 291; Mary [JENNINGS], 291
NIGH: Jeremiah, 424
NIGHTWINE: Elizabeth [CLANBAUGH], 97
NILES: David, 421; Erastus, 224
NIMMON: John S., JP, 209
NIMOCKS: F.B., 320
NIPPLE: Frederick, 421
NISBET: Alexander, 421; E.C., 206; Hugh, 204
NISBITT: James Jr., 582; James, JP, 215
NISWANGER: John, JP, 542
NIVER: Casper, 211
NIXON: Col., 357, 588; H., 432; James, 466, 619; Robert, 380, 410, 418; Robert Jr., 496; William, 401
NOBLE: Christopher, Capt., 559; Curtis, 211; Louisa [ROWLEY], 484; Margaret, 168; Silas, 615; Woolsey, 168
NOBLES: Azor, 421
NOEL: Jacob, 502
NOLEN: John, 424; Sarah E., 424
NOLEY: Susan [BAUGH], 32
NOLF: Barbara, 422; Catherine, 422; Conrad, 422; Elizabeth, 422; George, Capt., 422; Isaac, 422; Jacob, 422; Rachel, 422; Sarah, 422; Susan, 422; Susannah, 422
NORBURY: Heath, JP, 218

NORMAN: Eliza, 422; Eliza Jane, 422; Hannah, 422; Henry, 422; Joseph, 422

NORRIS: Benjamin F., 330; Elizabeth, 422; James, 226, 258, 558; John, 422, 512; Mary, 422; Rebecca, 422; Sarah, 422; Thomas, 422

NORTH: Caleb, 423; Caleb, Capt., 37; Capt., 66, 398

NORTHROP: Amos, 423; David, 423; Gideon, 423; Isaac, 423; Thankfull, 423

NORTHRUP: Capt., 122; Henry, 264

NORTHUP: David, 423

NORTON: A.C., 531; A.P., 182, 205, 336, 373; A.T., 531; F.I., 317; George, 530; Harriet [TILDEN], 562; James, 423; Jane, 423; Jared, 423; Lebbeus, JP, 402; Leroi, 240; Leverett, JP, 345, 365; Morris, 593; P.J., 317; Philander, 402; Rowland, 603; Sarah, 423; William, 423; William S., JP, 353

NORWOOD: Leander L., JP, 44

NOSSITER: Isabella, 110

NOTT: Jane, 424; Jonah C., 39; Thomas, 424

NOWLAN: John, 424

NURSS: Caleb, 424

NUSSER: Ely, Capt., 474

NUTTING: Capt., 433

NUTTLE: Robert E., 439

NUZUM: Thomas, 198

NYCE: George W., 481; William, 293

NYE: Amanda [GRISWOLD], 228; Andrew, 424; Hester, 424; Marvin, 228

O'BRIAN: Daniel, 424; Joseph, 424; Martha, 424

O'BRIEN: Andrew, 424; John, 424; Sarah, 424; William, 424

O'BRINE: Daniel, 424

O'CONNOR: Martin, 580

O'DOMER: Murty, 425

O'DONNELL: James, 425

O'DONNER: Murty, 425

O'NEAL: John, 426; Sarah, 426

O'NEIL: Henry, 426; Ruth, 427; Walter, 427

OAKLEY: Polly [JACKSON], 286; Samuel, 286

OAKS: John, 578

OBLINGER: Elizabeth [LYN], 351

OGDEN: Aaron, Capt., 358; Col., 218; John M., 304

OGG: David, 615; Jane, 615

OGILVIE: Samuel G., JP, 285

OGLE: Charles, 347; James, Capt., 268

OHL: Capt., 394; John, 425

OHLE: Henry, Lt., 425

OHLY: Henry, JP, 252

OHMET: John, 425

OKERSON: Nicholas, 425

OKESON: John, 425; Margaret, 425; Mary, 425; Nicholas, 425; Samuel, 425; Sarah, 425; William, 425

OKEY: Arthur, 119; Henry, 119

OLDEN: David, 425; Thomas, 425

OLDFIELD: William, 426

OLDHAM: Ann, 426; Isaac, 426; Richard, 426

OLDS: Capt., 43; James, Capt., 604

OLEMHOLTS: Elisabeth [IRELAND], 283

OLIN: D., 430; David, 334

OLIPHANT: Andrew, 426; James M., 445; Jonathan, Capt., 504; S. Duncan, 179

OLIVER: Anna [KRIDER], 320; E.C., JP, 241; George L., 447; J.B., JP, 349; James B., JP, 80, 436; Polly Gracy, 426; Stephen, 426; Thomas, JP, 588

OLLER: Jonathan, 6; Samuel, 6

OLMSTEAD: Edward, 539

OLMSTED: Henry, 208, 591; Waller, JP, 354

OLNEY: Nancy [GREENE], 223, 644; Richard M., 539; Stephen, 223

OLP: Daniel, 121

ONEAR: Angus, 426

ONWER: J.I., 127

OPP: Capt., 176

ORAM: Abigail, 427; Cooper, 427

ORGAN: Matthew, 427

ORMSLEY: Dyer, JP, 452

ORN: James, 112

ORNE: H., 86, 194, 251, 522; Herman, 49, 103, 191, 286, 458, 487; N., 16; William, 83

ORNER: Martin, 427

ORR: Alexander, 76, 579; Chambers, 184, 427; Joseph, 238, 427; Rachel, 427; Robert, 427; Robert Sr., 427; Sally [BOWMAN], 59; Samuel C., 70, 562; William H., 166

ORTON: Darius, 427; Dennis, JP, 209; J.B., 531

ORVIS: Jesse, 481

ORWIG: Henry, 428

OSBORN: George, 241; Gilbert, 270; James, 428; Josiah, 428; Lois [HORTON/HOUGHTON], 270; Louisa [HORTON/HOUGHTON], 270; Richard, JP, 116; S.S., 214; Sterling, 270

OSBORNE: Margaret, 428; Samuel, 428

OSBOURN: Joshua, 428

OSGOOD: Jeremiah, 428; Levi, 127

OSLER: Daniel, 250

OSMAN: William, 428

OSMUN: William, 428; Zilke, 428

OSTERHOUT: Peter M., 241; Thomas, 558

OSTERLOH: A.F., 208, 348; Albert F., JP, 68; Catharine, 348

OSWALD: B., JP, 246–47; John, Dr., 603; Susan [MILLER], 395
OTIS: William A., 312; William L., 312
OTT: John R., 369
OTTERSON: Hugh, 428
OTTO: Catherine, 429; Catherine H., 429; Daniel H., 429; Elizabeth O., 429; John, 429; John B., 429; Margareth, 429; Mary, 429; Sarah, 429
OURHAND: Catharine, 429; Dedrick, 429
OURY: Adam, 429
OVERDEER: Eli, 450
OVERLY: Christopher, 271
OVERMYER: Samuel, JP, 577
OVET: Peter, 81
OVIATT: Samuel, JP, 5
OVITT: Jacob, 329
OWEN: Griffith, 334; John, JP, 424; Samuel, 154; Thomas, 36
OWENS: Catharine, 429; G.P., 555; John, JP, 30, 386, 538, 545, 619; Mary Ann, 72; Robert, 429; Vincent, 429
OWERY: George, 430
OWREY: Adam, 430; Francis, 430; George, 429; Henry, 430; Mary, 430
OWRY: Adam, 430; Mary, 430
OX: Peter, 430
OXREIDER: Jacob, 392
OYSTER: Daniel, Capt., 588; George, JP, 339

PACE: Michael 3rd, 430; Michael Jr., 430
PACKARD: William, JP, 223
PACKER: Charles B., 430; Lucy T., 430
PACKHURST: Margaret [BALLARD], 23
PADDACK: Horace B., 32
PAGE: John, 310; Mary [KEELER], 305; Samuel, 295; William, JP, 18

PAIGE: Edmund, 280
PAIN: Rufus S., 611
PAINE: Charles C., 308; Clement, 18, 481; Edward, Capt., 430; Eleares, 203; Henry, JP, 265; Ira, 355; Ira C., 238, 358; Lovina, 430; Lydia [MAKEPEACE], 355; Thomas E., 272; William B., 46
PAINTER: Catherine, 430; Jacob, 11, 238, 371, 430; John, Lt., 430; Thomas, JP, 425
PAISLEY: John, 11, 254, 407
PALM: Eve [DUEY], 143; Michael, 143
PALMER: Daniel, 411, 430; James, 431; Jane [STEEL], 537; John, JP, 444; Joseph, 431; Mary, 431; Richard, JP, 489; Robert M., 386; Rundle, JP, 238; Strange N., JP, 386; Thaddeus, JP, 55; W., 418; Waterman, 212, 340; William, 119
PALMETER: Joshua, 431
PALMITEER: Mary Catharine, 431; William, 431
PALMITER: Eli, 431; Enos, 431; John, 431; Joshua, 431
PALSGROVE: Henry, 452
PALTZGRAEFF: John, 363
PANCOAST: David, Capt., 103
PANCOST: Capt., 110
PANGBORN: Elijah, 445
PARCEL: Stephen, 441
PARCHMENT: Mary, 431; Peter, 431
PARDEE: Allen, JP, 458; Elizabeth, 431; George K., 474; Hannah, 431; John, JP, 474; Mary, 431–32; Susanna, 431; Thomas, 431–32
PARISH: Cyprian, 432
PARK: Alexander, 207; Amaziah, 432; Berry B., 432; David E., 608;

James, 34, 45, 230, 309, 594; John Jr., 207; Joseph, 207; Lorana [GREGORY], 224; Sabre, 432; Theophilus, Capt., 524; W., 215
PARKE: Benjamin, 205; John, 267; Jonathan G., 246; Joseph, 376, 452; Joseph G., 7, 130, 178, 219, 224, 343, 419, 508, 511, 549, 561, 577
PARKENSON: Daniel Sr., 432
PARKER: Alice [JOB], 292; Andres, 432; Capt., 28, 502; D., Capt., 412; Daniel, JP, 613; Ed. A., 122, 167, 498; Elizabeth [GROVER], 228; Eunice, 433; Isaac Brown, 181; Israel, JP, 113; J., 382; Jacob, 313, 455; James, 94, 238; James W., 80; Jane, 432; John S., 432; Joseph G., 37, 385; Joseph, Capt., 432; Leonel E., JP, 230; Lovel E., JP, 292; *Lucy L.*, 116; Mary, 432; Nathan, 433; Robert, 432–33; Rufus H., 230; Samuel, 433; Stephen, 292; Thomas, 294, 544; Timothy F., Dr., 207; William, 94; Zenus, 177
PARKHILL: James, 433; John, 433
PARKHURST: Eben F., 433; Joel, 566; John, 433; Laetitia, 433
PARKISON: Daniel Sr., 432
PARKMAN: D., 165; Henry D., 355; Phebe [EDWARDS], 165
PARKS: Amarillis, 433; Amos, 433; Frederick H., 417; James, 5; Josiah, 433; Mary, 434; Michael, 433; Nathan, 434
PARMER: Charles, 434; Isabella, 434; Samuel, 434
PARNELL: Hiram, 339; Israel, 339

PARR: Capt., 386
PARRISH: Almira, 434;
Caroline, 434; Charles,
439; Ebenezer, 434;
Elihu, 434; Elihu W.,
434; Elizabeth, 434;
Isaac, 51; Levi, 250;
Martha, 434; Robert A.,
286; W.F., 614; Wayne,
434
PARROTT: Ellen, 434;
Samuel, 434
PARRY: Ely, 446; R., 156,
276, 313; Rowland, 51,
60, 82, 156, 430, 439,
503, 550; William, 187
PARSONS: A., 97; Achsah,
434; Capt., 113; Charles
C., 116; Dan K., 434;
Dorcas [WILLIAMS],
603; Eli, 434; Gen., 617;
George, 79; Huldah, 434;
J.L., 347; Jabez, 435;
James, 434–35; Justin,
435; L.H., JP, 412; Sally,
435; Solomon, 435
PARTORIUS: Charles
Macket, 352
PARTRIDGE: John, 435
PASSAVANT: C.S., 574;
P.L., 541; Sidney, 261
PASSELS: William, 482
PASSMORE: Benjamin J.,
378; James C., 503; John,
42
PATCHEN: Ira, JP, 578;
Seir, JP, 224
PATRICK: Capt., 242;
J.G., JP, 160; Matthew,
163, 599; Robert, 70;
William, 307
PATTEN: Christopher, 435;
George D., 531; Mathew,
JP, 433
PATTERSON: A., 284;
A.O., 335; Adolphus, 9;
Alexander, 435–36, 514;
Amy, 436; Andrew, 342;
Capt., 341, 452; Col.,
106, 452; David P., 340;
David W., 68; Duncan,
324; Eleanor
[ANDERSON], 9;
Elizabeth, 436; Elizabeth
[WHITE], 596; Emma,
436; Francis, 286;

James, 78, 268, 520, 660;
John, 4, 189, 273, 390,
436, 594; John E., 196;
Joseph, JP, 550;
Margaret, 436; Martha,
436; Mary, 436; Matilda,
436; Nicholas, Capt., 355;
R., JP, 402; R.M., 436;
Robert, 4, 6, 421, 436,
522, 594; Robert G., 78;
Robert M., Dr., 436;
Samuel, 78; Sarah, 436;
Stephen, 294; Thomas,
289, 436; W.D., 340;
William, 436; William G.,
JP, 64
PATTISON: George, 202
PATTON: D.W., 212, 240,
563; Frederick L., 355;
John, 314, 355, 436–37;
John C., 597; Jonathan
A., 355; Joshua D., JP,
317; Margaret, 436–37;
Margaret Jane, 437;
Richard, 135, 355;
Samuel, 436–37, 457;
Thomas, Capt., 124; W.,
304; William, 436
PAUL: Ellen, 506; Hosea,
JP, 506; Joseph S., 54;
Mary [HESTON], 257;
William S., 289
PAULES: Adam, JP, 214,
329; Jacob, 214
PAULHAMUS: Abraham,
437; Sarah, 437
PAULHEMUS: Abraham,
437; Sarah, 437
PAULIN: Hannah
[BACON], 19
PAULL: James, 437
PAULUS: Henry, 388
PAWLHAMUS: Abraham,
437
PAWLING: George H., JP,
195
PAXSON: Catharine
[BEECHER], 630; J.S.,
401, 495; Jonathan, 630;
Joseph, Col., 530; Louisa
[HESTON], 255; Richard,
255, 378, 585
PAXTON: Capt., 231;
Joseph, 535; Maria
[MILLER], 395, 397;
William M., 395, 397

PAYNE: Dan, 488; Electa,
437; George M., JP, 431;
J.C., JP, 57; Lucretia
[BIERCE], 46; Mary,
437–38; Noah, JP, 41;
Solomon, 437–38;
Solomon L., 437
PEACE: James, 309; Justin,
481
PEACHEY: John, 404
PEACOCK: Alexander H.,
592; Eli, 438; Neal, 438;
Susanna, 438
PEADRICK: Susanna M.,
423; Washington F., 423
PEALE: James, Lt., 438
PEARCE: Amiel P., JP,
228; Thomas, 438
PEARL: Lois [HUNT], 279
PEARSON: Charles, 562;
Isaac, 318; John L., JP,
316, 337; Nancy, 438;
Thomas, 438
PEAS: Elliott S., 153
PEASE: Ebenezer, 438;
Ebenezer N., 438;
Greham, 438; Isaac, 438;
Jesse, 438; Joel, 439;
Lydia, 439; Rhoda, 438;
Samuel, 439; Stephen,
438
PEAT: William, 218
PECK: Barbara, 439;
Benjamin, 439; Capt.,
480; Conrad, 439; Daniel,
439; Hannah, 439; Henry
A., 23; Hiel, 439; John,
439; Lyman, 439;
Margaret, 439;
Margaretta T., 192; Mary,
439; Samuel, 456;
William, 439
PECKHAM: H.M., 271
PEDDLE: Elizabeth A.
[RUGAN], 485
PEDDLEY: Margaret M.,
173
PEDEN: David, JP, 234
PEEBLE: Alexander, Capt.,
272; Capt., 61
PEEBLES: Samuel, 368
PEES: Andrew, 440; James
B., 440
PEET: Thaddeus, 440
PEGG: Daniel, 440

PELATE: Barbary, 440; Martin, 440
PELHAM: Martha C., 440; Peter, 440
PELING: Robert, 440
PELLING: James, 440; John, 440; Mary, 440; Robert, 440
PELLYER: John, 372, 406
PELTON: Alice, 441; Betsey, 441; Samuel, 441; Spelman, 441
PEMBERTON: Christian, 441; Deborah, 441
PENCE: Catherine, 520, 660; Sarah, 520, 660
PENDLETON: Col., 270
PENFIELD: A.C., JP, 435
PENNINGTON: Thomas, 297
PENNOCK: H.S., 216; Isaac M., 115, 337; Joseph, 115, 605
PENNYPACKER: Derrick, Capt., 621; Matthias, 10; Washington, 612
PENROSE: Clement B., 368
PENROW: Col., 573
PENSINGER: Henry, 441
PENTLAND: Capt., 596
PERCEL: John, 441
PERHAM: Joseph, JP, 309
PERKIN: Joseph L., JP, 190
PERKINPINE: Elizabeth, 441
PERKINS: Aaron, 441; David, 441; E.H., JP, 187; Isaac, JP, 228; Lucy [BABCOCK], 18; Luke, 306; Thomas, 36
PERRINE: Isaac, 442; Peter, 404, 442
PERRY: Benjamin, JP, 81, 544; J.H., 200, 620; Jane [SWAZE], 552; Joseph H., 219; Lucy [McCLOUD], 370; Rowland, 42, 300, 305, 496; Sally [HUTCHINS], 281; Silas C., JP, 308, 481, 557
PERSICO: Luigi, 637
PERSINE: Daniel, 292
PERSING: Jacob, 237

PETER: Michael, 442
PETERMAN: Elizabeth, 516
PETERS: Anthony, 442; Jacob, 442; John, 442; Rachel, 442; Richard, 45, 63, 377, 599; Richard Jr., 346, 468; Thomas R., 328
PETERSON: Conrad, 442; Henry H., JP, 264; John, 442; Lucinda, 442; Mary, 442
PETRICKEN: William A., 330
PETRIKEN: Jonathan D., 442
PETRIKIN: James, 310, 490; William, JP, 310, 457, 490
PETRY: Jacob, 443
PETTEBONE: Henry, JP, 290; Payne, 181, 529
PETTES: John, 317
PETTIBONE: M.D., 372; Sarah [BINGHAM], 46
PETTIGREW: Samuel, JP, 201
PETTIT: A., JP, 32, 66, 174, 301, 305, 421; Andrew, 11, 32, 77, 187, 282; Henry, 305; J., JP, 39; John, JP, 294; Robert, 186, 395, 563; Thomas M., 398
PETTY: John, 74
PETUKIN: Jonathan D., 377
PEW: Alice, 443; John, Jr., 4; William, 443
PEYTON: John, Capt., 615
PHALEN: James, 436
PHELPS: Alfred, 62, 281, 348, 438; Augustus, 443; D., 613; E.F., 97, 166, 568; Edwin F., 348; H.N., 438; Hiram, 228; Ira, 443; Jared, 443; Laura [GRISWOLD], 228; Timothy, 228
PHELSON: A.H., JP, 348
PHILE: George, 443
PHILIP: Capt., 3
PHILIPS: Abraham, JP, 390; Albert, 443; Anna, 443; Capt., 130, 240, 420; Darius, 519; Dorcas, 444;

Elisabeth [SMITH], 519; Esquire, 443; Jesse E., 96; Joel, 607; John, 444; Levi, 443; Martha [WILSON], 607; Peter, 444; Peter S., 384; Philip, 444; Samuel, 444; Spencer, 444; Sylvester, 445
PHILLER: George, 219, 285
PHILLIPPI: Abraham, 445; John, 205; Peter, 445; Susanna, 445
PHILLIPS: A.C., JP, 131, 296; Alvah C., 65, 290, 553; Ann, 290; Bathsheba, 444; Cathrin, 420; Clara [HILLYER], 261; Comer, JP, 444; Dan, 444; Elisha, 445; Elizabeth, 444; Enos, 288; Ewen, 256; George M., 58, 97, 159, 227, 560; Isaac, 445; Isabella, 444; Jacob, 444; John, 121, 143, 185, 444; Joseph, 444; Julia [JAMES], 288; Margaret, 444; Mary Ann, 444; Melinda, 445; Michael, 444; Peter, 444; Philip, 444; Samuel, 261, 444; Samuel B., 51; Sarah, 445; Spencer, 444–45; Stephen Jr., 445; Susan, 444; Susanna [IDLE], 281; Thomas, 376, 397, 591
PHILO: Azor, 445
PHILPOT: Hugh M., 220
PHILSON: Alexander H., JP, 293
PHIPPS: David Jr., 367
PHREANER: Benjamin, 274
PHYSICK: Caroline [JACKSON], 285; Philip, 285
PICKEL: Mary [GENTZERMAN], 208
PICKERING: Catherine [STALEY], 534; Timothy, Col., 529
PICKETT: John, 261, 446; John Jr., JP, 446; Nancy, 446

PICKING: Christian, 329; Henry A., 329; William S., JP, 278, 450, 553
PIEFFER: Samuel, 186
PIERCE: Abiram, 113, 206, 461, 528; Capt., 254; Chester, JP, 317; George, 97; James, 461, 512; John, 445, 657; John L., 445; Samuel, 314; Stephen, 491; Thomas, 446; Thomas F., 97; William, Capt., 77; Wm. K., 38
PIERCY: Lt., 171
PIERSOL: Sampson, 446
PIERSON: Col., 431; Margaret [CHAPMAN], 95
PIGSLEY: Paul, 446
PIKE: Charity, 446; James, JP, 181, 290; Jonathan, 446; Perry C., 316; Zebulon, Capt., 3
PILE: George, JP, 319
PILLINGTON: Eliza [KELLER], 305
PINKERTON: Andrew, 471; Catherine [RICHEY], 471; Elizabeth, 446; Henrietta, 446; Henry, 408, 446; James, 471; John, 446, 471; Mary, 446; R.A., 37; Samuel, 84
PINKITT: John, 446
PIPER: Edmund L., 339; Henry, 447; James, 75, 100, 164, 550; O.P., 580
PIPES: James, JP, 476; Joseph, 447; William, 447
PIPPINGER: John, Capt., 175
PIQUETT: Martin, 562
PITKIN: Betsey, 447; Stephen, 447
PITTMAN: Capt., 221
PIZER: George, 96
PLACE: C.H., JP, 271
PLANE: Jacob, JP, 313
PLANK: Abraham, 447; Elizabeth, 447; George, 447; Hetty, 447; Jacob, 447; John, 447; Mehitable [METCALF], 399; Polly, 447; Sally, 447

PLANKS: Sarah [TEVIS], 557
PLATT: Franklin, 130, 241; John, 447; Joseph, 447
PLAYFORD: Robert L., 276
PLEASANT: James, 324
PLEASANTS: Israel, JP, 343, 418; W.J. Pemberton, 142
PLONINGER: Jonathan, 52
PLOTTS: George, 447
PLOTZ: George, 447; Rachel, 447
PLUM: John, 448
PLUMB: H.A., 267; Ralph, 183; S., JP, 267
PLUMMER: Elisha, 448
PLUNKETT: Capt., 3
POAGUE: Robert, 373
POAK: James S., 448
POE: Adam, 448; Andrew, 448
POH: John, 448
POINDEXTER: Robert W., 486
POINT: Elizabeth [NORRIS], 422; J.M., 422
POK: John, 448
POLEY: John, Capt., 122
POLLACK: David, 448; Elias, 448; Ephraim, 157; James, 228
POLLARD: Abner, 349; Abner Jr., 390; John, 449; Mary, 449; Samuel, 449
POLLOCK: Ann, 449; Caroline, 449; David, 448–49; David Jr., 448; Elias, 448; Ephraim M., 256, 273; James, 95, 381; Polly, 449; Rebecca, 448; Thomas, 133
POLSTOW: Margaret [SINGLEY], 515; Thomas, 515
POMERCY: Medad, 449
POMEROY: Col., 12; D.F., 454; Daniel, 449; Medad, 449
POMERY: Daniel, 449
POMROY: C.W., 177
POND: Elijah, JP, 337; Paul, 449; Phebe, 449

POOL: Amos, 449; Jephthale, 449; Peter, 449; Peter S., 187
POOR: William, 450
POORMAN: Christian, 450; Elizabeth, 450
POPE: Adam, 450; Catharine, 450; Catharine [ANTRUM], 13; Conrad, 13; Ezra, 450; George, 450; John, 450; Margaret, 450; Mary, 450; Nicholas, 450; Salome, 450
POPHAM: William, Capt., 211
POPPLETON: Caroline, 450; Samuel, 450
POPST: Christian, 450
PORTER: Ann P. [MALCOLM], 355; Byron, 567; Col., 70, 445; Elizabeth, 451; Evaline [ANDERSON], 10; Frederic, 355; George B., 310, 414; Isabella [BONNER], 55; J.M., 590; James F., 267; James Holmes, 267; John, 61, 136–37, 343, 346, 409, 544, 564; Joseph, 451; P.H., 167; Robert, 451; S.H., 302; Samuel, 451; Samuel Jr., 451; Sarah [ZIEGLER], 624; T.J., 404, 458; Wells, 122, 451; William A., 424; William, JP, 353
PORTMAN: J., 191; John, 451
POSEY: Col., 596
POST: Albert L., 396; David, 22, 57, 93, 226, 254, 262, 398, 461, 497, 576, 593; Gideon, 451; Isaac, 262
POSTLETHWAITE: Thomas, 394
POTTER: Adam, 167, 350; Borden, 451; Col., 173, 366, 542; Elisha, 223; Elisha S., JP, 575; Gen., 260; Henry H., 56; James, 353, 381; Joseph, 78, 294, 452, 558, 579, 662; Lyman, 11; Oliver, Capt., 158;

(POTTER, continued)

R.L., JP, 130, 360, 377;
Robert, 452; S.A., 556
POTTEY: Charles, 15
POTTS: Col., 528; George
M., 78; Jonathan, 8;
Nathan, JP, 78; Noah,
352; Robert T., 27;
Thomas P., 528
POTTSGROVE: Henry,
452
POULSON: Erastus, 9, 178,
513
POUND: Mary
[GOODELL], 215;
William, 215
POUNDS: Stephen, 36
POWELL: Benjamin, JP,
243; David, 452;
Elizabeth, 452; Frederick,
452; John, 452; Polly,
452; R., JP, 7
POWER: Benjamin, 452;
Manasseh, 453; William,
271
POWERS: -----, Rev., 235;
Aaron, 453; Eliza
[HALLET], 235; Hazard,
JP, 189, 489; J.M., 272;
Sarah, 453
PRALL: Amelia, 453; John
J., 453
PRATT: Asa, JP, 4;
Elnathan, 453; Ephraim,
453; Ira, 144; Luther M.,
252; Mary [BALLARD],
23; Olive, 453; Polly
[BENJAMIN], 41;
Ransley S., 453
PRAY: Daniel, Capt., 330
PRAYME: Henry, 453
PREDIN: John, 384
PREISE: George, 454
PRENTICE: James, 484
PRENTISS: C., 18; Cyrus,
2, 22, 34, 81, 132, 161,
174, 191, 207, 259, 300,
324–25, 345, 365, 437,
447, 502, 559, 561–62,
579
PRESCOTT: Col., 433;
David W., 572
PRESTON: David, 454;
Edward, 376; Elizabeth,
454; Hannah, 454;

James, 454; L., 418; Levi,
454; Lucy [BALDWIN],
22; Samuel, 48, 88, 184,
189, 418, 551, 611;
Solomon, 454; William,
454
PRICE: Ann, 11, 454;
Barbara [WALTZ], 582;
Eli K., 170, 338, 410;
Elizabeth, 454; Henry,
454; Jacob, 454; James,
JP, 302, 318; Jane
[SMITH], 521; Jared,
518; John, 531; Thomas,
361; Thompson, 454;
Timothy, 455; William
H., 397
PRICHARD: Miles, JP, 597
PRINCE: Capt., 178;
Enoch, JP, 292; Frederick
O., JP, 286; James A.,
139
PRINDLE: Amasa, 200
PRINTICE: Capt., 617
PRIOR: Abigail, 455;
Abigail W., 455; Abner,
Major, 455; Ann, 455;
Erastus F., 455; Harriet,
455; Simeon, 455
PRITCHARD: Benjamin,
JP, 362
PROBST: J.A., 315
PROCTOR: Col., 385, 592;
Thomas, Col., 392, 419
PROSATER: John, 557;
Margaret [TEVIS], 557
PROSSER: Abraham, 455;
Daniel, 455; Daniel M.,
455; John, 455; Robert,
455; William, 455
PROTZMAN: Peter, 455
PROUDFIT: James A.,
455; John, 455
PROUDFOOD: James, 455
PROUDFOOT: James, 402,
455
PROVINCE: Joseph Y.,
456
PRUNER: D.J., JP, 205,
454
PRYFOGLE: Elizabeth
[MOORE], 402; Jacob,
402
PRYME: Henry, 453
PRYOR: J.K., JP, 270

PUDDING: Catharine, 456;
Conrad, 456; Elisabeth,
456; Peggy, 456
PUDING: Conrad, 456;
Elizabeth, 456
PUGH: George, JP, 225;
Isaac, 341, 387; John B.,
JP, 140, 265, 288, 324;
John D., JP, 541; John,
JP, 42, 169, 195, 538
PULMAN: Rufus, Col., 70
PUMROY: John M., 190,
263; Joseph, 190; William
R., 190
PURCELL: Edward, 315
PURDAY: Capt., 29
PURDON: Jonathan, 378,
539, 614
PURDY: Harvey, JP, 296;
J., 244; Murrillea, 155
PURNELL: John, 456, 611;
Martha Ann, 456; Sarah
Ann, 456
PURNEY: Joseph, 263
PURSELL: Joseph, 16
PURVES: John, 610;
William, 27, 115, 256,
266, 312, 324, 345, 364,
373, 397, 405, 439, 502,
515, 517, 539, 548
PURVIANCE: John N., 5
PURVIS: S.G., JP, 318; W.
William, 15; William,
245
PUSEY: William B., 6
PUTMAN: Rufus, Col., 89
PUTNAM: Col., 250;
Elijah, 456; Gen., 330,
504; Jesse, 456; Luman,
JP, 250; Schuyler, JP,
177, 315, 441, 484, 532;
Thomas, 318, 456
PYLE: B. Franklin, 166;
Ziba, 166
PYLES: Joseph, 456; Sarah,
456; Susannah, 456;
Thomas, 456

QUAIL: Capt., 405; Ellen
L., 457; William M.,
Capt., 457
QUAINTANCE: Hannah
[BENTLY], 457; John,
457; William, 457
QUAIT: William M., 457

QUARTERMAN: John, 457
QUEENS: John, JP, 101
QUEGGLE: Capt., 553
QUERY: Robert, 396
QUICK: Henry, 457; Mary [CAMPBELL], 85
QUIGGLE: Capt., 395
QUIGLEY: Cary, 458; Edward, 457; G.W., 79; John, JP, 452; Michael, JP, 152; Samuel, 457; Samuel Jr., 457
QUIGLY: Cary, 458
QUIMBY: E., 521; E. Jr., 566; Ephraim, 397
QUINBY: E., 221; Samuel, 221, 458, 589; William, 132

RAB: Capt., 123
RABER: Johannes, 458; John, 458
RABINSTINE: Duwalt, 477
RADCLIFF: John L., 309
RADEBAUGH: Jacob, JP, 113; Peter, 458; Thomas, 458
RADEEBACK: Peter, 458
RADER: David, 128
RADLE: John, JP, 22, 187
RAFE: Anna Maria [LYN], 351; Ellen [SIMMONS], 513; John, 513
RAFESNYDER: Catharine [COTSMOYER], 117
RAGUEL: William, 325
RAHM: Anthony, 500; E., 470; Mary [SCHATZ], 500
RAHN: Philip, 458
RAIGNEL: William, 39
RAIGUEL: William, 111, 282, 541, 599
RAINER: Robert, JP, 556
RAINEY: James, JP, 129; John, 556; Samuel, 578
RAIS: Johannes, 255
RAKE: Daniel P., 44
RALEY: R.F., 18, 146
RALSTON: Andrew, 458; John, 84, 284, 458; John, Jr., 458
RAMAGE: John, 459

RAMBACH: Jacob, JP, 493
RAMBLE: Catharine, 459; Samuel, 459; William, 459
RAMSAY: Albert, JP, 614; Capt., 25
RAMSEY: Ann Eliza, 27; Archibald, JP, 44, 399; Aseneth, 459; David, 264, 459; E., 3; F.M.W., 602; George, JP, 534; J.L., 325; James P., 104, 317, 478; Jeremiah, 459; Jesse B., JP, 608; John, 11, 171; L.D., JP, 459; Robert, 147, 610; W.D., 399
RANCK: John, JP, 48, 344; Luther, 48
RANDAL: Asher, Capt., 152; Nathaniel, Capt., 152; William, 495
RANDALL: Alexander, JP, 225; Archibald, JP, 23, 188, 282, 383; Charles, 390, 459; Marquis D., 459; Michael, 459; Richard, JP, 153
RANDOLPH: Ann [CAMPBELL], 85; Christian, 459; Dennis, 459; Jane A. [LLOYD], 342; Martha, 459; Michael, 459; Nathaniel, 85; Thomas, 459
RANK: David, 599; John M., 599
RANKIN: A.N., JP, 478; Andrew B., JP, 115, 258, 614; Catharine, 460; Jonathan, JP, 60, 116; Margaret, 460; Thomas, 460
RANSALL: Valentine, 460
RANSOM: Elizabeth, 460; George Palmer, 460; Joseph, 460; Mary, 460; Samuel, Capt., 605
RAPPERT: Jacob, 460
RARICK: Godfrey, 460
RASH: Charles, JP, 128, 132; John, JP, 496
RASWELL: Capt., 162
RATHBON: Ruth [CUMMINGS], 127

RATHBONE: Edmund, 460; Gannett, 23; Martha [BALLARD], 23
RATHBUN: Edmund, 460; Ezra, 461
RATHBURN: Thomas, 461
RATHMELL: J.G., JP, 56
RAUB: Capt., 343, 466
RAUCH: Jacob, 77
RAUCHER: Jacob, JP, 494
RAUER: Samuel, Col., 451
RAUK: John M., 111
RAUSCH: George, JP, 390
RAUSH: George, JP, 332, 428
RAUTH: John, 461; Rachel, 461
RAWDON: Abigail [WINSLOW], 610; Jeduthun, 29
RAWLAND: Henry, 461
RAWLINGS: Col., 194
RAWSON: Secretary, JP, 601
RAY: Alex, 54; Jane [WILSON], 608; Thomas P., 14
RAYBOLD: F.A., JP, 483
RAYEN: William, JP, 419
RAYMOND: Amos, 461; Benjamin, 299; C., 100; David, 461; Seth S., 461; Zaccheus, 461
RAYNSFORD: Hannah, 461; Joseph, 461, 656; Joshua W., 461, 656; Polly, 461
REA: Joseph, 69; Lenox, 462; Martha, 462; Mary Jane, 462; Noah, 462; Thomas, 389; Washington, 389; William Henry, 462
READ: Albert Abel, 200; Alexander, 312, 314; Capt., 410; Catharine, 462; David, 462; Elizabeth, 462; James, 462; Joel, 462; Margaretta [CONKLEN?], 462
READER: Capt., 474
READING: Capt., 172
READY: Abraham Jr., 462; John Abraham, 462
REAGAN: Alexander, 465; Alice, 465; Brice, 465;

(REAGAN, continued)

Esther, 465; Frances, 465; George, JP, 316; Philip, 465; Polly, 465
REAGER: Michael, 462
REAM: Curtis, 462, 536; Henry, 462; John, 462, 582; John F., 467; Mary [WAGNER], 577; Richard, 462; Sarah [WANN], 582
REAMER: Edward, 521
REBZ: Matthias, 463
RECHLINE: Col., 80
RECTOR: John, JP, 165
RED: Will, 464
REDDIN: Charles, Capt., 571
REDHEFFER: Andrew, Capt., 257
REDIFER: Jacob, 56, 127, 475, 500, 503, 518, 525
REDLION: Henry, 463; Mary Ann, 463
REDSECKER: Jacob, JP, 248, 505; Samuel, 505
REDSERKER: George, 414
REECE: Andrew, 463; Jane, 463
REED: A.B., 88; Alexander B., JP, 298; Amos, 463; Andrew, Capt., 344, 425; Benjamin, 463; C.F., 363; Charles M., 6, 128, 272; Col., 412; Colin M., 236, 456; David, 462; Esther, 464; Frederick, 463; Fulton, 58; G.P., JP, 164; George W., 283; George, JP, 177; Giles, 463; Henry, 394; James, 287, 352, 379, 421, 463–64, 608; Jane, 464; Jemimah, 463; John, 93, 153, 223, 458; Jonathan P., JP, 491; Joseph, 7, 464; Leah, 177; Margaret, 464; Margaretta [CONKLEN?], 462; Matthew, 60; Michael, 103, 326, 401, 584; Nancy [RUSSELL], 488; Parker, 10; Philip, 172, 464, 500, 518;

Rufus, 463; Samuel, 115, 279; Sarah, 464; Tabitha, 653; Thomas, 374, 464; Walker, 653; William, 98, 165, 488, 500; William B., 487
REEDER: A.H., 469; Merrick, JP, 315; Thomas, Capt., 156; William, 391
REEGAN: John, 478
REEGER: Ann Deborah, 464; David, 464; Elizabeth, 464; Frederick, 466; Jacob, 464; John, 464; Lydia, 464; Margaret, 466; Polly, 464; Samuel, 464; Thomas, 464
REES: Capt., 389; George, 464; George A., 478; Griffith, 464; Jacob, 573; Rebecca, 464; Thomas, 465
REESE: Lewis, JP, 353; Peter, 465
REEVES: Anna, 465; Benjamin, 465; David, 636; Hannibal, 465; Jonathan, 80; Lucian B., 465; Luther, 38, 465; Manassah, JP, 331; Mary, 465; Nancy, 465; Rumsay, 465; Sarepta, 465; Thomas Jr., 3
REFFY: William, Capt., 539
REGAN: Philip, 465
REGES: John W., JP, 41, 416
REICHART: Charles, 472
REICHENBACK: Adam, 471; Catharine, 471
REICHEY: Abraham Jr., 471
REICHSWICK: Conrad, 465
REICHWICK: Conrad, 465
REID: Franklin, 270; James, 466
REIFSNYDER: John, JP, 333
REIGART: Franklin, 217
REIGEL: John, JP, 17; Michael, 466
REIGER: Frederick, 466

REIGHTER: *John, 43*
REIGLE: Michael, 466
REILEY: Christopher, JP, 113
REILLY: John, 397; Owen, 190; Wilson, 416
REILY: Jane, 466; John, 466
REIMBOLT: Johannes, 530
REINECKE: Frederick, 336
REINER: Jacob, 466
REINHARD: Jacob, 59; Joel, 454
REINHOLT: Henry, 468
REINOR: Jacob, 466
REIS: Frederick, 469
REISHER: Samuel, JP, 539
REISINGER: George, 584; Polly [WARNER], 584
REISSNYDER: John, JP, 101
REISWICK: Conrad, 465
REITER: Jacob, 466
REITZ: Michael, 321
REITZEL: Maria [SHINDEL], 508
REMINGTON: Joseph N., 466; Josiah, 466; Ruth, 466
RENELS: Benjamin, 466
RENISON: John, 467; Mary, 467
RENSHAW: R., 590; Thomas N., 266
RENWICK: John, 273
REPPARD: William, 237
REPPLIER: Jonathan, 493; Jonathan G., 6, 227
REPSHER: Ann [SMITH], 520; James, 520; Peter, 520
RESSELL: Paul, 487
RETTINHOUSE: George D., JP, 266
RETZ: Matthias, 463
REUM: John F., 467
REX: Margaret, 467; Samuel, JP, 251; William, 467
REXFORD: Simon, 467
REYMER: George, 478
REYNELS: Jacob, 371
REYNOLDS: Abijah, 467; Alexander, 313, 485;

(REYNOLDS, continued)

Benedict, 467; Benjamin, JP, 178, 361; David R., 495; Gamaliel, 229, 467; George, 366, 468; Gurdin, 468; Gurdon, 568; Isaac, 196; Jonathan, 279, 402, 468; M.M., 85; Mary, 467; N., 108; R.W., JP, 53; Rebecca, 196; Reuben, 94; Robert W., JP, 222; Robert, Capt., 576; Shubel, 468; Simeon, 467–68; William, 468; Z., 236
RHEINER: Elizabeth [WOLF], 613
RHINEHOLT: Henry, 468
RHOADS: Daniel Jr., 630
RHODES: B.K., 124; George, 469; J., 341; J.V., 600; John C., 124; Nicholas, 469
RIBBETT: Abraham, 469
RIBERT: Cathrine, 469; Johannes, 469; John, 469; Lydia, 469; Michael, 469; Solomon, 469
RIBLET: Abraham, 469; Christian, 469; Daniel, JP, 469
RIBSON: Sarah [ERWIN], 173
RICE: A., 470; Chauncey, 469; Darius, 470; Edward, 28; Frederick, 469; George, 210, 312; Isaac, 470; John, 119, 393, 424, 470; Nathaniel, 470; Owen, 590; R.S., JP, 468; Robert S., JP, 250, 317; Samuel, 470; William, 468
RICH: Capt., 506; Elbridge, 300; Jane [JUSTICE], 300; T.W., 172; Virtulon, JP, 487
RICHARD: Capt., 343; Samuel, 302; T.L., 568
RICHARDS: Anna, 179; Edgar H., 179; Eliza V. [ANDERSON], 10; Elizabeth O. [OTTO], 429; G.W., 331; George, 166, 179, 393, 452, 528;

Isaac, JP, 527; Jesse, 470; John F., 393; Jonathan S., 592; Mark, 92, 179, 452, 528; Matthias, 180, 551; Matthias S., 213, 416, 551; Rachael [BOWMAN], 59; Warren, 611
RICHARDSON: *Braton,* 471; Caleb, 470–71; Caleb C., 470–71; Daniel, 470; E.T., JP, 597; Gershom, 470; Hollon, 534; Huldah, 470–71; John, 46; Lyman, 471
RICHE: Isaac, 471; William, 471
RICHENBECK: Adam, 471
RICHEY: Abraham, 471; Adelia [DUNHAM], 160; Catherine, 471; Elizabeth, 471; Paxson, 8; Robert, JP, 585
RICHIE: Eliah, 471; Martha, 471, 657; Rebecca, 471; Robert, 471, 657; Sarah, 471; Thomas, 471; William, 471
RICHMOND: Col., 420; Gideon, 599; Hannah [WHITNEY], 599
RICHTER: George, 139; Jacob, 202
RICHTMEYER: Abigail [CHURCH], 97; Nicholas, 97
RICHWINE: Daniel, 145
RICKETSON: C.W., 50
RICKETTS: E.G., 303
RICKEY: Benjamin, 471; Joseph, 472; Obededom, 472
RIDDELL: Francis, JP, 15
RIDDLE: George R., 201; J. Short, 3; J. Steward, 186; James J., JP, 95; James M., 51, 634; John W., 236; Michael, 562; W.B., 661; William B., 575
RIDEN: John, 471
RIDGE: Mahlon, 586; Susan, 341

RIDGWAY: J., 480; Mathew, 598
RIECHART: Charles, 472
RIFFERT: Christian, 472
RIFFLE: Elizabeth [JACOBY], 288; Jacob, 255
RIGDON: James, 472
RIGG: Rufus, 472; William, 472
RIGGS: C., 392; Capt., 615; David W., Dr., 275; Jonathan, 472
RIGHTER: Euphemia R. [WILSON], 609; J.K., 609
RIGHTMEYER: Adam, 193; David, 213, 443; John, Capt., 26
RIGHTMYER: David, JP, 347; J.L., 347
RILE: John, JP, 56
RILEY: Daniel, 473; Eleanor, 473; James, 473; James R., JP, 21; Joseph, 473
RIMMEY: Conrad, 473; Hannah, 473; John, 473; Margaret, 473; Nancy, 473; Rachel, 473; Ruth, 473; Thomas, 473
RINE: Joseph Jr., 101
RINEBERGER: Henry, 415
RINEHART: John M., 357
RING: George, 463; Walter, JP, 463
RINGER: Stephen, 155
RINGLAND: Phebe, 628; Thomas B., 628
RINKER: Abraham, 473
RIPLEY: Jacob, JP, 15
RIPPEY: William, Capt., 81, 338
RIPPLE: George, Capt., 191
RISDEL: Jane, 473; John, 473
RISDELL: John, 473
RISHELL: George, 473; Jacob, 473
RISING: Ben, 473
RISINGER: Peter, 511
RISLEY: Joseph L., JP, 19
RISSLER: Thomas, 434
RITCEY: William, 471

RITCHEY: John S., JP, 256
RITCHIE: Abraham, 471;
Catherine, 471; Elizabeth,
471; Elizabeth [JOB],
292; John, 292; Paxson,
175, 368; William, 91,
127, 236, 328, 402, 411
RITH: Samuel, 390
RITTENHOUSE: David,
89; David, JP, 103; Eliza
[NORMAN], 422; Jacob,
474
RITTER: Louis, 528
RIVELY: Frederick, 474
RIXFORD: Simon, 467
ROACH: William, 474
ROADS: Peter, Capt., 155
ROAN: John, 474
ROBB: Isaac, 246
ROBBINS: Brintnal, 474;
Mary, 474; Moses, 458;
Samuel, 474; Samuel J.,
14, 385; Silas, JP, 252;
Thomas, 474
ROBENSER: Henry, 419
ROBERSON: Lucretia
[TILDEN], 562; Morris
D., JP, 216–17
ROBERTS: A.B., 18; A.E.,
87; Amos, 475; Ann, 476;
Catharine, 476; David,
475; E.J., 51; Edward,
475; Edward J., 621;
Elisha, 476; Elizabeth,
476; Ephraim, 476;
George H., 44; Gideon,
475; Jerusha, 475; John,
143, 205, 393; Joseph,
475; Lydia, 475; Mabel,
476; Margaret, 475;
Mary, 475; Mary Ann,
475; Milicent, 476;
Nathan, 475; Owen, 475;
Rebecca, 476; Samuel,
82, 189, 360; Samuel A.,
98; Samuel C., 303;
Sarah, 476; Stephen, 476;
Thomas, 476; W.B., 248;
W.R., 105; William,
475–76, 600; William S.,
476
ROBERTSON: Andrew,
476; D.S., 453; Elizabeth,
165, 476; James, 165;
Nancy, 476
ROBESON: Morris D., 155

ROBINETT: A., 609;
Allen, 12, 414
ROBINETTE: George, 55;
J., JP, 55
ROBINS: Elias, 90; Isaac,
476; John, 583
ROBINSON: A.L., JP, 119;
Alexander, 477;
Alpheous, 230; Chandler,
477; E.A., JP, 326;
George, 645; James, 477;
James, Capt., 131;
Jedediah H., 477; John L.,
285; John R., 477; John
W., 81; Jonathan J., 359;
Lois, 477; Nancy, 516;
Nancy [BUTLER], 81;
Penrose, 36, 611; Polly,
477; R., 541; R.R., JP, 95;
Rebecca, 477; Richard,
361, 376, 537; Samuel,
452, 618; Silas A., 477;
Thomas J., 477; Timothy,
Col., 453; William, 477;
William R., JP, 479;
Zadock, 477
ROBINSTINE: Duvalt, 477
ROBISON: Charlotte, 367;
E.A., JP, 150, 336;
Ephraim A., JP, 36, 367;
James, 123; John, 109;
Mary, 421; R.N., JP, 356;
R.R., JP, 527; Samuel,
460
ROCK: Adam, 629
ROCKENDERFORD:
Elizabeth [SAILOR],
489–90
ROCKHILL: Thomas C.,
407
ROCKROTH: Jacob, 517
ROCKWELL: W.A., 57
ROCKWOOD: Simeon,
477; Simeon T., 477
RODDICK: Elizabeth, 550
RODDY: Nancy [BLACK],
49
RODEARMEL: Peter, 390
RODENBOH: Jacob, 266;
Rebecca [HOLGATE],
266; William H., 266
RODERMAN: Joseph, 584
RODES: Catharine, 478;
Frances, 478; Margret,
478; Mark, 478; Susan,
478

RODGERS: Amanda
[McCARTY], 368;
Elizabeth Jane, 478;
Joseph, 478; Mary
[WERTZ], 592; Mary
Ann, 478; Mary L., 478;
Sarah A., 478; William
H., 478; William R., 478
RODROCK: J., JP, 256;
Jonas, Dr., 256
ROEDER: Casper, 478;
Catharine, 478; Conrad,
478; John, 478
ROEMER: Eleanor, 478;
Elizabeth, 478; Julian,
478; Louisa, 478; Nancy,
478; Peter, 478; Philip,
478
ROGEN: John, JP, 49
ROGERS: A.G., 480; A.J.,
422; Ann, 479; Ann
[McBRIDE], 367; Anna,
479; Artimesia, 480;
Betsey [SCOVILLE],
498; Col., 244; Edward,
479; Elizabeth, 479;
Evans, 125, 219, 240,
251, 592; George A., 295;
Hannah [LIKENS], 337;
Harvey, 480; James, 264,
349, 380, 479; James A.,
143; James H., 207; Jesse,
460; John, 380; Jonah,
381; Joseph, 419; Joseph
B., 198; Josiah, 480;
Josias, 479; Lucy, 480;
Margaret, 479; Mary,
480; Milton, JP, 139;
N.T., JP, 292; Noah, JP,
499, 534; Polly, 480;
Rachel, 479; Richard,
479; Roine, 479; Roswell
R., 479; Ruby, 480; Ruth,
479–80; Samuel, 480;
William, JP, 460; Zelima
[SEELY], 499;
Zephaniah, 479
ROHRER: John, 480
ROHRMAN: John, 480;
Sarah, 480
ROLAND: Abraham, 6;
James, 243
ROLLINS: M., Col., 26
RONAN: David, 377

ROOD: Clement, JP, 105; Emeline, 269; Joseph W., 269; Norman, 86
ROOKS: Daniel, 480; John L., 480
ROONEY: John A., 376
ROOSA: Isaac, 299
ROOT: Abel, 481; Capt., 126; Henry, 300, 437, 481; Joseph, 481; Loyall L., 481; Lucy, 481; Lyman, 481; Mary, 481; Polly, 481; Reuben, 261; William R., 481; William, JP, 71, 165, 543
ROSE: Amanda [BRODHEAD], 66; Andrew L., JP, 118; Anson H., 118; Charlotte [ANDERSON], 9; Daniel, 481; Enos, 481; Henry, 481; Isaac, 481; James, 382; Jonathan, 387, 481, 544; Lydia, 481; Margaret Elizabeth [SCHNEIDER], 494; Martha [McKINLEY], 382; Rufus, 226; Russell, 481; William S., JP, 62
ROSEBROUGH: Isaac, 481; Rachel, 481
ROSENERANTY: Rozilla, 558
ROSENGRANT: George, 241
ROSER: Abraham, 481
ROSET: Jonathan, 35, 50, 108, 131, 253, 272, 452, 458, 488, 493, 516, 546, 548, 557, 573, 575, 605, 607, 613, 618
ROSHONG: Daniel, 624; Enoch, 624; Jeremiah, 624; John, 624; Magdalina, 624; Therisa, 624; Timothy, 624
ROSS: Benjamin, 223; Capt., 328; Catharine [HUM], 277; Catharine T., 482; Charlotte, 482; Elizabeth, 481; Esther, 482; F.C., 147; F.M., 283; Harvey, JP, 51; Isaac, 481; James, 277, 482, 614; James B., 426; John, 211, 482, 616;

John B., 50; Joseph, 23, 222; Lydia [ELDRIDGE], 167; Moses A., JP, 215; Nancy [RIMMEY], 473; Perrin, 167; Polly S., 482; Samuel, 358; Samuel M., 50; Sarah [BLACK], 50; Stephen, JP, 61; Thomas, 387, 482; William, 44
ROSSELL: Job, 600; Sarahann [WHITZELL], 600
ROSSITER: William, JP, 303
ROSY: Chapman, 153
ROTH: Catharine, 482; Daniel, 132, 482; George, 482; Joseph, 482; Juliana, 482; Margaret, 482; Mary, 482; Matthias, 482; Nicholas, 482; Rebecca, 482; Richard L., 482
ROTHENBERGER: Catharine [BARNHART], 28
ROTHROCK: Jacob, JP, 517; James, JP, 592
ROUNES: Charles, 483; Nathaniel, 483
ROUSE: Peter, 483
ROUSH: Samuel, JP, 329
ROVER: Elizabeth, 483; George, 483; Joseph, 483
ROW: George, 483; Jacob, 483; John, 483; Susanna, 483
ROWAN: Charles, 333; John, 483
ROWE: Amelia, 484; Milly, 483; Thomas, 483–84
ROWEN: John, 483; William, 484
ROWLAND: Aaron, 484; Anna, 484; Betsey, 484; Daniel, 484; David, 484; Elizabeth, 484; Emeline, 484; Esther, 484; Grace, 484; Henry, 461; Henry Sr., 658; Hezekiah, 484; James, 484; Jonathan, 240, 461, 658; Levi, 484; Luke, 484; Maria, 484; Mary, 658; Nancy, 484; Olive, 484; Polly, 484; Robert, 477; Samuel, 383;

William, 461, 658; William H., 382
ROWLEY: Capt., 569; Ichabod, 484; Lois, 484; Louisa, 484; Lovina, 484; Nathan, 484; Reuben, 484; Richard, 467; Susannah, 484; Ziba, 484
ROWSE: Z., JP, 382
ROXBOROUGH: Elizabeth [FRY], 199; William, 199
ROZET: John, 282, 296
RUBERT: Barnabas, 133; Michael, 133
RUCH: Francis, 53
RUCHER: Jonathan, 58
RUCKMAN: Sarah [JAMES], 288; Thomas, 288; W.D., 541
RUDOLPH: George, 7, 485; George Jr., 485; Jacob, 485; Mary, 485
RUFF: N.M., JP, 168
RUFIELD: A.C., JP, 591
RUGAN: Catharine, 485; Charles, 485; Elizabeth A., 485; George, 485; John, 485; Margaret, 485; Mary C., 485
RUGJAN: John, 485
RUMSEY: William, 66
RUNK: John, 485; Samuel, 485
RUNNION: Conrad, 485; Elizabeth, 485
RUNYAN: George, 485; Margaret, 485
RUNYON: E., 601
RUPERT: Adam, 486
RUPP: Andrew, 486; Daniel, 524; John, 486
RUSH: Adam, 486; Benjamin, 486; Calvin, 486; Emily, 486; James, 486; Jane, 486; Jesse, 615; Jonathan, 245; Julia, 486; Peter, 615; Rees, 615; Richard, 486; Samuel, 486; Sarah R. [BARNES], 27; William, 27, 486
RUSK: Daniel, 177; Jacob, 487; Jane [FALKNER], 177; Margaret, 487; Mary, 487

RUSSEL: Edward, Col., 263; James, 487; James B., 394; Magdelane [BEECHER], 630; Paul, 487; Thomas, 630

RUSSELL: Alexander, 487; Ashbell, 487; Asher, 487; C.W., 349; Catharine, 487; Charles, 558; David, 575; Esther, 487–88; Evan, 487; Gideon, 487; James, 488; Jemima, 487; John, 379; Joseph, 587; Judith, 488; Mary, 487; Moses M., 488; Nancy, 488; Paul, 487; Philip, 488; Philip M., 487; Rachel, 488; Rebecca, 488; S.L., 189; Samuel, 488; William, 488; William W., 292

RUSSILL: Esther, 488; Philip, 488

RUST: Henry, 186; Mary [FLAUGH], 186

RUTAN: Ellen, 488; Samuel, 488

RUTHERFORD: John, 17

RUTHFOR: Cathrine, 488; Elizabeth, 488; Fanny, 488; George, 488; Jacob, 488; Joseph, 488; Nancy, 488; Polly, 488; Susanna, 488

RUTHRAUFF: Henry, 147

RUTLEDGE: James, JP, 307, 380; John D., 532

RUTTER: Daniel, Dr., 489; Henry, 589; Mary, 587

RYAN: Alvan, JP, 595; G.G., 94; Hannah, 334; Isabella, 488; Jane [CAMPBELL], 85; John, 488; John 2nd, 489; John W., 129; Sarah [DAVIS], 133; Susan [TUBBS], 566; Thomas A., 16

RYBECKER: John, 489

RYBURN: James, 489

RYERSON: Mary, 489; Thomas, 489

RYMAN: Theodore, JP, 88, 120

RYNEARSON: Isaac, 489; Okey, 489

SABIN: A., 479; Hiram, 441; William H., JP, 549

SACKETT: Jonathan Y., 285; Samuel, 135, 384; Zavin, 489

SADLER: Isaac, 489

SAEGER: Daniel, JP, 89, 185, 390; Edward, 89, 167; Eli J., JP, 129, 139, 301, 332; H.B., 218; Jonathan, 139, 462; Josiah, 139; Nicholas, JP, 139, 230, 473

SAFFORD: Capt., 178

SAGE: John, 106

SAILOR: Catharine, 489; Elizabeth, 489, 492; Jacob, 489, 492; Magdalina, 489; Nancy, 489; Peter, 489–90; Samuel David, 489; Sarah, 489

SAINT: Joseph, Col., 520

SALEHAMMER: Nicholas, 490

SALISBURY: Anna [MARTIN], 361; John, 361; William, 490

SALLADA: J.M., 324

SALLADE: Jacob, JP, 357

SALLIDAY: Daniel, 490; Mary, 490

SALMON: John, JP, 85

SAMPLE: Isabella [MOSHER], 408; John, 441, 490; Margery [CHAMBERLAIN], 92; William M., 490

SAMPSON: Bristol, 75, 490; Henry, 490; Phebe, 75; Sally, 490; William, 490

SAMSON: Benjamin P., 529; Henry, 490; John, 529

SANBORN: J.S., 274

SANDERLAND: Samuel, 491

SANDERS: Jacob, 491; John, 56; Mary, 491; Peter, 248; William, 491

SANDERSON: Anna, 491; Fanny, 491; George, 154, 459, 613; Jabez, 611; John J., 117;

Rebecca, 491; William, 491; William H., 568

SANDS: Andrew, 491

SANFORD: E.S., 299; Giles, JP, 79, 179, 586; Gus, JP, 591; Lavinia S., 79

SANNER: Michael, JP, 104

SANTEE: Alexander, 402; John, 180, 491; Polly [MOORE], 402

SANVERS: Michael, JP, 276

SARBOLDT: John, 319

SARGEANT: Ebenezer, 499; Richard, 491

SARGENT: Bridget, 504; Jonathan, 432; Nathan, 438; S.N., 14

SARTWELL: C.K., 127

SARVIS: Mary Ann [JOHNSON], 293; Moses, 293

SARWILL: John C., 503; John, JP, 503

SATTERLEE: Capt., 371; Dezire, 491; J.F., 613; James, 491

SATTEROLE: James, JP, 122

SAUL: Joseph, 205

SAUNDERS: Abraham, 492; Abraham Jr., 492; John, 491

SAVAGE: Abijah, Capt., 437; L.W., JP, 406, 449; S.W., JP, 95

SAVIDGE: John, Capt., 492

SAVILLE: George, 492; Mary, 492

SAW: Benjamin, 602; Polly [WILKINSON], 602

SAWTELL: Benjamin, 492; M.M., 234

SAX: Andrew, 492; John Andrew, 492

SAXTON: James, JP, 281; John, 89; Rebecca, 281

SAYER: Eli J., JP, 132; Lem, JP, 1

SAYERS: E.M., 619; William, JP, 216

SAYLER: Jacob, 492

SAYLOR: Catharine [WEAVER], 587; Charles, JP, 218, 551;

(SAYLOR, continued)

Elizabeth, 492; Jacob,
492; John, 492
SAYRE: Benjamin, 72;
Rauel, 492; Sealy, 51
SAYRES: James, 578;
Taylor, 578
SCHAEFFER: E., 462,
523; Emanuel, JP, 305,
437; Lambert, 493
SCHAFFNER: Jacob, JP,
379
SCHALL: Jonathan, 43,
428
SCHANABLE: Joseph, 493
SCHATZ: Elizabeth, 500;
George, 500; Henry, 500;
Jacob, 500; John, 500;
Magdalena, 500; Mary,
500; Peter, 500; Sarah,
500; Susan, 500
SCHAUER: John, 27, 569
SCHEAT: Capt., 7
SCHEETZ: Justus, 319
SCHEIB: Catharine, 493;
William, 493
SCHEIBELER: Jacob, 506
SCHELL: Abraham, 141;
E.D., 491
SCHELLEHOMER:
George, 493
SCHENCK: Elizabeth, 493;
Jacob, 493; Jane, 493;
Mary, 493; Susan, 493
SCHIEB: Catharine, 493;
Elizabeth, 493; John, 493;
Sarah, 493; William, 493
SCHLEMM: Edmund, 156
SCHLEPPY: Jacob, 493
SCHLEPY: Jacob, 493
SCHLERUM: Edmund,
483
SCHLICKER: Molly
[IRELAND], 283
SCHLIKER: Frederick, 494
SCHLOTT: Adam, 494;
John, 533
SCHMALTZ: Elizabeth,
494
SCHMUCK: John, 494;
Michael, 494
SCHNABLE: Jonathan, 493
SCHNEBLY: Jacob, JP,
202

SCHNEIDER: Christiana,
494; Eva Elizabeth, 494;
Jacob, 176, 347, 494, 544;
Johannes, 494; John, 494;
Margaret Elizabeth, 494
SCHNELL: Henry, 582;
Samuel, 193
SCHNELLY: G.W., 118
SCHOCH: George, 141
SCHOENER: D.G., Dr.,
316; F.B., 460; Henry,
416; William B., 311;
William, JP, 6, 27, 38, 99,
138, 220, 227, 311, 416,
493
SCHOFIELD: G.C., 192;
William, 494
SCHOLFIELD: Lane, 494;
William, 494
SCHOONOVER: Daniel,
551
SCHOSS: Jeremiah, 351
SCHRACK: Capt., 259
SCHRADER: Henry, 511;
Philip, 511
SCHREIBER: Frederick,
511; Susana, 511
SCHREINER: Henry J., JP,
607
SCHREIVER: Daniel, 585
SCHRIVER: Anna Maria,
494; Daniel, 318; Philip
Peter, 494
SCHRUM: George, 495
SCHRYVER: Allen L.,
237; Charity
[HAMMOND], 237;
James P., 237
SCHUCKERS: J.W., JP,
30, 221; Jacob W., JP,
221, 227
SCHULLER: John, 500;
Magdalena [SCHATZ],
500
SCHULTZ: George, 250;
Margaret, 512; Michael,
512
SCHULTZE: Henry F.W.,
323
SCHUTZ: Rosana, 147
SCHUYLER: S., JP,
260–61, 359; Simon, JP,
173
SCHWAB: Julius, 495

SCHWARTZ: Francis P.,
346; George, 208;
Nicholas, 208
SCHWARTZER: John, 38
SCHWETER: Harriet
[KRIDER], 320
SCOTT: Agnes, 497;
Alexander, 477; Amos,
426; Andrew, 495, 497;
Ann S., 497; Anna, 495;
Asa, 495; C.S., 317;
Capt., 430, 438;
Christopher, 495; David,
394, 495; Elizabeth, 479,
496; Freeman, JP, 358;
George, 495; George W.,
52; H.L., 648; Hannah,
495; James, 331, 488,
497; James P., Dr., 361;
James R., 159, 411; Joel,
496; John P., 303, 502;
Jonathan, 495–96, 503;
Joseph, 497, 551; Joshua,
496; Josiah, 104, 497;
Lucius, 496; Margaret,
496; Margaret
[ROGERS], 479; Mary,
495–97; Micah, 496;
Nancy, 479; Nehemiah,
146; Oliver, 496; Peter
Coe, 104; Robert, 9, 67,
125, 159, 187, 496–97;
Robert C., 497; Samuel,
497; Sarah, 496–97;
Sarah [ROBERTS], 476;
Thomas, 248, 497;
Thomas R., 22; William,
253, 479, 495, 497–98;
William 2nd, 497;
Wilson, 427
SCOUTEN: Jacob, 498
SCOVILL: Amasa, 498;
Westol, 498
SCOVILLE: Betsey, 498;
Orlan, 498; Orpha, 498;
Persis, 498; Sylvester P.,
19; Westol, 498
SCOWDEN: Sarah, 498;
Theodorus, 498
SCULL: Edward, Capt., 96;
John, JP, 385
SCULLEN: Philip, 261
SCULLY: D.S., 295; John,
JP, 346
SEABROOK: George, JP,
36

SEAGER: H.B., 218
SEAGRAVES: Alexander
J., 322; Elizabeth
[KURTZ], 322
SEAL: Margaret
[STEEVER], 537
SEALS: James, 341, 498;
Sarah, 498; William, 111,
134, 216, 296, 312, 341,
345, 351, 364, 387, 498
SEALY: Jane
[CHAPMAN], 95;
William, JP, 95
SEAMAN: Catharine, 498
SEARCH: Edwin K., 499;
Elizabeth, 499; James,
499; Lot, 499; Mary A.,
499
SEARGENT: Ebenezer, 499
SEARLE: Daniel, 46, 257,
489; Isaac W., 226;
James, JP, 327
SEARLES: George S., 499
SEARS: Charity, 602
SEATON: Andrew, 210
SEAVER: Ichabod, 499;
Philene, 499
SEBASTIAN: Philip, 410
SEBLE: John, 69
SEBOLT: Abraham, 499
SEBORN: F.A., JP, 552
SEBOTT: Abraham, 499
SECHERLING: Joshua,
486
SECHLER: D.M., 417;
John F., 245; Rudolph,
JP, 417
SECKLER: Abram, 512;
John, 512; Michael, 512;
Rebecca, 512
SEDWICK: George C., JP,
329
SEEDOM: Catharine
[SIMMERS], 513; John,
513
SEELEY: Abigail, 499;
Capt., 541; Samuel, 499
SEELING: Anthony, Capt.,
63
SEELY: Abigail, 499–500;
Alanson, 500; Anna, 500;
Benjamin 1st, 499–500;
Capt., 417; Charlotte,
499; E.S., 330; Ebenezer,
500; Eleazer, 500; Esther,
500; Harvey, 500;

Isaac D., 499; J.H., 386;
Lorana, 500; Mabel, 500;
Mahitable, 500; Mary,
499; Nathaniel, 94, 566;
Permelia, 500; Phebe,
499; S.D., JP, 500;
Samuel, 499; Samuel C.,
500; Samuel Sr., 500;
Sarah, 500; William *M.,*
JP, 73; Zelima, 499
SEGNER: Elizabeth
[BEECHER], 630;
George, 630
SEHATZ: Henry, 500
SEHILD: George, 629
SEIBERLING: Frederick,
500; Jonas, 265, 500;
Joshua, 265
SEIBERT: Henry, 500;
John, 500; Mary, 500;
Rachel, 500; William, 6
SEIDEL: Michael, 630;
Peter, 501
SEIFER: B.G , 153
SEIGLER: Benjamin,
Capt., 520
SEILLE: Godfried, Capt.,
155
SEILOR: Levi, 233
SEIP: Charles, 308, 394,
649
SEIPE: John, 402
SEIPLE: Martin, 469
SEITSINGER: William,
501
SEITZINGER: Erastus B.,
501; George, 501; Jacob,
JP, 143, 398, 501; Maria,
501; Nicholas, 501;
William, 501
SEIVERT: Jacob, 501
SELBY: Brainard Jr., JP,
89; Ira, JP, 21, 181, 408,
579; Thomas B., 89
SELEY: John, 501; Marcy,
501
SELIN: Capt., 416
SELL: Henry, 124
SELLARS: John, 486
SELLERS: Catharine
[MILLER], 395; James
M., 305; John, 395;
Joseph, 308; Robert B.,
133; William, JP, 305
SELLS: Abraham, JP, 185

SELSER: Isaac, 315; Mary
[KIRK], 315
SEMPLE: William M., 464
SERENA: Joseph, 501;
Nancy, 501
SERGEANT: David R.,
107; Thomas, 88, 453,
519
SETER: John, 270
SETTLEMYER: Godfrey,
501
SEVERANCE: Azulen,
502; Benjamin, 501;
Rebecca, 501; Samuel,
502
SEWARD: Amos, 502;
Jehu, Col., 581; John,
502; Lucinda, 502;
Martha, 502; Nathan,
502; Persis, 502; Sylvia,
502; Timothy G., 502
SEWELL: F.H., JP, 12;
Hurlbut, JP, 372
SEYBERT: John, 500
SEYFERT: Elizabeth
[MANEBECK], 356;
Simon, 356; William M.,
356
SEYMOUR: A.J., JP, 499;
Capt., 18; Isaac, 57
SHACKLEE: Peter, 502
SHADE: Capt., 149, 224;
Charles, 510; Sarah, 288
SHADLER: George, 181
SHADOW: Deadlove, 502
SHAEFFER: Charles, 650;
Jacob, 582
SHAFER: John, 502;
Margaret [CRAMER],
120
SHAFF: Frederick, 502
SHAFFER: Adam, 502;
Catharine, 503; Elizabeth,
503; Frederick, 502–3;
Henry, JP, 183, 346;
Jacob, 503; John, 150,
503, 512, 596; Lavinia,
503; Margaret, 503; Mary
"Polly," 503; Peter, 504;
Philip, 503; Sally, 503;
Samuel, 603; Sarah, 503;
Susannah, 503; Thomas,
503
SHALER: Charles, JP, 441
SHALES: Lyman, JP, 40
SHALLCROSS: Isaac, 387

SHANDLER: Robert, 503
SHANE: John, 84
SHANK: Christian, 544;
George, 308; Jacob, 493;
John, 67, 578; Margaret
[BROWN], 67; Mary,
493
SHANKLAND: Alexander,
503; Vententia, 503
SHANNEN: John, JP, 469
SHANNON: Amos V., 503;
E.P., JP, 60; James R.,
514; James, JP, 74; Jane
[WILSON], 607; John,
607; Robert, 503; Robert
E., 503; Wilson, 288
SHANTZ: Catharine, 504;
Henry, 504; Jacob, 504;
Magdalena, 504
SHARADIN: Catharine
[MANEBECK], 377;
David, 356
SHARMAN: Col., 545
SHARP: Amos, 504;
Andrew, 164, 504; Ann
[FALKNER], 177;
Cephas, 394; James, 324,
349; John, 177, 499;
Phebe [SEELY], 499;
Sarah [WEAVER], 587;
William M., 157
SHARPE: Jacob L., 121,
157, 298; Lodewyk, 328
SHARPLESS: John, 172,
428
SHARPLY: Enos, 354
SHARRY: Michael M., 101
SHARSWOOD: George,
580; William, 278
SHARTLE: Capt., 624
SHASTER: Andrew, 504
SHATINGER: John, 550
SHATTS: Nancy
[HARTMAN], 246
SHATTUCK: B., JP, 272,
314, 490; Benjamin, JP,
114
SHAVER: Peter, 504
SHAW: Bridget, 504; Capt.,
70; David, JP, 442; Eli,
504; Henry, 504; John,
382; M.P., 296; Margaret,
504; Richard, 491, 504;
Robert, 56; Samuel C.,
JP, 298; Sarah, 504;

Tryphena [BINGHAM],
46; Upton, 504; Victor,
504; William, 504–5
SHAWKE: Jacob, 505
SHAWLEY: Simon, 166
SHAY: Col., 612; John,
Col., 593
SHEAFFER: Frederick,
369; Peter, 505
SHEARER: David, 505;
Hannah, 505; Henry, 329;
Jacob, 176, 505; Susanna
[DAVIS], 134
SHEARMAN: Col., 50
SHEARS: Peter, 505
SHEAVER: Jacob, 505
SHEBLEY: Margret
[RODES], 478
SHECKLER: Eve, 505;
Frederick, 505; Jacob,
505
SHEELER: Martin, 421
SHEELY: Sally [PLANK],
447
SHEETS: George, 506;
Henry, 506; Mary, 506;
Philip, 506
SHEETZ: John, 506
SHEFFER: Daniel, 6
SHEFFLEN: George, 506
SHEFFLER: Catharine,
506; George, 506
SHEIBLER: Frederick, 506
SHELAN: J., 49
SHELBY: James, 227;
Peter, JP, 334
SHELDING: E., Col., 364
SHELDON: Almira, 203;
Caroline [BALDWIN],
22; Col., 78, 131, 211,
345, 611; Israel B., 554;
Jonathan, 647; Rhoda
[EDWARDS], 165;
Thomas, 165
SHELHAMMER: Philip
Jacob, 506
SHELLEHAMER: Philip
Jacob, 506
SHELLER: Christian, JP,
469
SHELLEY: Elizabeth, 506;
Jacob, 506; John, 124;
Lewis, 506; Rosanna, 506
SHELLHAMMER: Philip
Jacob, 506

SHELLHORN: Baltzer H.,
506; Elizabeth, 506
SHELMIRE: David, 460
SHELTER: George M., JP,
456; Jacob H., 456
SHENCK: Daniel, 353
SHENEFELT: Henry, 506;
Nicholas, 506
SHENGLE: Peter, Capt.,
448
SHEPARD: Isaiah, 507;
Nathaniel, 608
SHEPHARD: William,
Col., 564
SHEPHERD: Benjamin,
507; David, 507; James,
479; Jesse M., 479;
Joseph, 507; Levi, 105;
Moses, 131, 507; Phineas,
507; Ruth, 507; Sarah,
507; Thomas, 340;
William, 507
SHEPLEY: Ann S.
[SCOTT], 497; Richard,
497; Samuel, JP, 75
SHEPPERD: Robert, 507
SHERARD: Samuel, 368
SHERBAND: David, 205
SHERBONDY: David, 465;
Frances [REAGAN], 465
SHERBURN: Col., 580
SHERE: Ann
[DENNISON], 140;
Samuel, 505
SHERER: David, 505;
Hannah, 505; Henry, 505;
James, 505; John, 505;
Mary A., 505; Robertson,
505; Samuel, 505
SHERETT: Robert, 550
SHERIDAN: Hannah
[McELROY], 377
SHERMAN: Christopher,
507; Col., 167, 268, 428;
Comfort [KALLAM],
301; D., JP, 403; J.C.,
440, 507; Jonathan C.,
301; Jonathan G., 526;
Laban S., JP, 583; Labon
L., JP, 148
SHERRADEN: Paul, JP,
452
SHERRED: John, Capt., 25
SHERRER: Christian, JP,
250; Christopher, JP, 318
SHERROD: David, JP, 115

SHERTZER: Isaac, JP, 439
SHERWIN: Abigail, 507;
Ahimaar, 23, 412;
Ahimaas, 507; *Alymaas,*
507; Daniel, 507; Jane,
507
SHERWOOD: Capt., 89
SHEWELL: Thomas, 381,
388
SHIELDS: Daniel, 339,
370, 410; David, 507
SHIFFERSTERNE:
Andrew, JP, 198
SHILAM: Col., 18
SHIMER: Elizabeth, 508,
515; Isaac, 508, 515;
Sylvanus, 289
SHINABARGER: George,
125
SHINDEL: Catharine, 508;
Elizabeth, 508; John, JP,
45; Maria, 508; Peter,
508; William H., JP, 138
SHINE: John, 538
SHINGLE: Peter, 508
SHINN: Benjamin, 403;
William, 403
SHIP: Thomas, 517
SHIPLEY: Adam, 508
SHIPMAN: John, 14, 454,
508, 628; Sarah, 508;
Silas, 508; Silas S., 508;
William, 109
SHIPPEN: Charles, 50;
Henry, 160, 552;
Jonathan, 50
SHIPPLY: Isaac, 592
SHIPTON: John, 508, 584
SHIRK: Cyrus, 489–90;
Jacob, 508
SHIRLEY: Daniel, 508;
Thomas, 508
SHIRTS: Matthias, 509;
Susana, 509
SHITZ: John, 214, 509;
Mary, 509
SHIVE: Lewis, 147, 509
SHIVELEY: Catharine,
509; Christiana, 509;
Daniel, 509; Jacob, 509;
John, 509
SHIVELY: Catharine, 509;
Daniel, 317; David P.,
176; Jacob, 509; Mathias,
Capt., 425

SHIVERS: Adam, 509;
Ann, 509; Thomas, 30
SHOALS: Capt., 379
SHOCK: Alfred, 351;
Jacob, 340; Nancy
[LITTLE], 340
SHOCKEY: Christian, 509;
Levi, 509; Mary, 509
SHOEMAKER: Abraham,
510; Anthony, 53;
Anthony, JP, 53; C.D., JP,
296; Henry, Capt., 141;
Peter, 359; Robert M.D.,
574; Rosanna, 313;
Samuel, 196, 313, 330,
340, 354, 471
SHOEMAN: Adam, 510
SHOENER: Henry, 510;
Mary M., 510
SHOLES: Capt., 597;
Lyman, 53, 84, 211, 363,
380, 433, 612, 623
SHOLL: Capt., 103
SHOME: John, 510
SHOMO: John, 510;
Joseph, 510
SHOOK: Daniel, 277; John,
277; Susannah [HUM],
277
SHOOP: Martin, 510
SHORE: Abraham, 387
SHORTS: Elizabeth, 525
SHOTT: A.H., 23
SHOTZ: John, 494
SHOUFLER: Valentine,
510
SHOUP: Elizabeth, 510;
Henry, 510; Henry Sr.,
510; Ludwig, 510
SHOUSE: Christian, 511;
J.A., 624; Mary, 511
SHOVER: Francis, 511
SHOW: William, JP, 339
SHOWBERGER: G., 161;
J.H., 161
SHREDER: Philip, 511
SHREFFLER: Henry, 511
SHREFLER: Henry, 511
SHREVE: Israel, Col., 511;
John, 511; Solomon, 511
SHRIBER: Frederick, 511
SHRIVER: Philip P., 511;
William J., 48
SHROTT: Samuel, 511
SHROYER: Matthias, 511

SHRUM: George, 495;
Henry, 512; Margaret,
512; Sarah, 495
SHRYOCK: Christian, 512
SHUBERT: Elizabeth, 512;
John, 512
SHUGERT: Samuel T., 473
SHUGHRUE: John, 302
SHULER: Henry, 512; John
R., JP, 176; John, Capt.,
344; Richard, 512
SHULTS: Anna
[MORGAN], 404
SHULTZ: David, 173, 395;
John, 110; Margaret, 512;
Mary, 110; Michael, 512
SHULZ: David, 110
SHULZE: Christian, 520
SHUMAN: George, JP, 55
SHUMWAY: Peter, 512
SHUNK: Francis R., 201
SHUP: Martin, 510
SHUPP: Elizabeth, 510;
Martin, 510
SHURE: Daniel F., 443
SHURK: -----, Mrs.
[KEIFFER], 304
SHURLUN: Henry, Col.,
437
SHUSTER: John, 518
SHUTTELL: Daniel, 512;
Maria, 512
SHUTZ: Matthias, 340;
Rosana, 147
SHUYER: Thaddeus B., 80
SIBNEY: Pamela, 9
SICHTING: John, 316
SICKLER: Michael, 512
SIDMAN: Eliza, 512;
Henrietta, 512; Isaac,
Col., 512; Maria, 512
SIEGER: Michael, 265, 486
SIEGFRIED: Col., 171;
Joseph, Capt., 224
SIELEG: Anthony, Capt.,
363
SIEMERS: Frederick M.,
513; Hannah, 513
SIGLE: Henry, 513
SILK: James, 513; Nancy,
513; Thomas, 29;
William, 29
SILL: Richard, 426, 576;
Thomas, 210
SILLY: Col., 177
SILVAS: Benjamin, 521

SILVERS: Benjamin, 334
SILVIS: Benjamin, 279
SIMISON: Boyd D., 216
SIMKINS: William, 204
SIMMERS: Catharine, 513;
  George, 513; Jacob, 513
SIMMONDS: William, 513
SIMMONS: Augustus, 513;
  Benjamin, 513; Daniel,
  513; Elizabeth, 513;
  Ellen, 513; George, 513;
  James, 513; Jeremiah H.,
  JP, 145; Jeremiah, Capt.,
  513; John, 245, 513; Julia
  Ann, 513; Margaret, 513,
  659; Mulvina L., 513,
  659; S.H., 191; Sarah,
  513; Stephen H., 426;
  Stephen, JP, 191;
  William, 399, 513
SIMMTON: William,
  Capt., 575
SIMON: Col., 536
SIMONS: Frederick, 514;
  Henry W., JP, 261
SIMONTON: Alexander,
  514; James H., 307;
  Mary, 514; Robert, 514;
  Thomas, 514
SIMPSON: A., 20;
  Alexander, 514; Capt.,
  56, 241; Edward, 560;
  J.D., 399; Mary, 514;
  Samuel, 82, 99, 111, 260,
  346, 433, 528, 613, 615;
  Silvanus, 514; Stephen,
  514; W.W., 284; William
  A., 140
SIMS: Catharine [MYERS],
  415; John, 514
SINCLAIR: Col., 389
SINGER: H.M., 107
SINGLEY: Barbara, 514;
  Catharine, 515; Elizabeth,
  514; George, 514; George
  W., 515; Jacob, 514;
  Margaret, 515; Nicholas,
  514; Peter C., 514;
  William, 514
SINK: Abraham, 515; Ann,
  515; Ellen, 515
SINNICKSON: Thomas,
  JP, 462
SINTER: Henry, 456
SINTON: J., 91, 261, 315,
  542, 556

SISK: Sally [BISBEE], 47
SITER: John, 100, 453
SITGREAVES: F.R., 469
SKEER: Albert, 427
SKELLY: William, 273
SKELTON: Hannah [LEE],
  330; John, 330
SKIFF: J.A., 544
SKILES: Elizabeth
  [RICHEY], 471; Hugh
  M., 186; Isaac, 105;
  Margaret [FLACK], 186;
  William, 368, 471
SKIMER: Elizabeth, 515;
  Isaac, 515; Mary, 515;
  Nancy/Ann, 515; Sarah,
  515; Susanna, 515
SKINNER: A., 94;
  Archibald, 451; C.K., JP,
  561; H.L., 95; Luther H.,
  JP, 33; Luther, JP, 395;
  Samuel, JP, 487
SKIPTON: Matthew, 515
SLACK: Henry, 499
SLANTON: Capt., 453
SLATER: Alanson, 213;
  William, JP, 49, 210
SLATHOM: Anthony, 515
SLATHOUR: Anthony, 515
SLAUGH: *Bernard*, 515
SLAUGHTER: William,
  515
SLAUTER: Jared, 6
SLAYMAKER: Nathaniel
  E., JP, 20
SLENTZ: Elizabeth
  [BOWMAN], 59
SLICK: William, 515
SLOAN: James, 516; John,
  JP, 31; Walter, 516;
  William, JP, 83
SLOANE: John R., 484
SLOCUM: William, 28
SLONAKER: Elizabeth
  [PHILLIPS], 444; Isaac,
  444
SLOTTERBACK: George,
  516; Margaret, 516;
  Michael, 516
SLOTTERER: Therisa
  [ROSHONG], 624;
  William, 624
SLOUGH: *Barnhart*, 515;
  Jacob, 515–16

SLUMP: Elizabeth
  [REEGER], 464; John,
  464
SMALL: David, JP, 216,
  559; Philip A., 71, 589;
  Samuel, 287
SMALLWOOD: Col., 438
SMECK: Henrietta
  [MANEBECK], 377;
  Samuel R., 356
SMETHEN: Waitel, 516
SMETHERS: Lowrey, 474
SMETZLEE: Elizabeth
  [WAGNER], 577
SMILEY: John, 95; John
  H., JP, 71; John H./N., JP,
  71, 89; Mary, 516;
  Samuel, 516; Susannah
  [MORGAN], 405
SMITH: Abraham, 289,
  516; Abram, Capt., 541;
  Adam, 516; Alexander,
  517; Ann, 520; Anthony,
  517; B.B., JP, 19, 56,
  105; Baltzer, 311;
  Barbara, 520, 660; Bela
  B., JP, 271, 389;
  Benjamin B., JP, 5, 99,
  129, 131, 224, 285, 560;
  Benjamin F., JP, 135,
  450, 622; Betsey, 521;
  Brig. Major, 548; C., 606;
  Capt., 36, 225, 381, 599;
  Catharine, 517, 520–21,
  660; Charles, 95, 339;
  Christian, 517; Clarinda
  [HICKOCK], 258;
  Clement, 382; Clifford,
  375; Col., 126, 528;
  Conrad, 517; Cornelius
  S., 268; Daniel, 47, 50,
  240, 335, 355, 401, 414,
  457, 494, 604–5, 620;
  David, JP, 232, 251;
  Davis, JP, 146; Deborah
  [GRANT], 220; Edward,
  166, 517–18; *Elhanan W.*,
  167; Elijah, 232, 565;
  Eliphald, 518; Eliphalet,
  518; Elizabeth, 484,
  517–20; Elizabeth
  [JAQUET], 289;
  Elizabeth [THOMPSON],
  560; Elizabeth S., 519;
  Emeline [ROWLAND],
  484; Eve Elizabeth, 518;

(SMITH, continued)

Frances [WEAVER], 587; Francis A.L., 116; Francis H., JP, 593; Franklin B., 623; Frederick, 267, 405; Frederick E., JP, 587; Frederick K., JP, 624; George, 8, 207, 518; Gideon, 518; Griffith, 518; Hannah, 517, 519; Henry, 179, 518, 521; Henry M., 225; Henry Sr., 519; Homan, 535; Hugh, 522; Hulet, 399; J., 190; J.W., 468, 517; Jacob, 362, 519, 541; James, 210, 239, 519; James 1st, 519; James 2nd, 519; James E., 519; James H., 56; James M., 520; James S., 158; James S. Jr., 519; Jane, 519–21; Jemima, 519; Jerusha C., 74; Johannes, 660; John 3rd, 520, 660; John 4th, 520; John A., 517; John Boyd, 60; John F., 106, 241, 310, 395; John K., 16; John N., 519; Jonathan, 21, 41, 53, 198, 311, 315, 320, 379, 382, 439, 514, 517–20, 660; Joseph, 163, 516, 520, 564; Joseph L., 522; Joseph W., JP, 52; Joshua, 383; Josiah W., 298; Julia J., 74; Kenderton, 220; Lenas, 468; Leo, JP, 156; Lewis W., JP, 256; Lloyd, JP, 215; Lucy, 521; Lucy W. [JONES], 297; Magdalena, 519; Margaret [DIXON], 147; Margaret [POPE], 450; Mary, 52, 207, 518–21; Mary [ELDRIDGE], 167; Mary [HARRAR], 243; Mary [THOMPSON], 559; Matthew, Capt., 589; Merrit, 376; Nathan, 91, 479; Nehemiah L., 560; Peter, 521; Philip, 512, 517, 521; Philip J., 147; Polly, 366; Polly [HEWIT], 257;

R. Rundle, 521; Rachel, 518; Rhoda [JONES], 297; Robert, 45, 200, 521; Robert M., 373; S. Mervin, JP, 152, 291; S.T.W., 258; Sally, 522; Sally [COREY], 114; Sally [ELDRIDGE], 167; Sampson, 519; Samuel, 106, 287, 521, 602; Samuel A., 251, 576; Samuel F., 545; Samuel Jr., 521; Samuel S., 519; Sarah, 494; Sarah [TOWNSEND], 564; Simeon, 521–22; Simon, 271; Theodore H., 400; Thomas, 108, 260, 366, 522, 618; Thomas 1st, 522; Thomas 2nd, 522; Thomas A., 518; Thomas D., 226, 283; Thomas P., 63; Townsend, 564; W.R., JP, 60; William, 69, 232, 517–18, 520, 522; William 2nd, 522; William B., 559; William F., 283; William H., 454; Wilson, 183; Ziba, 286
SMITLEY: Michael, 271
SMOCK: Capt., 443
SNAVELY: Capt., 4
SNEDICKER: Garret, 523
SNEDIKER: Garret, 523
SNELBAKER: David T., JP, 162
SNELL: David, 523; Mary, 523
SNETHEN: Nancy, 516; Waitel, 516
SNEVILY: John, 5
SNIDER: Isaac, 253; John, 523
SNIVELY: Capt., 347; Matthew, 344
SNODGRASS: Robert, 25, 176, 251, 303
SNOOK: Cornelius, 244
SNOW: Eunice, 523
SNOWDEN: James R., 7, 156; James Ross, 51, 475; Samuel, 188; Sophia, 11
SNYDER: Abram, 145; Adam, 523; Andrew, 523; Capt., 113, 620; Catharine, 523–24;

Catharine [FRAZER], 195; Charles A., 46; Daniel, 524; David, 68; Dieter, 524; E.G., 216; Elizabeth, 524; Elizabeth [CARNES], 87; Elizabeth [WEAVER], 587; Elizabeth [WEIGELL], 589; Eugene, 62; George, 87, 387, 524; Henry, 459, 524, 581; Jacob, 524; James, 597; John, 449, 474, 523–24; John J., JP, 107, 276; John L., 205; John P., 524; Jonas, 75, 392; Joseph, 187; Joshua, 61; Margaret, 523; Mary [WALTERS], 581; Michael, Capt., 123, 176; Peter, 276; Philenah, 71; Simon, 46; William, JP, 68
SOCKMAN: Henry, 524
SOHN: Alberdina, 525; David, 524; George I., 525; Jacob, 524
SOLLADAY: John, 525
SOLLIDAY: Catherine, 525; Daniel, 525; George, 243, 273, 525; John, 525; Margaret, 525; Mary, 525
SOLT: Daniel, 525; Eve, 525; John, 525; Maria, 525; Paul, 525
SOMERS: Samuel, 19
SOMMERS: Elizabeth, 525; Leonard, 525; Margaret, 525
SONDAY: Adam, 525; Hannah, 525; Mary E., 525
SONEENS: Michael, 526
SONES: Amos, 526; Jackson, 526; Peter, 526
SONTAG: Elizabeth [WANN], 582; Jacob, 582
SOODER: Eva, 526; John, 526
SOPER: David, JP, 498
SORTER: Peter, 526
SOUTH: Allen, 586; Benjamin, 526; Delilah, 526
SOUTHERLAND: John, 526

SOUTHWELL: Asahel, 526; Dolly, 526; Hannah, 526
SOUTHWICK: Amasa, 232; Arnold, 527; David, 527; Jonathan, 527; Lemuel, 527; Mary, 527
SOUTHWORTH: William, 527
SOWDER: Christopher, 527
SOWERS: John C., JP, 231; Michael, 527
SOWERS: Michael, 526
SPAHN: George, JP, 49
SPALDING: Howard, JP, 408; John, 527; Simon, Capt., 579
SPANGENBERG: Mary [GANGWER], 203; Thomas, JP, 1, 263, 277, 306
SPANGENBURG: Catharine, 527; Daniel, 527; Elizabeth, 527; Frederick, 527; Jacob, 527; John, 527; Rebecca, 527; W.H., 527
SPANGERBURG: Elizabeth, 527; John, 527
SPANGLER: Basil L., 472; C., 282; C.E., 351; Capt., 216; Daniel, 88; George, 527; Harriet, 528; Joseph K., 528; Mary Ann, 527; Rudolph, Capt., 123; Sarah, 527; Zachariah, JP, 77, 120, 321, 440, 530, 533, 578, 590
SPARHAWK: Thomas P., 434
SPARR: John, 528
SPARROW: Lydia, 528; Stephen, 528
SPARRY: John, 528
SPATZ: Michael, 528
SPAULDING: Charles, 528; John, 105, 528; John G., 477; Sarah, 528; Simon, Capt., 42, 90, 605; Wealthy Ann, 528; Zebulon B., 528
SPAYA: Joseph D., 40
SPEAR: Isaac, 376; Joshua, 528; Robert, JP, 110, 343;

Samuel, 71; William, JP, 247
SPECHT: Adam, 528; Christian, 528; William, 28
SPEER: Abraham, 529; David, 255; Robert, 136
SPEERS: Susannah [SPONG], 531
SPELMAN: H.B., 99; Luther, JP, 106, 407, 617
SPENCER: Amandus, 529; Daniel, 529; Elam, 529; Elam Willis, 529; Eunice, 529; George T., 543; Hiram, 529; John, 529; Joshua G., JP, 331; Lovina [ROWLEY], 484; Orange, 529; P.R., 140; Peter, 529; Russel, JP, 543; Samuel, 530; Sue [WHEELER], 595
SPENGLER: Capt., 33
SPENSLER: A., JP, 307; A.L., JP, 368
SPERA: William, 530
SPERD: William, 530
SPERING: John, 530; Joshua, 530; William, 2, 196, 308
SPERRY: Bethiah [WINSLOW], 610; Catherine [IDLE], 282; Joy, JP, 522
SPETH: Jacob, 530
SPICER: Amos Jr., 210; John, 530; Samuel, 530
SPICKLER: Samuel, 258
SPIEGEL: Lawrence, 530
SPIEHLMAN: Henry, 537
SPIELMAN: George, 107
SPIER: Margaret [SHAW], 504
SPIGELMYER: Shem, 608
SPIRES: John, 530
SPOHN: Catharine, 531; Philip, 531; William, 110, 295, 315, 612
SPOKN: Philip, 531
SPONG: Catherine, 531; Elizabeth, 531; Jacob, 531; John, 531; John Leonard, 531; Margaret, 531; Susannah, 531; William, 531

SPONK: Elizabeth, 531; Jacob, 531
SPONSLER: A.L., JP, 194
SPOON: Abraham, 531
SPOOR: Abraham, 529, 531; David, 529; Rebecca, 531; Rebekah, 529
SPORTZ: John, 494
SPOUG: John Leonard, 531; Margaret, 531
SPRAGUE: Eleanor, 614, 663; Elizabeth, 531; Ezra, 228; Gideon, JP, 405; Harriet A. [GRISWOLD], 228; Henry, 531; John, 531
SPRING: Joseph, 188
SPRINGER: Capt., 261; Crawford, 532; J.D., JP, 367; J.S., 337; Jacob, 532; James, 389; Jonathan D., JP, 615; M., Capt., 566; Martha, 532; Uriah, 532
SPRINGFIELD: William, 532
SPRINGUM: John, 532
SPROTT: S.W., 465
SPROUGHT: Col., 122
SPROUT: Col., 492, 534; Ebenezer, Col., 74, 107
SPURREL: Edward, Capt., 361
SPYKER: Samuel, 367, 429
SQUIB: Abram, 70
SQUIER: James, 199
SQUIRE: Elisha, 532; Ezra, 532; Huldah, 532
ST. CLAIR: Col., 164, 264, 609; Daniel, 536; Daniel P., 536; Isabella, 536; William, JP, 33
ST. JOHN: Chancelor, JP, 597
STABB: John, 533
STABLER: Lohrens, 471
STACEY: Davis B., 481
STACKHOUSE: Henry, 533; John, 533; Joseph, 533
STACY: Joseph, JP, 333, 499
STADDEN: William, 533
STAFFORD: David, 533; Job, 448–49; Sarah, 533
STAGE: Benjamin, 533

STAGER: John S., JP, 145
STAGG: Benjamin, 533
STAHL: Abraham, 483
STAHLE: Barbara, 534;
Jacob, 534
STAHLER: Daniel, 624;
Lohrens, JP, 624
STAHLEY: Jacob, 534
STAIDINGER: David, 541
STAKE: Capt., 100
STALEY: Catherine, 534;
George, 534; Jacob, 534;
John, 534; Mary, 534
STALFORD: J.P., JP, 168
STALL: Elias, 208
STALLSMITH: Israel, 61
STALY: John, 443
STANCLIFT: Comfort,
534; Lemuel, 534;
Samuel, 534
STANDEFF: Russell, 261
STANDLY: Lucinda
[SEWARD], 502
STANLEY: Andrew, 84,
284; Sylvester, JP, 398
STANNARD: Claudius,
534; Eliahim, 365
STANSBURY: W., JP, 167
STANSON: Hugh, Capt.,
578
STANTON: Affa
[BISBEE], 47; Capt., 78,
211; Col., 234; Edwin M.,
591; Emily, 534; Jason,
534; Jason D., 534; Sally,
534
STAPLES: John, 535;
Luke, 535; Lydia, 535;
Margaret, 535
STAPLETON: William Jr.,
246; William, JP, 246
STARBIRD: Franklin, JP,
535; John, 535
STARBRID: John, 535
STARK: Adam, 268; D.S.,
619; David, 300; Enos,
321; J. Duane, JP, 416;
Samuel, 445
STARKEY: Esther, 535;
Joseph, 535
STARKS: Charles, 535;
Elizabeth, 535; Samuel,
535
STARKWEATHER: D.A.,
156
STARLIN: Gen., 243

STARMAN: Col., 236
STARN: Smith, JP, 112
STARNER: Samuel, 420
STARR: Abigail, 536;
Elijah, 535; Moses, 535;
Samuel Moore, 536;
Smith, JP, 325, 484
STATSER: David, 536
STATTLER: Samuel Jr.,
152
STATZER: David, 536;
Elizabeth, 536
STAUB: Christiana, 533;
John, 533
STAUFFER: Ann C., 545;
Christian, 255; George,
545; Henry, 545; Sarah,
545
STAUNTON: Robert, 536
STEACY: John, JP, 8
STEADMAN: John C., 111
STEAMON: Richard, 211
STEARNS: John, 536;
Mary, 536
STEBBINS: James H., 299
STEBER: Capt., 274
STECK: George, 393–94;
Jacob S., JP, 329
STECKEL: William, 420
STEED: James, 536
STEEL: Archibald, 537;
David, 537; Geoge F.,
345; Isaac, 138; Jane,
537; John, 537; Leah
[DECKER], 138; Mary,
328; Mary [BEATTY],
35; Rebecca, 537;
Richard, 537
STEELE: Capt., 570;
David, 537; Jane, 537;
Richard, 537
STEEN: Catharine, 537;
John, 537; Robert, 202,
402, 594
STEENBACK: Cyrus, 78;
Dolly [BARNES], 78
STEENE: John, 537
STEEVER: Daniel, 537;
Leonard, 537; Margaret,
537
STEFFE: Jacob, 304
STEG: Capt., 263
STEIGER: Abraham, 537
STEIN: A.G., 163; John,
108; John, JP, 96

STEINBURGH: Dolly
[SOUTHWELL], 526
STEINHIZER: Christopher,
537
STEINHYSER:
Christopher, 537
STEINHYZER:
Christopher, 537
STEINMAN: George, 274
STELL: William S., 265
STENGEL: Catharine
[Breneze], 63; Conrad,
63; Mary, 63; Peggy, 63
STENTZ: Philip, 382
STEPHENS: Chester, 461;
David, 539; Esther, 538;
George A., 38; Giles,
538; Isaac, 538, 600;
Joshua, 461; Paul, 538;
R.T., JP, 505; Reuben T.,
JP, 19
STEPHENSON: Capt.,
428; Elijah, 539; John,
342, 538; Jonathan G.,
236; Lt., 594; Margaret,
538; W.M., 119; William,
538
STERICHER: Justus, 538
STERIGERE: Jonathan B.,
464, 538; Justus, 538
STERLING: Elizabeth
[KELLER], 305; Gen.,
77; James, 548; John,
505; Levi, 538
STERMER: George, JP,
123; Joseph, JP, 563
STERN: David, 301;
Samuel, 306
STERNER: Christian, 538
STERPER: Daniel Jr., 593
STERRETT: Joseph M.,
469
STEVENS: Almon, 424;
Asa, JP, 64, 91, 535;
Benjamin R., JP, 100,
312; David, 424; E.L.,
432; Ebenezer, 539;
Elijah, 424; Eliza
[CUMMING], 126;
Elizabeth, 424; Fitz H.,
145; Hannah [TUBBS],
566; Irad, JP, 555;
Jonathan, 30, 57, 424;
Lucy, 518; Mary, 538;
Mary [MYERS], 415;
Nathaniel, 538;

(STEVENS, continued)

Phebe [McCLOUD], 370; Rachel, 539; S.S., 524; Samuel, JP, 41; Simon, 64, 436, 523; T.A., 577; Vincent, 539; William, 539
STEVENSON: A., 52, 175, 474, 620–21; Alexander, 539; Augustine, 25, 179, 294, 303; Augustus, 91, 380; George, 539; H., 211; Hugh, 646; James, 175, 539; James B., 250; John, 378; John B., 445, 476; John M., 539; Joseph, 249; Maria, 539; Nancy, 487; Nathaniel, 539; Rebecca, 614, 663; Reuben M., 56; Sarah, 539; William, 242, 540
STEWARD: A.B., 303; Col., 340–41; Walter, Col., 94
STEWART: Absalom, 104; Andrew, 47, 176, 394; Ann [YOUNG], 621; Archibald, 302, 540–41; Berekiah, 185; Catherine, 541; Charles, 540, 547; Christopher, 540; Col., 61, 149, 224, 343, 594; D.H., 279; David H., 540; Elizabeth, 540; Franklin, 226; Frederick, 238; G., 37; George, 540; Hugh, 540; James, 541; James 1st, 541; James 2nd, 541; John B., JP, 145, 550; Jonathan, 159, 246, 541; Lydia [HUNT], 279; Mary, 540, 547; Mary [FISHER], 185; Mary [RUSK], 487; Rebecca, 540; Robert, 73, 167, 291, 578, 622; Robert G., 137; Ruth Ann, 541; Samuel, 29; Thomas, 469, 541; Walter, Col., 171, 412; William, 238, 332
STICKEL: Hannah, 541; Valentine, 541
STICKNEY: Charles B., 307
STIDINGER: John, 541

STILES: Jonathan D., 132, 139, 332; William L., 560
STILL: Samuel W., 102; William, 541
STILLÉ: W. Gray, 63, 436, 551, 592; William G., 450
STILLING: Benjamin, 542
STILLWAGGON: Frederick, 542; Margaret, 542
STILLWELL: Capt., 337, 577
STILWAGON: Philip, 542
STILZ: J. George, 332
STIMMEL: Fanny, 542; Isaac, 542
STINE: Daniel, JP, 39, 282
STINGERE: Jonathan B., 509
STINGFELD: Elizabeth, 532
STINSON: Elijah, 542; Elizabeth, 542; William, 542
STINTZEN: Jack, Col., 93
STIVERS: Samuel B., 15
STOCK: George, 542; Henry, 488; Richard, 357
STOCKDALE: James, JP, 158, 365
STOCKER: Elizabeth [KESSLER], 310; Jonathan, 310
STOCKING: A.W., JP, 259
STOCKTON: Joseph, Rev., 385; Robert Clark, 123
STOCKWELL: Charles, JP, 228
STODDARD: Capt., 200
STOEVER: Frederick Jr., 260; William H., 329, 376
STOKELEY: Joseph, 543; Nehemiah, 543; Polley, 543; Susannah, 543
STOKELY: J., JP, 379, 542; Joseph, 51, 62, 117, 271, 310, 501, 587
STOKES: Capt., 235; Charles, 579
STOLL: Adam, 543; Andrew, 543; Catharine, 543; Frederick, 543; Valentine, 239
STONE: Abigail, 543–44; Axy, 543; Baltus, 543; *Battus*, 543; Bille, 543;

Col., 327; Dorothea, 544; Earl, 543; Ebenezer, 543; H.W., 529; Hannah, 543; J., 508; John B., JP, 243, 532; Mary, 543; Nelson B., 191; Prudence [COLVIN], 108; Rachel, 543; S.M., 116; Susan [DUEY], 143; W.R., 220, 543; Westcott, 543–44; William, 544
STONEBRAKER: Adam, 544; Valentine, 544
STONER: Henry, 143; Jacob, 544; John, 142, 544; Lydia [DEUTZLER], 142
STOOPE: Andrew, 544; Israel, 544; Sarah, 544
STOOVER: Maria [BARNHART], 28
STOPE: Jacob, 544; Mary, 544
STORER: Richard W., 250
STORMBAUGH: Eliza [LINDY], 338
STORY: John, 544
STOUFFER: Ann C., 545; Henry, 545
STOUGH: Andrew, 545; Elizabeth, 545; George, 173–74; Jacob, 173; Jacob Jr., 174; Margarett [EATINGER], 173; Samuel, JP, 209; Susan [EATINGER], 173
STOUGHT: Andrew, 545
STOUGHTON: Augustus, 545
STOUT: Abraham, 545; Charles M., 300; Christian, 524; Jacob W., 463; John, 545; Joseph, 152; Mary, 545
STOVER: Abraham, 369, 493; Abraham F., 361
STOW: Hiram S., 325
STRAHAN: Gregory, 545; Joseph, 545; Margaret, 545; Mary, 545
STRAIN: Alexander, 7; Elizabeth [ALSWORTH], 7
STRAIT: Samuel, JP, 114
STRANG: Francis, JP, 249
STRANT: Col., 1

STRATTON: Charles, 486; Franklin, 3; John R., JP, 389; Lot, 545; Rebecca, 274; Samuel, 545; Samuel T., 274; Thomas, 545

STRAUCH: Capt., 482

STRAUS: John, 367

STRAW: Catharine, 546; Christian, 546; Elizabeth [DUEY], 143; George, 143; Nicholas, 546; Rachel, 546

STRAWBRIDGE: George, 87

STREET: Zadok, 60

STREETER: Adams, 546; Nancy, 546; Naphtali, 546; Rufus, 546

STREMBECK: Catharine, 546; Jacob, 546

STRICKER: Jacob, 546, 639

STRICKLAND: Polly [DEWITT], 140

STRICKLER: John N., JP, 219; Sarah, 219

STRIGHT: Apphia [JONES], 297

STRINGFELLOW: Sarah [McCARTY], 368

STRINGFIELD: William, 532

STROCK: Moses L., JP, 245

STROHECKER: G.W., Dr., 150

STROHL: Christian, 544; George, 544; Henry, 544; Jacob, 544, 546; John, 544; Mary, 544, 546; Samuel, 544

STROKE: Michael, Col., 176

STROMAN: Catharine, 546; Jonathan, 546; Jonathan R., 67, 546

STRONG: Abel, JP, 109; David, Capt., 277; John, 546; Lydia, 546; Walter, 412

STROOP: Elizabeth, 547; George, 547; Henry, 547; John, 547

STROUD: Col., 391; Daniel, 404; Fanny [ELDRIDGE], 167;

George M., 547, 571; Jacob, Col., 15, 141, 322–23

STROUGH: Nicholas, 547

STROUP: Elizabeth [HARTCHY], 245; Ellen [BRODHEAD], 66

STROUS: Jacob, 547

STRUMPH: W.W., 47

STRUNK: Amos K., JP, 589; Barbara, 547; Jacob, 313, 547; John, 547; Jonas, 547; Joseph, 547; Mary, 547; Sarah, 547; William, 547

STUARD: Charles, 547

STUART: Col., 7; James P., 587

STUBER: Charles, 491

STUDELLMAN: John, 547

STUDER: Philip, 548

STULL: Andrew, 279; Henry, 177; Sarah [FALKNER], 177

STULLS: Daniel, Capt., 59

STUMP: George, 548; George A., 548

STUMPF: W.W., JP, 557; William W., JP, 255; William, JP, 261

STURDIVANT: John, 127

STURGEON: Robert, 548

STURGES: Charles M., 548; George, 548; Isaac, 548; Joseph, 548; Lewis, 548, 551; Lewis B., 48, 184, 189, 418, 611; Lewis N., 88; Lucinda, 548; Maria, 548; Mary Ann, 548; Thaddeus B., 484

STURGIS: John P., 100

STYER: John, 379

STYLES: Catharine, 548; Henry, 548

STYVERS: Daniel, 548

SUBER: John, JP, 414

SUGART: Eli, 549; John, 549

SUHLER: Rudolph, JP, 150

SUITE: James, 647

SULLIVAN: Capt., 431; Gen., 337; John, 387

SUMMER: Margaret [CLANBAUGH], 97

SUMMERS: Andrew, 555; Anna, 549;

Benjamin, JP, 112; Calvin, 549; David, 549; Ira, 549, 583; James, 549; Mary, 549; Peter, 549; Polly, 549

SUMMERSON: Elizabeth [SHAFFER], 503; Sarah [SHAFFER], 503

SUNDERLAND: Joseph, 549; Mary, 549; Samuel, 549; Thomas, 549

SUNDERLING: Sarah [WOLF], 613

SUNDERLN: Elizabeth, 491; Samuel, 491

SUPLER: John, 549; Rachel, 549

SUPPLEE: John, JP, 48; Peter, JP, 110

SUSSLER: Peter, JP, 10

SUTCH: George, 549; Jane, 549

SUTER: Charlette, 122; Solomon, JP, 122

SUTHERLAND: Alexander, JP, 455; Christiana [McCOY], 373; John, 526; Thomas C., 417; William, 488

SUTLIFF: A.C., JP, 145; Samuel, 81

SUTPHIN: John H., 549

SUTTON: A.G., JP, 20; Albert G., JP, 307; Barbara, 550; Catharine, 550; Daniel, 550; Ephraim, 550; Hannah, 550; Isaac H., 550; Jane [BROWN], 71; John, 550; Levi R., JP, 463; Myers, 71; Philip, 550; Sarah, 550

SWABLY: Hunter, 270; Peter, 270

SWAGER: Adam, 550

SWAGERS: George, 550

SWAIN: Anthony, 550; John, 38

SWAN: John Sr., 550

SWARTAGA: Henry, 551

SWARTOUT: Capt., 17

SWARTS: Phineas, 551

SWARTWART: Mary M. [ALDEN], 3

SWARTWOOD: Barnabus, 551; Barnardus, 551;

(SWARTWOOD, continued)

Daniel, 551; John, 551;
Mary M., 551; Moses,
551; Peter, 551
SWARTZ: Ludwick, 551;
Mary [STENGEL], 63;
Nancy, 551; Philip, 551;
Phineas, 551
SWATGA: Henry, 551
SWAVELY: Catharine
[HARTMAN], 246;
Hunter, 270; Peter, 270
SWAYER: Capt., 538
SWAZE: Alice, 552;
Betsey, 552; Daniel, 552;
David, 552; Edith, 552;
Jane, 552; Sarah, 552;
William, 552
SWEARIGAN: Capt., 6
SWEARINGEN: Joseph C.,
419
SWEARINGIN: Andrew,
Capt., 93
SWEARNGEN: L.W., 131
SWEEDS: John, 478;
Joseph Rodgers, 478
SWEENEY: Capt., 101;
Hugh, 552; T., Capt., 379
SWEENY: Edward, 552;
Joseph, 552; Joseph Jr.,
552
SWEERT: Reuben, 552
SWEET: Joshua, 552
SWEIER: Thomas, 270
SWEIR: Isaac, 132
SWENEY: John, JP, 576;
Samuel, 90, 487
SWENK: John B., 316
SWENSON: Andre, 75,
118, 169, 179, 184, 189,
505, 554; Andrew, 131,
285
SWENTZEL: Christian,
552; Frederick, 552
SWENTZELL: Frederick,
552
SWESY: Daniel, 553; Mary,
553
SWETLAND: Luke, 553;
William, 553
SWETZE: John, 414
SWIFT: H., Col., 57;
Herman, Col., 183
SWINK: Elizabeth, 553;
Jacob, 553

SWISHER: Abraham,
Capt., 263
SWITZEN: George, 553
SWITZER: George, 553
SWOOPE: John, 266
SWOPE: Col., 494, 553,
590; Michael, Col., 263
SYBERG: Capt., 347
SYKES: Henry, 553
SYLVUS: Jacob, 464; Lydia
[REEGER], 464
SYMMES: Capt., 178, 231,
609
SYPE: Catharine, 553;
Charles, 553; Christopher,
553; Jacob, 553; Jonas,
553; Mary, 553; Philip,
553; Susannah, 553;
Tobias, 553
SYPERT: Henry, 500, 554;
Mary, 500, 554

TAFT: Matthew, 554
TAGGART: Cardiff, 129;
Samuel, 576
TAINTOR: Erving, 211–12
TALBERT: Capt., 21, 97
TALBOT: B.W., JP, 424
TALCOTT: Eleazer, 554;
Sally, 554
TALLER: Capt., 141
TALLMAN: George, 9;
Jeremiah, JP, 363
TALOR: Caleb, JP, 88
TANNER: Archibald, 39,
207; Edmund T., 554;
Polly, 554; Ruth, 554;
Tryal, 554; William, 554
TANNYHILL: Agnes
[NEWELL], 419; James,
419
TANTTINGER: John, JP,
185
TAPPAN: C.W., 21
TAPPIN: John, Col., 468
TARBELL: *Jno.,* 192
TARMEN: Mary
[ANDERSON], 9
TARPENING: Lawrence,
554
TARPERNNING:
Lawrence, 554; Lucy, 554
TARR: Casper, JP, 597;
Esther [REAGAN], 465;

Gasper, JP, 205; James
R., 597; John B., 465
TASSEY: James, 169, 562;
John, 5
TASSY: John, 617
TATE: Hannah
[ZEIGLER], 624; Ruth
[RIMMEY], 473
TATHAM: George N., 192,
221, 469
TAUGHINBAUGH:
Margaret [LEAS], 329
TAYLER: Aaron, 292;
Amy [JOB], 292; John,
259, 536, 560; M.B., 348,
402, 435, 438
TAYLOR: Abraham, 330,
555; Alanson, 408, 655;
Alle [WILKINSON],
602; Amos, 186, 285;
Andrew I., JP, 285; Ann,
555–56; Ann [INSKEEP],
283; Azuha, 555; Capt.,
102; Charlotte [JAY],
207; Cyrus, 602; Daniel,
595; David B., 576;
David, JP, 11, 135;
Edward, 555; Elisha, 555;
Elizabeth [LOWE
GREEN], 555; Elizabeth
[NEWELL], 419; Ethel,
555; Ezra B., JP, 437;
George, 216, 356, 384,
419; Israel, 448; James,
555; James D., 404; Jesse,
376; John, 44, 63–64,
73–74, 143, 177, 198,
216, 230–31, 261, 285,
307, 336, 373, 388, 398,
419, 429, 431, 441, 457,
471–72, 484, 523, 552,
555, 560, 569, 582, 591,
593, 617; John A., 556;
Joseph, 379; Joshua,
Capt., 418; Lucinda
[KALLAM], 301; Mary,
556; Matthew, 419;
Moses, JP, 285; Peggy,
555; Reuben, 556;
Robert, 283; S., 140;
Samuel W., 377; Sarah,
556; Simon, 556;
Susannah [DEWITT],
139; T.J., 552; Thomas,
190, 555;
Timothy, Capt., 15;

(TAYLOR, continued)

William, 556; William
2nd, 556
TEAFFE: Henry, 556; John,
556; Mary, 556
TEAL: Adam, 556; Cathrin,
556; John, 556
TEATS: Hugh H., JP, 237
TEEL: Mary, 36
TEEPLE: Elijah, 76
TEESE: Christina [DYER],
162; John G., 162
TEETER: Jacob, Capt., 263
TEEZDALL: Emily R., 342
TEGHTMYER: Henry, JP,
227
TEIN: George, 562
TELLER: Rufus, 68
TEMPLE: Archelaus, 557;
Eunice, 557
TENANT: Isaac M., 56;
John C., 54; Robert, 71
TENERY: Sarah, 557;
William, 557
TENNATE: Ami, 230
TENNEY: Daniel, JP, 6
TERPENNING: Lawrence,
554; Lucy, 554; Rachel
Ann, 554
TERREL: Elihu, 557
TERRELL: Annis, 238;
Elihu, 557; Harry, JP, 37,
238, 335, 404, 557;
William, 184; William J.,
169, 189, 342, 554;
William P., 477
TERRY: Benjamin, 557;
Daniel, JP, 404; George,
557; Henry R., JP, 97;
Lucily [METCALF], 399;
Seth, JP, 106; Uriah, 42,
479; Warner, 135;
William, 557
TETER: Samuel, Capt., 591
TETTERS: Elizabeth
[WILT], 592
TEVIS: Elizabeth, 557;
John, 557; Joseph, 557;
Julia Ann, 557; Margaret,
557; Mary, 557; Rezin,
557; Sarah, 557
TEWKSBURY: Lucinda
[FULLER], 200

THACHER: Arthur, 557;
Obadiah, 503; Peter O.,
JP, 64
THARP: Huldah
[WOODMANCY], 615;
James, 588, 615; Paul,
557; Reuben, 557
THARPE: Lodewyk, 576,
583
THATCHER: Thomas, 558
THAYER: Esick, 558;
Esther, 558; Hiram 2nd,
593; James, 558; Jane,
558; Joel, 558; John, JP,
586
THOLES: Lyman, JP, 137
THOMAS: A.E., 242, 459;
Asa, 558; Caleb, 43, 117,
168, 402, 558, 590; Capt.,
422; Daniel, 384, 414,
445; David, 434, 558;
Ephraim, 558; Francis,
559; George, 4; James,
640; Jesse, 169; John,
559; Jonathan W., 29,
220; Joseph, 559; Mary,
271; Morgan J., 417;
Owen, 559; Phebe, 559;
Polly, 558; S., Capt., 362;
S.J., 162; Sally, 499;
Samuel H., 113; Thomas,
559
THOMMAN: Frederick,
69, 113, 514
THOMPKINS: Phineas,
563
THOMPSON: Adam, JP,
196; Alexander, 95, 117,
168, 266, 331, 449, 527;
Anthony, Capt., 190;
Benjamin, 543; Capt.,
469; Charles, 309, 600;
Col., 91, 428, 537; David
K., JP, 299; Elizabeth,
560; Epaphras, 559;
Esther, 560; J., Capt.,
588; J.G., JP, 239; James,
50, 177, 390, 404, 448,
532, 559; Jared, 560; Job,
559; John, 204, 213, 331,
415, 602; John 2nd, 560;
John B., 191; Joseph,
560; Josiah, 457; Lucy,
560; Mabel, 560; Marcy
[WILKINSON], 602;
Mary, 559–60;

Nancy, 331; Peter, 560;
R., 560; R.P., 462;
Robert, 71, 309, 585, 600,
610; Sally, 560; Samuel,
447; Seth, 432, 560; Seth
Jr., 560; Thankfull B.,
560; W.O., 56; William,
410, 419, 560, 602;
William J., JP, 219, 267,
355, 385; William O., 19
THOMSON: Alden, 560;
Cyntha Lorinda, 560;
James, 559; Joseph, 560;
Rebeca, 50; Thomas, JP,
50; W.P., 155; William,
JP, 235
THONSON: Joseph, 560
THONY: Capt., 345
THORNE: John, JP, 208
THORNTON: J.R., 647; R.,
140
THORP: *Aches* [GOLDY],
215; Anna [COVERT],
180; Col., 324; James,
557; Jonathan, 180;
Pharis, 203; Reuben, 557;
William, 232
THRALL: Reuben, 548;
Walter, 548
THROCK: Elijah, 367
THROCKMORTON:
Joseph, 561
THROP: Aches [GOLDY],
215, 643
THRUSH: Jacob, 561
THULER: T.F., 656
THURBER: Amos, 561;
Harriet N., 29; Maria, 561
THURNLER: George, 120
THURSTON: Nicholas, 31
THUYER: Ebenezer V.,
151
TIBBEN: Catharine, 561;
Henry, 561
TIBBET: Jemima
[YOUNG], 622
TIBBETS: E., 2, 59–60
TIBBIN: Henry, 561
TIBBS: J.W. Jr., 392
TIDD: James, 5; Joseph,
270
TIERNAN: -----, 157
TIFFANY: Alfred, 561;
Anna, 561; Anna
[SCOTT], 495; Aranah,
366; Ason, 78;

(TIFFANY, continued)

Chandler, 561; Dalton, 561; *H.,* JP, 200; Hosea, 561, 564; John, 561; Laura [BARNES], 78; Lewis, 561; Melo, 561; Orvil, 561; Peletiah, 561; Preston, 561; Thomas, 561; Tingley, 561; Virgil, 561; William C., JP, 314
TILDEN: A.P., 41; Daniel, 562; Esther, 562; Harriet, 562; Josiah, 562; Lucretia, 562; Lydia, 562; Mary, 562; Mason, 562; Sabin, 562; Stephen D., 562
TILLEY: Capt., 125
TILTON: James A., 562; John, 562
TIMMS: Absalom, 562
TINDALL: Elizabeth, 562; Margaret, 562; Sarah, 562; Thomas, 562; William, 562; Zachariah, 562
TINE: George, 562
TINGLEY: Charles, 574; Mason, 19; Sabra [YEOMANS], 621
TIPPER: Andrew, 562, 610; Charles, 562; Mary, 562
TISDEL: Silas A., JP, 105, 238
TITUS: James, 583; John, 539; Patty [WARNER], 583
TOBIAS: Rachel [RUSSELL], 488
TOBIN: Isaac, 563; Thomas, 563
TODD: Andrew, JP, 235; Isaac, 112; James Jr., 36; Samuel, JP, 194; Thomas, 386; William, 32, 88, 416, 495, 563
TOLAND: *George W.,* 67; Jane, 411; John, 6; Robert, 29, 67, 207, 214, 328, 387, 522, 530, 578
TOLBERT: Samuel, Capt., 131
TOME: Henry, 563

TOMLINSON: Giles H., JP, 309; Samuel, JP, 405
TOMPKINS: Filor S., 495; Joseph, 233; Phineas, 563; William, JP, 59, 407
TONER: Catharn [WAGNER], 577; James, 563
TOOPS: Leonard, 563; Margaret, 563
TOPHAM: Reuben, 563
TOPPIN: Col., 431, 460
TORBETT: Mary Ann [BORROW], 56; Samuel, 313
TORRANCE: Hutchman, 79
TORRENCE: Joseph, 16
TORREY: Hermon, JP, 325, 421
TOUSLEY: P.H., 170
TOWER: Nathaniel, 564; Richard, 564
TOWLE: Oliver, Col., 520
TOWN: B.C., 274; Bester C., 475; Isaac E., 202; Mehitable, 570
TOWNER: Elijah, 564; Isaac P., 564; Joseph, 564
TOWNLEY: Robert, 190, 314
TOWNSEND: Elizabeth, 564; Hannah M. [CUMMINGS], 126; John, 259; Noe, 564; Sarah, 564; W., 127, 145; W.H., 356, 595; William, 86; William H., 299, 350; William P., 474, 582
TOWSON: Capt., 11, 510
TOZER: Peter, 564
TRACY: Elijah G., 608; Elijah S., 96, 113; H.W., 281; Irene H., 422; J.A., 119; Linus, 26, 69, 158, 198, 228, 422, 454, 554, 595, 610, 613; Marion B., 595; Michael, 40, 137, 514; Myron, 215
TRAGO: Eli, JP, 319
TRAISTER: Catherine [SOLLIDAY], 525
TRAKER: David, 575
TRASEY: Charles, 334
TRASK: R.E., 378; Retire, 564; Rufus, 564

TRAVIS: Sally [WOODCOCK], 615
TREES: John, 564; Peter, 564; Thomas, JP, 354
TREMBLEY: Henry, JP, 152
TREVOR: G.B., 543; George B., 69; Henry S., 622; J.B., 64, 306; Jonathan B., 30, 60, 139, 164, 227, 229, 241, 321, 335, 341, 347, 376, 391, 425, 431, 506, 523, 534, 541, 551, 616; Jonathan B., Jr., 126, 329; Joseph, 104
TRIMBLE: James, 461; John, 377, 565; Margaret, 565
TRIPLETT: Thomas, Capt., 449
TRIPNER: George, 565; Mary, 565
TRIPPER: Col., 49
TRITT: Peter, 565; Samuel, 565
TROTH: Henry, 176, 319, 481, 509, 519
TROTTER: J., 572; William, 88
TROUBAT: John Jr., 294
TROUT: Boltzer, 565; Elizabeth, 565; Henry, 565
TROUTMAN: Catharine, 565; G.M., 399; George, 25, 58, 81, 108, 150, 172, 185, 188, 208, 247, 251, 275, 283, 314, 332, 471, 516, 523, 531, 561; George M., 183, 187, 443, 500; George W., 243; Lewis M., 550; Peter, 565
TROWBRIDGE: Benjamin H., 565; Daniel, JP, 565; Ebenezer, 565; Elihu, 565; Lyman, JP, 583; Pamela [BRUSH], 72; Parnel, 565; Seelye, 72; Stephen, 565; William D., 72
TROWLING: Lyman, JP, 328

TROXELL: Charles, JP, 250; Susan [ZIEGLER], 624
TRUAX: Ann [HOLLENSHEAD], 266; Joseph, 566; Nancy [HOLLENSHEAD], 266
TRUBY: Henry, 151
TRUE: L.B., 407
TRUESDALE: Samuel W., JP, 339
TRUESDELL: Samuel W., 535
TRULY: Susan, 411; William, JP, 411
TRUMBOWER: Philip, 195
TRUMP: A., 77, 454, 456, 610; Augustus, 597; Betsey, 566; Elizabeth, 566; George, 566
TRUXAL: Jacob, 138
TRYER: Andrew, 566
TRYON: Ezra, 566
TUBBS: Benjamin, 566; Catharine [STRAW], 546; Cynthia, 566; George, 546; Hannah, 566; James 2nd, 566; Polly, 566; Robert, 52, 566; Samuel, 566; Susan, 566
TUCKER: Allen, 325; Charles, 322; James, 566; William D., JP, 297
TUDOR: George, Capt., 593; John, 566; Rachel, 566; William, 558
TUMAN: Peter, 567
TUNISON: Anthony, 567; Mary, 567; Susannah, 567
TUPPER: Hannah [CHERRY], 95
TUPPS: Major, 496
TURK: John, 412
TURNBAUCH: John, 151
TURNER: A.W., 567; Abraham W., 567; Alexander, 567; Asaph, JP, 206, 295, 306; Benjamin, 568; Catharine, 567; Charles, 567; Daniel, 567; George, 144, 567; Hannah, 568; Harriet, 567; Henderson, 87; Honey, 568;

James, 567–68; Jane, 567; Jesse, 586; John, 61, 568; Mary, 567; Mary Sophia R., 567; P.F., 79; Patrick, 567; Phebe Ann, 567; Rebecca [BIRCH], 47; Rhenhanah [CARNES], 87; Samuel, 411; Sarah, 567; Simon, 516; Thomas, 567; William, 3, 97, 567; William G., 568; William R., 568
TURNEY: Asa, 568; Hannah, 568; Henry, 568; Polley, 568; Simon, 516
TURPENNING: James, JP, 326
TURRELL: William, 286; William J., 78, 285, 615; William P., 75
TURRILL: Betsey, 568; David O., 568; Hannah, 568; Isaac, 568
TUTTLE: Amos, JP, 483; Barnet W., 258; Capt., 529, 577; Isaiah, 568; Jerry, 574; John, 574; Jonathan, JP, 213; Lorana [SEELY], 500; Mariah [HICKOCK], 258; Moses, 574; Myron, JP, 165; Polly [GREENE], 223, 644; Sally, 574
TYE: William, 568
TYEMAN: Thomas, 568
TYLER: A., 249; Aby, 568; Asahel, JP, 46; Bezaleel, 569; Capt., 2; Col., 452; H.C., 569; Jacob, 568; Joab, 91; John A., 569; Julia A., 4; Lynden E., 569; Lynder E., 569; M.C., JP, 184; Martin, 4; Moses, 569; Nathaniel, 569; Rachel, 569; Robert G., 569; Sarah, 569; Silas, 569
TYREMAN: Thomas, 568
TYRRELL: Betsey, 298

UBAN: John, 570; Joseph, 570
UDREE: Daniel, Col., 26, 482

UFFINGTON: Ann [HALLET], 235; Thomas S., 235
UHLER: Jonathan, 44
ULLERY: Capt., 230
ULMAN: Jacob, 64
ULRICH: John, 569
UNANGST: Philip, 488
UNDERHILL: David, JP, 599; R.L., 573
UNDERWOOD: Isaac, 569; Lybin, JP, 94; Morrison, 133, 152
UNKLE: Elizabeth [SCHATZ], 500; Henry, 500
UPDEGRAFF: A., 575; Isaac, 570; Joseph, 275; Uria, 495
UPDIKE: Thomas B., 464
UPJOHN: James, 569
UPP: George, JP, 124
UPSON: Allen, 583; Joseph, 569
UPTHEGROVE: Isaac, 570
UPTON: Ezekiel, 570; Mahitable, 570
UPWRIGHT: Philip, Capt., 548
URBAN: Joseph, 570
URD: Sarah [COLLINS], 107
URSELL: Frederick, 570
URY: Col., 555
UTLEY: Hamilton, JP, 203
UTT: Elias, 570; Lucretia, 570; Sarah [STRUNK], 547

VALENTINE: Bernard, 570; Capt., 170; Thomas S., JP, 457; William, 480
VANAKEN: Benjamin, 570–71; Margaret, 570–71
VanANKEN: Abraham, 571; Benjamin, 571; Daniel, 571; Elke, 571; Gideon, 571; Hannah, 571; Jacob, 571; Margaret, 571
VanARSDALEN: Aaron, 571; Hannah, 571; John, 571

VanARTSDALEN: Alice E., 571; Garret, 571; Isaac, 571; Jacob C., 571; Sarah, 571
VANATA: Samuel, JP, 402
VanATTA: Capt., 556
VanAUKEN: J.W., JP, 539; Margaret, 571
VanBENSCHOTTER: Aaron, 571; Daniel, 571
VanBRICKE: William, Capt., 53
VanCAMP: J.C., JP, 341, 395; James, 428; John C., JP, 33, 523
VanCAMPEN: Moses, Lt., 337
VANCE: James, 571; William, 585
VanCORTLAND: Philip, Col., 620
VANDERBELT: Sarah G., 219
VANDERBILT: David, 572; Elizabeth [MORGAN], 405; P. Jr., JP, 385
VanderCOOK: Daniel, JP, 304; James, JP, 65
VANDERGRIFT: Jonathan, 572
VANDERHOOF: Cornelius, 572; Mary, 572
VanderSMITH: D.B., 215
VanderVINDER: Christopher, 382; Sarah [McKINLEY], 382
VandeVENTER: Mary, 572; Peter, Capt., 572
VandeVNTER: Mary, 572; Peter, 572
VandeVOURT: Joseph, 312
VanDYKE: Achsah, 479; Betsy [CORNELIUS], 115; Davis, 572; Henry, 53, 457; J. Jr., 619; J.W., 619; John, 479, 572; Martha, 572; Polly, 572; William, 572; Wilson, 572
VANEMAN: Andrew, 572
VANETTER: Cornelia [LABAR?], 322; John, 322

VanFLEET: Abraham, 573; Cornelius, 573, 606
VanFOSSEN: Leonard, 573
VanGARDNER: Hannah, 573; John, 537, 573
VanGORDEN: Isaac P., 194; John W., 194; Moses, 573; Samuel, 573
VanGORDON: Agnes, 573; John, 573; Tunis, 573
VANHARES: Capt., 30
VanHEER: Capt., 193, 197
VanHERE: Capt., 194
VanHORN: Benjamin, 573; Christian, 40; Cornelius, 574; James, 574; Jane, 574; John T., 321; Margaret, 524; Sarah, 574
VanHORNE: Pattison, 23
VanHORNE: Hannah, 574; William, 574
VanKIRK: Elizabeth, 574; Elizabeth [LUKER], 349; Isaac, 349; Jemson, 574; John, 349; William K., 609
VanKLEECK: Peter, 498
VanKLEEK: Catharine [SEAMAN?], 498; Peter, 498; Rebecca, 498; Sarah, 498
VanLEAR: Matthew S., 284
VanMATRE: Jesse, JP, 391
VANNAMBURGH: Isaac, 19
VANNATTA: Sally [THOMPSON], 560
VanNESS: Capt., 570
VANORMER: Levi, 163
VanPOOL: Anthony, 317
VanRANSLIER: Robert, Col., 575
VanSANT: Jane M., 35
VanSCHOCK: Goos, Col., 467
VANSCI: Col., 181
VanSCIVER: Rachel [SEIBERT], 500
VanSCOY: Cornelia, 574; Samuel, 574
VANSICE: Hiram, 574; James, 574; John C., 574
VANTZ: Jacob, JP, 12
VANUXEM: James Jr., 82

VanWINKLE: Elias, 574; Hannah, 574
VanZANDT: B., JP, 9
VanZANT: George, 575
VARNER: Thomas, JP, 575
VARNUM: Catherine, 575, 661; Enoch, 575, 661; Philip, 575, 661; William, 575, 661
VASTBINDER: Philip, 566
VAUGHAN: Thomas, 575
VAUGHN: John, 575; John Jr., 575; S., 97; Stephen, JP, 31, 226, 454, 604; Thomas, 575
VEECH: James, 476, 549
VENEMAN: Nicholas, JP, 255
VERGASON: Abigail [BREWSTER], 64; David, 64
VERGESON: Anna, 575; Daniel, 575
VERNER: John, 575
VERNUM: Enoch, 661; Philip, 661; William, 661
VESEY: Capt., 112; Edward, Col., 112
VIALL: Elizabeth [HUMPHREY], 278; Ezra B., 278
VICKERS: Richard, 575
VIETS: Tacy [HILLYER], 261; Zopher, 261
VINCENT: Bethuel, 576; G.A., JP, 410; John, JP, 133; Mary [CORNELIUS], 115; Sarah, 464; William, JP, 564
VOCE: Col., 330
VOGEL: Capt., 569; John, 1, 48, 149, 185, 198, 203, 308, 462, 500–501, 518, 524; Joseph, 576; Maria Anna, 576
VOGHT: Rebecca [SPANGENBURG], 527
VOGT: George, 188
VOLANS: Samuel, 353
VOLK: Catharine [WOLF], 613
VOLLMER: Frederick, 340
VOLTZ: Philomena, 415
VonderSMITH: D.B., 235, 256, 305, 488;

(VonderSMITH, continued)

Daniel B., 352; Eli W.,
274
VONHEER: Capt., 577
VOOREE: Joseph, Col., 68
VOORIS: Capt., 156
VOREES: Thomas, Capt.,
467
VORSE: D.W., JP, 449
VOSBURGH: Nancy
[BROWN], 71
VOSE: Capt., 238, 244;
Col., 76, 235
VOUGHT: Godfrey, 576;
Joshua, 576; Lawrence,
576
VROMAN: Bartholomew,
576; Hannah, 576
VROOMAN: Bartholomew,
576

WACK: Frederick William,
576; Martin, 576
WADDLE: Thomas, JP,
364; William, 576
WADE: Abner, Capt., 46;
Andrew, JP, 360, 414;
B.F., 261; Daniel H., 576;
Edward, JP, 230; Jane,
576; Joshua, 576;
Rebecca, 576; Silvanus,
328, 576; *Sylvanus,* 576;
Thomas J., 576
WADHAM: Noah, JP, 496
WADSWORTH: Ann
[PRIOR], 455; Capt., 432;
Col., 358; Edward, Capt.,
577; Epaphrus, 577;
Freeman C., 577;
Hezekiah, 577; Kezele,
577
WAGER: Capt., 381; James
B., 395
WAGGONER: Adam, 577;
Capt., 118; Daniel, 577;
George, 577; John, 577;
Mary, 577; Michael, 578;
Rhoda, 578; Sarah, 577
WAGNER: Barbara, 577;
Barnet, 577; Catharn,
577; Daniel, 577;
Elizabeth, 577; Levi N.,
257; Mary, 577; Philip,
578; Snowden S., 477;

Susan, 414; William, 228,
577
WAGONER: John, 578
WAIF: Catharine
[HARTMAN], 246
WAINRIGHT: C.B., 134
WAIT: Asa, JP, 13, 290
WAKEMAN: Thomas, 118
WAKLEE: Elizabeth, 578;
John, 578
WAKLY: John, 578
WALBRIDGE: Capt., 439;
Henrietta, 578; Joshua,
578; Priscilla, 578
WALDHAM: Noah, JP,
582
WALDRON: Daniel, 578;
Samuel, 578
WALER: Benjamin, 584
WALKER: Anthony, 372;
Asher, 476, 578; Charles,
JP, 209; Daniel, 76, 579;
David, 610; Edward, 579;
Elizabeth
[ROBERTSON], 476;
Enoch P., 146; Gideon,
136; Isaac, 357; J. Blair,
381; James, 76, 260, 317,
421, 478, 579; John, 579;
Joseph, 543, 579; Lewis,
484; Lewis M., JP, 108;
Nathaniel, 579; Orin, 248;
Owen, 300; R., 24, 558;
Rachel, 579; Robert J.,
248; Robert M., Dr., 367;
Samuel, 159; William,
330; Z.F., 187
WALL: Isaac, 579
WALLACE: A.C., 199;
Abigail, 579–80; Andrew,
580; Anna, 580; Capt.,
84; Charles, 199, 579–80;
George, 210, 580; George
W., 579–80; George Y.,
JP, 446; Herman, 441;
Joseph, 109, 580;
Sophronia, 580; William
F., 580
WALLER: David, 580;
Henry, Col., 25; Jesse,
580; Lewis, 580; Mary,
580; Sarah, 580; William,
580
WALLEZE: Michael H.,
580
WALLIS: Sobrina, 580

WALLISER: Michael, 580
WALLS: Isaac, 579, 662;
Jonathan, 44, 101, 333
WALSH: Robert, U.S.
Consul, 436
WALTAR: John, 581
WALTER: Barbara, 581;
Daniel, 231; David, 581;
George, 260; H., 290,
509; Jacob L., 86; John,
581; John B., 400;
Nicholas, 581; Peter, 581;
Philip, 581; Samuel, 570;
Wesley, 570
WALTERS: Ann
[McKINNEY], 382;
Edwin, 165; Eleanor, 581;
Elizabeth, 581; Henrietta,
581; Henry, 581; Isabella,
581; Jacob, 581; Jacob
2nd, 581; John, 581; Julia
Ann, 581; Margaret, 581;
Mary, 581; Peter, 382,
581; Sarah Jane, 581
WALTHOUR: Conrad, 239
WALTMAN: Lewis, 586
WALTON: J.H., 270;
James Jr., 189; James O.,
322; James, JP, 189;
Samuel, 231; Wells, 274;
William, 581
WALTZ: Barbara, 582;
Michael, 582; Simon, 582
WALWORTH: A.W., JP,
200
WAMBACK: Barbara, 582;
Mary, 582; Philip, 582
WAMP: Capt., 101
WAMPLER: Capt., 477
WANDEL: James, 582;
John, 582
WANN: Barbara, 582;
Catharine Ann, 582;
Elizabeth, 582; George,
582; Michael, 582; Sarah,
582
WANNER: Peter, Capt.,
588
WARD: Anna, 582; Betsey
[EATINGER], 173;
Christopher L., 461; Col.,
390; Dolly [LEE], 330;
Edward, 583; Elijah A.,
JP, 278; Elizabeth, 583;
Elizabeth H.
[WHEELER], 595;

(WARD, continued)

Hezekiah, JP, 262;
Ichabod, 583; James M.,
523; John, 330, 582;
Jonas, Capt., 112; Joseph,
583; Lyman, 582; Mary,
582; Obadiah, 583; Peter
C., 424; Samuel, 582;
Thomas, 583; W.W., 555;
William, 173, 235, 523,
561, 582–83, 620;
William C., 523, 620
WARDEN: David M., 107;
John B., 9, 404, 591
WARDS: Edward, 583
WARE: Marvin, 234
WARFEL: John, 488
WARNE: Amy, 373;
Joseph, 373
WARNER: Alfred, 583;
Almira, 583; Ann, 586;
Betsey, 583–84; Col.,
178; David, 583; E.,
Capt., 57; Eliza, 583;
Emanuel, 584; F.G., 286;
Fanny M., 583; George,
584; Harriet, 583; Jane,
583; Jane M., 72; John,
583–84; Loring, 583;
Mary, 583–84; Michael,
584; Milo, 583; Noah,
583–84; Norman, 583;
Patty, 583; Polly, 583–84;
Rebecca, 583; Rhinehart,
584; S., Col., 544;
Samuel, 51, 583; Seth,
Col., 158, 454; Walter,
583; William, 584;
William H., JP, 480;
Zachariah, 584; Zelates,
583
WARNOCK: James, JP,
356–57; John L., 357;
William Shaw, 357
WARNSHER: Margaret
[BOYCE], 59–60
WARRELL: John R., 339
WARREN: Abraham, 584;
Thomas, 228; William,
378
WARRICK: Charles D.,
584; James, 584; Jane,
584
WARTMAN: Alphram, 149

WASHBURN: Catharine,
191; Eliza, 34; Joseph, JP,
93, 144, 452, 503
WASHINGTON: Col., 113,
329
WATER: Laura
[HILLYER], 261; Lester,
261
WATERMAN: Eleases, JP,
23; Isaac S., 586;
Jedediah, Capt., 455;
L.S., 469; Reuben R., 126
WATERS: Aaron, 301;
Abner, 584; Benjamin,
584; Eliza [WARNER],
583; George, 585; Mary,
585; Philip, 217; Rosina,
583
WATKINS: Abigail
[GAYLARD], 206; Ann,
585; Julia Ann
[SIMMONS], 513;
Truman, 206; William,
585
WATMOUGH: Caroline,
585; John G., 585;
Margaretta, 585; Mary
M., 585
WATROUS: Allen, 585;
William C., 585
WATSON: Amariah, 585;
Ann, 585; Benjamin, 585;
Capt., 601; Daniel, 184;
David, 172, 217, 305,
404, 488, 568, 570, 622;
George, 441; George, JP,
118, 162; H.G., Capt.,
399; Hannah [TURRILL],
568; James, 420, 585;
James D., 400; James Jr.,
457; John L., 199, 219;
Johnston, 107; Jonathan,
34, 272; Marmaduke,
405; Noah, 585; Sarah
Ann [HUBLEY], 441;
Thomas J., JP, 257;
William, 496; William G.,
JP, 252
WATT: Capt., 102; Col.,
82; David, 281, 600; Isaac
M., JP, 239, 405; James
F., 203; Joseph, 456;
Peggy [PUDDING], 456;
Susan E., 200
WATTAMYER: David,
585

WATTEN: Peter, 581
WATTERS: Joseph, 541;
Ruth Ann [STEWART],
541
WATTLES: A., JP, 260
WATTMAN: Lewis, 586
WATTS: Alexander, 586;
Henry M., 84; M.P., 84;
Margaret, 586
WATTTENBAUGH: Polly
[HARTMAN], 246
WAUGH: Robert M., 71,
327, 596
WAY: Abisha, 288; *H.M.*,
267; Parmelia, 330;
Samuel, JP, 217
WAYNANT: Jacob B., 284
WAYNE: Col., 37, 66;
Gen., 243, 247, 341, 466
WEAMER: John, 61
WEAR: Cornelius, 586
WEASEY: Elizabeth, 586;
John, 586; Phebe, 586;
Samuel, 586; Sarah, 586;
William, 586
WEASNER: John, 322;
Sarah [KURTZ], 322
WEATHERBEE: A.A., JP,
125
WEAVER: Adam, 530,
586; Anthony, 586; Capt.,
483, 511, 618; Catharine,
587; Catharine [SYPE],
553; Christiana, 587;
Conrad, 587; Daniel, 457;
Elizabeth, 587; Elizabeth
[CAMPBELL], 85; Eve,
587; Feronica, 587;
Frances, 587; Garret, 587;
George, 156; Hannah,
587; Henry, 587; Jacob,
169, 409, 587, 650; John,
157, 457, 587; John H.,
140; Joseph, 587; Joshua,
327, 497; Mary "Polly"
[DUCK], 156; Michael,
587; Robert F., 288;
Samuel, 587; Sarah, 587;
Susannah, 587; Tharaba,
587; William, 587
WEBB: Burkett, 127;
Charles, Col., 446; Col.,
577; J.L., 41, 423; John
L., 497; Josiah, 588;
Keziah [BOWMAN], 59;
Laura Ann, 588;

(WEBB, continued)

Mathias, 588; William
T.E., JP, 102
WEBBER: Daniel, 4; David
G., JP, 86; Hannah, 588;
Jeremiah, JP, 284; Polly
[ALLEN], 4; William,
588
WEBER: Jonathan, 111;
Jonathan C., 91, 362, 366,
520
WEBSTER: Betsey, 588;
Capt., 181; Catharine
[RANKIN], 460;
Elizabeth, 588; Francis
C., 39; James, 129, 237;
Margaret [RANKIN],
460; Michael, 588;
Moses, 588; Spencer S.,
228; Sylvia [BELDEN],
39
WEDDELL: P.M., 200
WEIDA: Michael, 588
WEIDLE: Jacob, 45
WEIDMAN: Jacob B., 277
WEIGELL: Catharine, 589;
Christopher, 589;
Elizabeth, 589; Michael,
589
WEIGHT: John M., 3
WEIGLE: Christopher, 589
WEIL: Solomon, 501
WEIMER: Peter, 183
WEIR: Andrew, 158; Anne
[DULIN], 158; James,
600; Jane, 158; John, 600;
Robert J., 294; Thomas,
Capt., 600; William D.,
158
WEIRICH: David, JP, 142
WEIRICK: Elizabeth, 589;
Michael, 589; Valentine,
589
WEISE: Adam, 111, 589;
Catharine, 589; George,
368
WEISER: George, JP, 17;
John, 589; Justina, 589
WEISNER: Capt., 130
WEISS: Elizabeth, 589–90;
Francis, JP, 61; Jacob,
589–90; Maria [SOLT],
525; Michael, 524;
Rebecca, 590; Thomas,
590; William, JP, 599

WEITZEL: Elizabeth, 590;
John, 590; Tabitha, 590
WEITZELL: Elizabeth, 590;
John, 590
WELCH: David, 413;
Francis, JP, 483; John,
590; Oscar, 433; William
C., 166, 457
WELD: John, JP, 567
WELDON: Joseph, 449;
Lawrence Johnson, 408;
Thomas C., 243
WELDY: Christine, 13, 301
WELLER: John, 590;
Juline, 348; Roswell, JP,
430
WELLHOUSE: George,
JP, 357
WELLINGTON: James G.,
271; Jonathan, 590;
Rachel, 590
WELLIVER: Christian,
590
WELLMAN: Abraham,
591; Comfort, 591;
Rebecca, 591
WELLS: Alles, 591; B.L.,
343; Charles D., 591;
Elisha, 183, 197, 225,
270, 281, 323, 328, 353,
416–17, 483, 623;
Elizabeth, 591; Ezekiel,
591; G.H., 204; James,
591; James E., JP, 592;
James *N.*, 648; John, 55,
64, 97, 153, 220, 648;
Laws, 591; Nathan, JP,
252; Perrin, 193; Robert,
591; Sarah
[SPAULDING], 528;
Theodore, 253; William
A., JP, 445
WELSH: A., JP, 282;
Benjamin, JP, 180;
Henry, 77; John, 11, 152,
591; Joseph, 592; Moses,
JP, 545; Patrick, 592
WELT: Barbara, 592;
Thomas, 592
WELTNER: Catharine
[HERTZOG], 355;
Thomas, 355
WELTON: Phio, JP, 582
WELTS: Barney, 592

WELTY: Henry, 379;
Jacob, 133; John, 346,
586
WENTLING: George, 592;
Mary, 592
WENTWORTH: Ariel, JP,
467
WENTZ: Magdalena
[MITCHELL], 399;
Robert, 351
WERDEBAUGH: John G.,
41
WERKHEISER: Catharine
[KESSLER], 310
WERNTZ: Philip, 592
WERSLER: Jonathan G.,
133; Maria [DAVIS], 133
WERTS: Jacob, 592–93
WERTZ: Catharine, 592;
Elizabeth, 592; Jacob,
592; John, 592; Margaret,
592; Mary, 592; Peter,
592; William, 592
WESCOTT: George B.,
277, 314
WESLEY: Salinda
[GROVER], 228
WESNER: John, 322; Sarah
[KURTZ], 322
WESSINGER: Ludwick,
612
WEST: Ann, 642; Ann
Eliza, 348; Benjamin,
Capt., 460, 468; Capt.,
431; Charles, 25; David,
Col., 25; Hilborne, 494;
Jacob, Col., 191; John,
593; John A., 614; John
H., 124; Margaret, 593;
Nathaniel, JP, 200;
Thomas, 593; William A.,
335
WESTBROOK: Abraham,
593; Cornelius B., 593;
Gideon, 593; John, 66;
Solomon, 66
WESTBURY: William, 221
WESTCOAT: George W.,
593; James, 593; Phebe,
593
WESTCOTT: Sophina, 108
WESTFALL: Abraham,
593–94; Abram, 268;
Ann, 594; Dinah, 593–94;
Eunice, 594;

(WESTFALL, continued)

Hannah, 594; James, 594; Levi, 594; Simeon, 594
WESTGATE: A.G., JP, 608
WESTLAKE: Josiah, 594; Sarah, 594
WESTON: John, 594; Salmon, JP, 601
WESTOVER: Jonathan, JP, 451, 577
WETHERBY: Benjamin, JP, 113, 198, 285, 516; Henry C., 71
WETHERILL: Charles, 459
WETMORE: Lansing, 407; Loven, 19
WETSTONE: Jacob, Capt., 155
WEYAND: Daniel, 293; Henry, 24
WEYANT: Samuel, JP, 237
WEYGANDT: J., JP, 139, 469; Jack, JP, 289; Jacob, JP, 91, 164, 184, 225, 261, 436, 542, 556, 622
WEYMAN: Col., 324; Daniel, 26, 180, 386; George, 122
WEYNARD: Matthias, Capt., 581
WHALEY: David M., 261; James, 240
WHARTON: Samuel, 594; Samuel Jr., 594; T.L., 231; Thomas L., 92, 238, 348
WHATELY: Samuel, Capt., 324
WHEATON: Jonathan, 594
WHEDON: Harvey, 155; Harvey, JP, 169
WHEELAND: Michael, 594
WHEELER: Ambrose, 595; Amos, 165; Belinda, 595; Benjamin, 595; Cathrin, 420; Charity, 595; Elizabeth, 595; Emily B., 595; Henry, 595; Herman J., 595; Isaac, 595; James I., 595; John, 595; Loby, 595; Loly, 595; Nathan, 595; Nicholas, 116; Randal, 595;

Sivia R. [EDWARDS], 165; Smith, 227; Susannah, 595; Truman, JP, 330
WHEELON: Harvey, JP, 22
WHERRY: Susannah [PYLES], 456
WHETSTONE: George, 518; Mary [ALLISON], 6
WHIPPLE: Elijah, 595; James, 441; Joseph, 596
WHISEN: William, 451
WHITAKER: Abraham, 38, 598; Henry, 598; J.C., 94, 566; Mary [BOYCE], 59–60
WHITAMOYER: Nancy [SAILOR], 489–90
WHITCOMBE: T.M., JP, 12
WHITCRAFT: Elizabeth, 596; Lydia, 175; William, 175, 596
WHITE: Alby, 597; Alexander, JP, 603; Amanda, 597; Ambrose, 171; Ann, 596; Barbara [MYERS], 415; Benjamin, 535, 596; Capt., 95; Charlotte, 597; Col., 109; D., 603; David, 128, 369, 493, 545, 596; Drucilla, 596; Edward, 162; Eleanor, 596–97; Elizabeth, 596; Elizabeth [ROBERTS], 476; Elizabeth [SCHENCK], 493; Ephraim, 596; Fanny, 597; George, 597; Hanford, 597; Henry, 597; Henry K., JP, 270; Hosea, JP, 518; Isaac, 596; J.R., 565; James, 541, 597; John, 187, 249, 306, 325, 484, 596; John A., 165, 286; John C., 102; Joseph, 294; Josephine, 597; Margaret, 596–97; Margaret A., 597; Martha, 597; Mary, 596–97; Nancy, 597; Nathan, 597; Olive, 518; Phebe, 597; Philenia, 597; Polly [POLLOCK], 449; Potter, 597; Rosannah, 596; Samuel, Capt., 597;

Sarah, 596; Sarah [CORNWELL], 116; Susannah, 596; Thomas, 1, 65, 67, 69, 155, 174, 191, 193, 215, 217, 299, 313, 463, 488, 518, 580, 584, 593, 601; William, 322, 338, 476, 597; William W., 456
WHITEHEAD: Charles, JP, 614; J., 249; Samuel, 598
WHITEKER: Abraham, 598
WHITELEY: Betsey, 598; Elisha, 598; John, 598
WHITEMAN: Woollery, 598
WHITER: Nancy [BALDWIN], 22
WHITESIDE: John, 637; Thomas, Dr., 201; W., 637
WHITESIDES: James, 96
WHITESTONE: Mary [ALLISON], 627; William [ALLISON], 627
WHITING: Bathsheba T. [HESTON], 257; John, 598; Nathan, 598
WHITLACH: William, 598
WHITLATCH: William, 598
WHITMAN: Hannah, 599; Henry S., JP, 398; John, 599
WHITMORE: James Jr., JP, 232; Joseph F., 350
WHITMYER: Philip, 599
WHITNEY: A.J., 599; Alanson, 599; Alvin, 598–99; Benjamin 3rd, 599; Benjamin Jr., 599; Elisha, 598–99; Enos, 599; Esther, 598–99; Hannah, 599; James, JP, 69, 420; John, 599; Molly, 599; Nathan, 599; Reuben M., 558
WHITROW: Col., 1
WHITSON: James H., JP, 186
WHITTLESEY: E.M., 181; Elisha, JP, 34; John, 18
WHITTLESY: Asaph, JP, 116; C.M., 143; E.M., 438, 615; J., 408;

(WHITTLESY, continued)

John, 21, 57, 116, 161, 181, 414, 579
WHITTON: A.T., 304; Charles, 304
WHITZELL: Daniel J., 600; John, 600; Sarahann, 600; Stephen, 600; William, 600
WICK: Calvin C., JP, 439; James, 313; James R., JP, 35, 268, 272, 475; John D., 206; William, 600
WICKE: Archibald, 410
WICKHAM: B.C., 346; John, 600; Sarah, 600
WICKIZER: Isaac, 654; Peggy [MILLER], 654
WICKLEIN: Jacob, 517
WICKS: James, 192
WICOFF: William, 221
WIEGAND: John Jr., 454
WIER: John, 600
WIES: Frederick, 124
WIESNER: Godfrey, 600
WIGGINS: Capt., 241; Cuthbert, 446; Job, 19; Philip, 298
WIGHT: Aaron, 618
WIGHTMAN: A.J., 230; Samuel, 178, 399; William, 600; William H., 600
WIGLE: J.H., 391
WIGTON: William, JP, 614, 621
WILBER: John, 601; Rueben, 443
WILBUR: John, 601; N.F., 367
WILCOX: Amos, 448–49; Calvin, JP, 390; Hosea, 601; Josiah, 601
WILDER: Austin, JP, 473; Horace, JP, 14, 234; Horan, JP, 584; Loisa [JONES], 297; Reuben W., 601
WILDON: Austin, JP, 259
WILEY: Bernard H., 601; Capt., 195; Elizabeth, 601; James, 153; Jane, 601; John, 245, 473; Mary, 601; Rebecca, 601;

Robert, 550; Thomas, 601; William B., 77, 255
WILFONG: John, 601
WILGUS: Ann, 605; Elias, 605
WILHELM: George, 602; Mary Ann, 602
WILKES: John, Capt., 427
WILKIN: John, JP, 9
WILKINS: A., 39; A.P. Jr., 197, 403, 430, 536, 560; George, 602; H., 43, 197; H.B., 3, 279; Horace, 70, 434; James, 602; John, 197
WILKINSON: Abel, 602; Alle, 602; Amos, 602; Ann T., 602; Anna Taylor, 602; Benoni, 602; Elizabeth, 602; Hannah, 602; Ichabod, 602; Ira, 602; Joel T., 602; Lanson, 602; Marcy, 602; Mary, 602; Mercy, 602; Murwine, 602; Polly, 602; William L., JP, 527; William S., JP, 600
WILKS: Luke, 244
WILL: Conrad, 606; Elizabeth, 342, 606; George, JP, 458; Henry, 103
WILLANER: Samuel, JP, 420
WILLARD: Easter, 603; Oliver, 20; William, 603
WILLCUTT: Rebecca, 2
WILLET: Col., 196
WILLETT: Col., 101
WILLIAMS: Aaron, 603; Abraham, 280, 534; Alice [SWAZE], 552; Amos, 604; Anna, 604; Barbara [WANN], 582; Benjamin, 377, 394, 457, 623; Betsey, 603; Caleb, 603; Capt., 538; Catharine, 603–4; Catharine [EATINGER], 173; Charles, 604; Chester, 68; Daniel, 603; David, 107, 201, 550; Dorcas, 603; Ebenezer, 603; Elias, 605; Ephraim, 457; Eunice, 603; F.M., 165; Frederick, 603;

H.D., 207; H.K., 454; Hannah, 603; Harvey D., JP, 268; Hector, 603; Henry, 603–4; Henry I., 486; Honor, 605; Isaac, 604; J.D., 102, 307, 336, 353, 515; J.H., 132, 617; J.P., JP, 456; J.R., 605; Jane, 604; Joel, 162; John M., 10; Jonathan, 29, 604; Jonathan Jr., 110; Joseph, 79, 212, 604; Joseph F., 602; Joshua, 55, 604; Julia [RUSH], 486; Leah [MASSEY], 364; Lewis, 238, 603; Lucy [GEER], 210, 642; Mary, 604; Nathan, 604; Polly [BROWN], 68; Rachel, 604; Reuben, 415; Rock, 210, 642; Roxeina, 603; S., Capt., 18; Samuel, 79, 604; Sarah, 604; Stacy, 604; Susannah, 604; Thomas, 141, 454, 605; Thomas C., 15; William, 173, 419, 582, 605; William Jr., 381
WILLIAMSON: Elizabeth, 605; George, 295; James, 605; John, 326, 605; Joseph, 249; Mary Agnes [YOUNG], 622; Thomas, 605; William, 166, 605
WILLIGUS: Elias, 605
WILLIS: Anne, 606; Fanny, 606; Grace, 605; Joseph, 605; Robert, 605; Thomas, 606
WILLITS: George H., JP, 142
WILLMAN: John, 576
WILLOUGHBY: Alfred, 435
WILLS: Conrad, 606
WILLSON: George, 338; Nathaniel A., 314
WILLYARD: John, 542
WILMARTH: Clarinda [BABCOCK], 18; Lewis P., 19
WILMOT: D., 615
WILNER: David, 606; Henry, 606; Margaret, 606

WILSON: A.D., 215, 643; Adam, 30; Alexander, 290, 306, 311, 450, 601, 606; Allen, 49; Amy, 292, 609; Andrew, 606–7; Ann F., 609; Arthur, 606; Asa, 413; Ashbel B., 609; Barbara, 607; Barton, 385; Benjamin, 607; Betty, 606; Capt., 262, 594; Christiana [BROWN], 67; Clayton, 292; D.S., 10, 394; David, 607; Edward, 45, 142, 329, 581, 619; Eleanor, 607; Elnathan, 607; Euphemia R., 609; F.F.A, 146; Fletcher, 248; Francis, 572; Frank, 178; Gilbreth, 607; H., 47; Isaac, 13, 350, 580; J.J., 608; James, 11, 35, 107, 109, 128, 183, 205, 310, 372, 550, 607–8, 616; Jane, 607–9; Janet, 607; John, 15, 29, 44, 52, 119, 149, 187, 189, 255, 280, 310, 324, 339, 356, 360, 370, 450, 467–68, 489, 497, 534, 608–9; John A., JP, 63, 287, 332, 589; John C., 607; John M., 223, 321, 472, 597; Joseph, 355, 367, 382, 535, 608; Lydia, 653; M., 47; M.D., 420; M.S., 18, 57, 75, 86, 109–11, 122, 134, 146–47, 224, 342, 468, 470, 558, 593; Mahlon, JP, 518; Mark, 166; Martha, 607; Mary, 607, 653; Mary [SHEETS], 506; Mary M., 607; Mason S., 226; Matthew, 608; Nancy, 608; Nehemiah, 608; Patrick, 444; Peter, 608; R.P., 550; Robert, 607; Robert 2nd, 608; Robert K., 45, 85; Robert M., 607; Robert M. 1st, 609; Robert M. 2nd, 609; Robert Sr., 608; *S./G.*, 226; S.D., 26, 52, 72, 208, 420, 468, 558, 561, 569; Samuel, 36, 46, 66, 142, 170, 184, 310, 321, 389, 393, 542, 581, 608–9; Samuel C., JP, 273; Sarah, 606, 609; Thomas, 62, 183, 565, 653; Valentine, 609; W.H., 27; William, 51, 60, 69, 115, 126, 139, 217, 230, 239, 265, 276, 280, 287, 316, 369–70, 377, 383, 411, 420, 439, 473, 572, 607, 609–10; William H., 609; William Jr., 15, 98, 161, 180, 263, 337, 339, 372, 399, 419, 423, 428, 440–41, 446, 450, 487–88, 503, 607, 610, 617; William T., JP, 66, 195

WILT: Barbara, 592; Catharine, 592; Daniel, 592; David, 592; Elizabeth, 592; George, 592; George W., 610; Jacob, 592; John, 592, 608; Margaret, 592; Mary, 592; Mary V., 610; Peter, 592; S.C., JP, 337; Samuel, 610; Susannah, 592; Thomas, 592

WILTBAHN: -----, Rev., 357

WILTBANK: James, Rev., 225

WILTZ: John, 612

WINBRENER: D.S., 218

WINDER: James, 611

WINDHAM: George, 610; Mary, 610

WINDOLPH: Elizabeth, 610; Jacob, 610

WINDSOR: Col., 125

WINEBAUGH: Nicholas, 185

WINHAM: George, 610

WINKELMAN: Caroline, 77; William, 77

WINKLEMAN: Caroline, 77

WINN: John, 610

WINNING: James, 610

WINNOCKS: F.B., 309

WINSLON: Stephen, 610

WINSLOW: Abigail, 610; Bethiah, 610; John, 610; Kenelon, 611; Keniton, 611; Kesiah, 610; Lois, 610; Stephen, 610; William A., 610

WINTER: John, 39; John Sr., 611; Jonathan W., 611

WINTERS: Jacob, 611; Samuel, 389

WINTON: Nathan, 611

WIPPLE: Joseph, 611

WIRE: Rhinehart, 611

WIREBACH: J.C., JP, 404

WIREMAN: Charles, JP, 321

WIRT: Henry, 589; Jacob, 180, 477

WISE: Col., 452; David, JP, 104; Frederick, 193; Jacob M., JP, 10; Jacob, JP, 506; Samuel, 379

WISECARVER: George, 611–12

WISEMAN: George, 612; George Jr., 612; Joseph P., 595

WISLER: Michael, 612

WISNER: Jacob, 612; Sarah, 612

WISSENGER: Ludwick, 612

WITHEROW: John W., 209; John, JP, 562, 612; Mary, 612

WITHERS: Joseph N., 413; Samuel, 546

WITHERSPOON: Susan [KOLLOCK], 319

WITHROW: Samuel, 612

WITMAN: Abraham, JP, 249; Charles, JP, 24, 458; Collinson R., 429; Jacob, 193; Margareth [OTTO], 429; William Jr., JP, 74, 275, 437

WITMER: Capt., 455

WITTE: C.H., 137; Mary [DEAN], 137

WITTENMYER: Jacob, 272

WITTES: Jasper, 24

WITTMAN: Andrew K., JP, 7, 393, 454

WITZ: John, 612

WOHLFANT: Philip, JP, 304

WOLCOT: Oliver, Col., 167

WOLCOTT: Benjamin, 613; Fanny M. [WARNER], 583; Horace, 583; John R., 613; Josiah, 613; Leona, 613; Margaret, 613; Mary, 613; Minerva, 613; Silas, 613

WOLCUT: Silas, 613

WOLDHAMS: Hetta, 52; Noah, JP, 52

WOLF: Adam, 613; Anna, 613; Capt., 551; Catharine, 613; Catharine [ROBERTS], 476; Elizabeth, 613; Horace E., JP, 300; Jacob, 125, 613; John, 337, 613; John P., 491; Joseph, 519; Magdalena, 613; Mary, 613; Mary Magdalen [MILLER], 392; Peter, 613; Sabina G., 300; Samuel, 476; Sarah, 613; Stephen, JP, 562

WOLFE: Adam, 614; David, 73; Joseph, 614

WOLFENBERGER: George, 303

WOLFERSBERGER: George, 305

WOLFF: Abraham, 260; Christian, 73, 159, 343, 530; Daniel R., 209; Joseph, JP, 286

WOLFINGER: John, 128; Jonathan F., 321, 533

WONDER: Andrew, 614; Hannah [SCOTT], 495; Jacob, 495; Mathias, 614

WONDERLICH: David, 331

WOOD: Alvah, 614; Catherine [OTTO], 429; Charles, 615; Clement, 26, 73, 100, 107, 109, 335, 383, 389, 397, 427, 484, 596; Col., 118; Consider, 614; Elizabeth, 614; Emma, 614; Ezra, 484; Gideon H., 175; Harman, 335; Harry, 105; James, 614; James W., 527; Jehu, 579;

Jesse, 289; John Jr., 397; Jonathan, 98, 372, 479, 614; Joseph, 565; Joseph P., 94; Josiah, 615; Levi, 615; Lodice, 614; Lucretia E. [KINGLEY], 314; Lucy, 614; Mary, 615; Moses, 98; Nancy M. [KINGLEY], 314; Polly [ROBINSON], 447; Robert, 615; Samuel C., 71; Samuel, JP, 98; Sarah [LEWIS], 335; Sarah L. [KINGLEY], 314; Smith, Capt., 578; *Syene,* 614; Theodore, 614; William, 481; Zilpha, 614

WOODARD: William, 600

WOODBURN: Esther [WHITNEY], 599; J.W., JP, 598; Jane, 378; John W., JP, 564; Moses, 615; Samuel, 181; Sena, 615; William, JP, 378

WOODCOCK: Alanson, 615; Albert, 615; Anna, 615; Hiram B., 615; Polly, 615; Sally, 615; Samuel, 615; Samuel H., 615

WOODEN: Charles, 615; Erastus, Col., 365; Isabella [KELLY], 307; Lucy [BENNETT], 42; Thomas, 307

WOODHAM: Noah, JP, 47

WOODHOUSE: Henry, JP, 574; M.P., 574

WOODMAN: Edward, 615

WOODMANCY: David, 615; Elizabeth, 615; Josephus S., 615

WOODMANSEE: David, 616; Gideon, 616; J.M., 616

WOODRING: Henry, 44

WOODRUFF: Almira, 616; Clarrissa W., 616; Elias, 616; Ephraim, 616; Fanny, 616; Frances, 616; Isaac, 616; Jesse, JP, 399; Samuel, 616

WOODS: Azariah, 617; Benjamin, JP, 153; Fanny, 614, 663; G.C., 2, 106;

James, 443, 614, 663; Jeremiah, 614, 663; John, 536, 614, 617, 663; John Jr., 614, 617; Joseph, 377, 614, 617, 663; Peter, 614, 663; Presley, 614, 663; Sarah, 614, 617, 663; William, 58, 191, 400, 442, 548

WOODWARD: Abisha, JP, 42, 128, 299, 561; Charles, 296; Experience, 296; Griswold, JP, 18; James S., 204; Mary A., 306; Nathaniel A., 277, 290; Olive, 42, 47, 128

WOODWORTH: Ezekiel, 617; Ezra, 617; Horatio, 617; Luther, 617; Priscilla, 617

WOOLCOT: Benajah, 617

WOOLCOTT: Benajah, 617

WOOLF: Henry L., 68, 460; Lewis, 617; Mary, 617

WORDHAM: Noah, JP, 297

WORK: David, JP, 550; George C., 26; John, 82, 300; John D., 258; William, 477

WORKMAN: Hugh, 617; James, 179, 618; Jane S., 617; Sarah, 14, 628; Shannon R., 401

WORLEY: Samuel, JP, 501

WORMAN: Samuel, 251

WORRAL: Benjamin, 618

WORRALL: Benjamin, 618; J.P., JP, 547; Jonathan, 69, 403, 618; William, 80

WORRELL: Jonathan, JP, 370; William, 512, 570

WORSTALL: Jane [HESTON], 257

WORTMAN: Abigail, 618; Abraham, 618; Smith, 618

WORTZ: John, 618

WRAY: James, 415, 540, 618; James A., 25; Robert, 159; Sarah, 618

WREN: Joseph, 618

WRIGHT: A.K., 491; Aaron, 618; Absalom, 619; Anna [LINE], 338; Betsey, 619; C., JP, 598; Capt., 393, 427; Charles, 619; Charles W., JP, 554; Chauncey, 498; Cyprian, 52, 489; David A., 19; Edward, 619; Elijah, Capt., 12; Elizabeth, 619; George, 619; H., 529; H.B., 151, 452, 609; Harriet B., 489; Hendrick B., 604; Henry, 366; Isabella [PHILLIPS], 444; Jacob, 619; James, 93, 254, 502; Jane [MITCHELL], 399; Joab, 619; John, 3, 619; Joseph, 16, 164; K., 606; Lewis, 619; Mary, 619; Matilda, 498; Moses, JP, 16; Neri, JP, 364; *Peninnah*, 619; Peter, 20, 68; R.E., 129; R.S., 301; Rensselair, JP, 323; Selah, 203; Stephen, 586; W., 444; William W., 17

WRIGHTMIRE: George, 620

WUNDER: Ann, 620; George, 620

WUNDERLICH: Jacob, 409

WURLS: William, 65

WURTS: Charles S., 296, 500

WURTZ: Charles S., 263, 428

WYGANT: James, 620; John, 620

WYLIE: Simeon, 620; William, 659

WYMER: Margaret [WALTERS], 581

WYNCOOP: Col., 37; David, 87

WYNKOOP: Abraham, 422; Hannah [NORMAN], 422

WYNN: Mary, 134; Thomas, JP, 134; Webster, 639

YABLE: Henry, 620; Mary, 620

YALE: Seth, JP, 46

YANGER: Catharine, 620; Henry, 620

YARDLEY: Samuel, 322; Thomas, 535

YARNALL: Benjamin H., 489, 558, 603; Elijah, JP, 303, 524

YATES: Walter, 408, 655

YAXTHIMER: Henry, 620; Henry Jr., 620

YEAGER: Capt., 155; Michael, 8

YEAKEL: George, Dr., 546

YEATS: Hugh, JP, 586; Nancy, 586

YEBEL: Henry, 620

YENGLING: John F., 621; Margaret, 621

YENTZER: John, 621; Mary, 621

YEOMANS: Joseph, 621; Sabra, 621; Samuel, 621

YERKES: Joseph, 410; Titus, 410, 461

YETTER: Anna [WOLF], 613; Lewis, JP, 173

YOCUM: Peter, 621

YOHE: George, 621; Peter, JP, 151

YONELLS: B.M., 100

YORK: Amos, 129

YORKE: G.M., JP, 497

YOST: Benjamin B., 179; Capt., 394; H.B., 48; Henry, JP, 586; Theodore, 278

YOUNG: Adam, 269; Andrew, 621; Ann, 621; Ann [HOOVER], 269; Capt., 496; Charles, 175, 621; Clorinda [HANKS], 238; Deborah Ann [ARMITAGE], 14; Elizabeth, 622; Esther [HANKS], 238; George B., JP, 429; H., JP, 342; Henry, 621; Isaac, 622; J.C., 62; J.J., 410; Jacob, 622; Jacob Jr., JP. 136; Jacob N., 478; James, 71, 238, 575, 622, 661; James S., 485, 537; Jane, 622; Jemima, 622; John, 622;

Josiah, 614; Lewn., JP, 542; Lydia [TILDEN], 562; Marks, 622; Mary Agnes, 622; Mary L. [RODGERS], 478; Philip, 623; Prudence, 622; Robert, 623; Samuel, JP, 266; William, 122, 478, 622

YOUNGMAN: George N., JP, 351; Thomas, JP, 315

YOUSE: John, 623

YOUTZ: Jeremiah, 227

YUNGST: Peter, 623; Samuel, 623

ZAHM: Matthias Jr., 408

ZAHN: Mathias, 274

ZAHNISER: Jacob, 8, 277, 378, 603

ZEANS: John, 623

ZEARING: Henry, 524

ZECHMAN: George, 624; Johannes, 550

ZEEMS: Jacob, 309

ZEGAR: Casper, 624

ZEIGENFUS: Charles, JP, 422; Susan [NOLF], 422

ZEIGLER: George, 624; Manuel, 624; William, JP, 4

ZELL: John, 201

ZELLER: Christena, 623; Michael, 623

ZELLNER: John, 624; Maria Elizabeth, 624

ZENDER: Catharine [DOWDERMAN], 154

ZEPP: Jacob, 624; Magdalina, 624

ZERCHER: Jacob, 338

ZERFASS: Capt., 390

ZETTLEMOYER: Martin, 624

ZIEGENFERS: Charles, JP, 198

ZIEGENFUS: Charles, 139

ZIEGLER: David, 624; Emmanuel, 624; Hannah, 624; Jacob, 624; John L., 624; Margaret, 624; Sarah, 624; Susan, 624; W., 624

ZIEKSMAN: George, 624

ZIEMER: John, 632